APOSTLE OF PEACE

To Dennis —
With every blessing
of peace,
John Dear, S. J.
September, 1998

APOSTLE OF PEACE
Essays in Honor of Daniel Berrigan

Edited by
JOHN DEAR

ORBIS BOOKS
Maryknoll, New York 10545

The Catholic Foreign Mission Society of America (Maryknoll) recruits and trains people for overseas missionary service. Through Orbis Books, Maryknoll aims to foster the international dialogue that is essential to mission. The books published, however, reflect the opinions of their authors and are not meant to represent the official position of the society.

Manufactured in the United States of America

Library of Congress Cataloging-in-Publication Data

Apostle of peace : essays in honor of Daniel Berrigan / edited by John Dear.
       p.   cm.
    ISBN 1-57075-062-9
    1. Berrigan, Daniel.   2. Catholics—United States—Biography.
I. Dear, John, 1959-   .
BX4705.B3845A66   1996
282'.02—dc20
    [B]   95-45430
                                                                            CIP

Father Dan Berrigan is an altogether winning and warm intelligence and a man who, I think, has more than anyone I have ever met the true wide-ranging and simple heart of the Jesuit: zeal, compassion, understanding, and uninhibited religious freedom. Just seeing him restores one's hope in the church.

—Thomas Merton in *Conjectures of a Guilty Bystander*

Dear Father Dan, I woke up thinking of you this morning with love and regret at not having been at the meeting to see you. With love, and gratitude too, for all you are doing—for the way you are spending yourself. Thank God, how the young love you. You must be utterly exhausted too, yet you keep going. Thank God, you are truly bearing the cross, giving your life for others.

—Dorothy Day in *The Catholic Worker*
(December 1972)

A Christian does what he or she must do as a Christian. Daniel Berrigan is our friend and is always welcome in our home. Any visit from him is an honor for us because he is a priest of uncommon conscience, he is a citizen of urgent moral purpose, and he is a human being of exemplary courage.

— William Stringfellow, statement to the press after Daniel Berrigan's arrest on Block Island, Rhode Island, August 11 1970

Contents

Daniel Berrigan, Apostle of Peace

An Introduction (of Sorts)

JOHN DEAR, S.J.

I first met Daniel Berrigan in the early 1980s. Dan was leading a retreat in the mountains of northeastern Pennsylvania. We stayed up late into the night talking about life in the Jesuits, peacemaking, civil disobedience, and the gospel. The next morning, I sat transfixed as Dan reflected on the scriptures, in this case, Paul's letter from prison to the Philippians. Dan wore a striped shirt that radiated every color in the rainbow. On one of the walls of the basement room where we met hung a billboard-size Corita Kent work of art screaming brightly: "POWER UP."

Dan spoke of "death as the social method of society." The world, he said, was a "kingdom of death, where everything is meshing and dying." Into this world walks the great yes of God, the Christ, "bringing trouble and all sorts of dislocations, unmaskings, lawbreakings, and truth. God comes to us unarmed. The disarmed God in Christ is the great scandal of history," he explained. "We are not yet a disarmed church because we are not yet worshipers of a disarmed God." This nonviolent Christ does "the wrong things, in the wrong places, at the wrong time, to the wrong people." Today, he concluded, "we are being asked to live out the drama of the disarmed Christ in a world armed to the teeth. To confess Jesus these days is to be working for peace."

Afterward, I met Dan in the hallway. "Thank you," I said in amazement. "I've never heard anyone speak that way about Jesus." "Well," he shrugged his shoulders and said with a smile, "sometimes you make a buck." With that, he proceeded to chuckle. For all the years I've known Dan, he has been laughing and making me and his friends laugh, whether over dinner, talking late into the night, enjoying the company of friends, sharing retreat time, sitting in a police station under arrest, or walking on Block Island or in a park. Dan keeps things light with his marvelous humor. His laughter amid the struggle keeps me and a wide circle of our friends going. We all thoroughly enjoy his company. Dan is a delight to be with.

After all these years, having lived and worked among the poor, studied the scriptures, traveled into warzones around the world, resisted war, and spent time in jail for "beating swords into plowshares," I view that first encounter with Dan as a turning point in my life. Dan was then a living ikon and mentor, but quickly became something even more profound, a dear friend. In 1984, as a Jesuit novice, I was nearly kicked out of the Society of Jesus for committing an act of nonviolent civil disobedience against U.S. warmaking at the Pentagon. "Congratulations," Dan wrote afterward. "You're in the best of companies, Company of Jesus. You've done something momentous, though humiliating and lost on most, for that Society which exists, like Christ, a 'ragged figure flitting from tree to tree at the back of the mind' (Flannery O'Connor). For this I thank you with all my heart"— and here he penned in red ink the outline of a heart. Shortly afterward, I was living in New York City, studying philosophy as part of the Jesuit course, working in a soup kitchen, and planning demonstrations with Dan's *Kairos* peace community against nuclear war preparation at the Riverside Research Institute (R.R.I.) on 42nd Street. For a few months, I lived in his Upper West Side community and shared his excellent cooking, wonderful humor, and love of life. Over the years, I was arrested repeatedly with him at R.R.I. and joined him on retreats in Pennsylvania, Virginia, Nevada, Michigan, California, and Washington, D.C. Slowly, I found myself in a new rhythm—under arrest, in jail, facing trial, on probation for resisting the imperial war machine, or planning the next action. Always, Dan is there with a smile, with a reason to laugh, a willingness to listen, and an interest in my journey. One night, after telling him my troubles and my latest adventures, he said, "Well, John, at least it ain't dull!"

In the autumn of 1993, we led a retreat for young people in the Shenandoah mountains of Virginia. Our text was the gospel of Mark. Once again, I sat transfixed, listening to Dan break open the word. He spoke of Jesus' place on the margins, on the edge, in the wilderness, away from the culture. That's where God acts, Dan quietly pointed out. A few weeks later, with Phil Berrigan, Lynn Fredriksson, and Bruce Friedrich, I walked into the Seymour Johnson Air Force Base in Goldsboro, North Carolina, into the midst of full-scale wargames, onto a tarmac with sixty F15E nuclear-capable fighter bombers. Our Pax Christi–Spirit of Life Plowshares group hammered on one of the death machines, was arrested, thrown into jail, and convicted on a felony charge. For eight months, we endured the narrow confines of a dingy county jail cell. Dan came to visit us, stood by us in court, and sent us glorious poems. One morning in our tiny cell, as I was bracing myself for another monotonous day, a television commercial for Ben and Jerry's ice cream came on. I walked into the small cell where my cellmates were watching TV and laughed aloud. Daniel Berrigan, the resister, peacemaker, truthteller, contemplative, smiled at us from the television screen. As he says no to death, he knows how to enjoy life.

When we first came to court in Elizabeth City, North Carolina, the judge and the prosecutor issued an order preventing us from discussing anything relevant, such as "nuclear weapons, U.S. foreign or domestic policy, war, peace, God, international law, Nuremberg principles, or any religious principles." In an effort to protest this charade, the four of us spoke out and then turned our backs on the court. As we did, twenty-one friends in the courtroom, including Martin Sheen, my brother Steve, and Dan, stood and turned their backs as well. Months later, after we were all found guilty, Dan wrote to me in jail: "I gotta secret for yez—which is prob'ly no secret at all. Jawe departed that pseudo temple in fury. It was the carnivores were on trial. So were all high authorities of the air force. They were self-condemned, convicted, shamed before the world. They await sentencing. The judgment may possibly be mitigated, but only on the plea of the four, whose expert testimony was taken seriously and attentively and at great length by Judge Jawe. Then he departed the court for chambers. Disgust and anger on his face bodes ill for the defendants. Can the Judge be placated? The four Noble Experts will plead night and day for those 'dwellers on the earth' who 'worship the works of their hands,' who 'abuse the widow and orphan,' whose deeds are 'the works of death.' They may perhaps prevail and win mercy, the Judge so loves them." Dan's sublime court analysis put the whole nonsensical event into perspective and buoyed my sagging spirit.

Needless to say, I would not have entered the Jesuits or remained in the Jesuits; I would not have begun struggling for justice and peace or continued that struggle today; and I would not now be a convicted felon who still longs to follow the troublemaking Jesus—if it were not for my friend and brother, Dan.

One night in jail, as I thought of a way to say thank you to Dan for all his gifts to me and to the church, it occurred to me that I should gather our friends together in one book to celebrate Dan's seventy-fifth birthday on May 9, 1996. This book, then, offers our thanks to Dan and to God for Dan's life witness. It celebrates Dan's life and pledges to carry on with Dan our ongoing resistance to the forces of death.

As I ponder Dan's life and our friendship, I turn again to the prison letters of Paul, to his epistle to the Ephesians, a text that sums up not only Dan's life, but the whole Christian calling in a world of imperial violence. Paul warns us that the life-and-death spiritual struggle we wage demands our lives, as it required Jesus' life. "Therefore," Paul concludes, "Draw your strength from the Lord":

> Put on the armor of God so that you may be able to stand firm against the tactics of the evil one. For our struggle is not with flesh and blood but with the principalities, with the powers, with the world rulers of this present darkness, with the evil spirits in the heavens. Put on the armor of God that you may be able to resist on the evil day and having done everything, to hold your ground. So stand fast with your loins girded in truth, clothed with justice as a breastplate, and your feet shod in readiness for the gospel of peace. In all circumstances, hold faith as a shield, to quench all the flaming arrows of the evil one. And take the helmet of salvation and the sword of the Spirit which is the Word of God. With all prayer and supplication, pray at every opportunity in the Spirit. To that end, be watchful with all perseverance and supplication for all the holy ones. (Ephesians 6:10-18)

Dan understands this biblical mandate to resist the principalities and powers and to live out the gospel of peace. He struggles to keep this Word and invites the rest of us to do likewise. I wish to reflect on my friend's life in the context of this Word as a way to learn from his life, his commitment, his faith in the God of life, and his steadfast resistance to the forces of death. As I grapple with the text from the vantage of Dan's life, I hope not only to learn from Dan's resistance to evil and to invigorate our commitment to resisting evil, but to celebrate Dan's love of life and refresh our own spirits for the long haul journey ahead. Through his story and the appreciations that follow in these pages, I hope that we will all be renewed in the Spirit of God to continue that great pilgrimage along the way of peace and justice.

RESISTING THE PRINCIPALITIES AND POWERS: THIS MAN IS DISARMED AND DANGEROUS

Dan was born on May 9, 1921, in Virginia, Minnesota, the fifth of six children (all boys), to Thomas and Frida Berrigan. His family moved to Syracuse, New York, where the boys grew up attending Catholic grade schools. In high school, Dan applied to the Society of Jesus. On August 14, 1939, along with his childhood friend Jack St. George, Dan entered St. Andrew-on-the-Hudson, the Jesuit novitiate (now owned by the Culinary Institute of America) near Poughkeepsie, New York. He made the Spiritual Exercises of St. Ignatius, a thirty-day silent retreat; spent several years studying philosophy and the humanities; taught at St. Peter's Prep in Jersey City, New Jersey (1946-1949); and studied at Weston School of Theology in Massachusetts (1949-1953). He was ordained a priest on June 21, 1952. In 1953, he traveled to France for the traditional Jesuit sabbatical year known as tertianship. There, his worldview expanded as he met the French "worker priests." He returned to teach at Brooklyn Prep until 1957, when he moved on to LeMoyne College in Syracuse, New York, where he taught New Testament until 1962.

Denied permission to accompany his younger brother Philip, a Josephite priest, on a Freedom Ride through the South, Dan went to Paris on sabbatical in 1963 and then to Czechoslovakia, Hungary, the Soviet Union, and South Africa. On his return, he began to speak out against U.S. military involvement in Vietnam and co-founded the Catholic Peace Fellowship. In 1964, along with his brother Philip, A. J. Muste, Jim Forest, and others, he attended a retreat on peacemaking hosted by Thomas Merton at the Abbey of Gethsemani. Merton's urgent reflections on the life and faith of Franz Jaegerstaetter, the Austrian farmer beheaded in 1943 for refusing to kill for the Nazis, made a profound impact on Dan. Together, they pledged to oppose war. In 1965, Dan marched in Selma, became assistant editor of *Jesuit Missions*, and co-founded Clergy and Laity Concerned about Vietnam. He traveled the country speaking out against the war. In November, a young Catholic Worker named Roger LaPorte immolated himself in front of the United Nations. Because Dan spoke at a Catholic Worker liturgy shortly afterward, reflecting on Roger's life and death, his Jesuit superior and New York's Cardinal Spellman ordered Dan to leave New York immediately and go to Latin America. Dan obeyed and headed south. Thousands voiced their outrage over this treatment of Dan, and he was allowed to return from exile five months later. Late in 1967, he began teaching at Cornell University. On October 22, 1967, at the Pentagon in Washington, D.C., Dan was arrested for the first time for protesting the war. "For the first time," he wrote in his journal in the D.C. jail, "I put on the prison blue jeans and denim shirt; a clerical attire I highly recommend for a new church."[1] In February 1968 he traveled with Boston University history professor Howard Zinn to North Vietnam, took cover with others in a shelter as U.S. bombs fell around them, and assisted in the release of three U.S. air force personnel.

Then, as all the world learned, on May 17, along with his brother Philip and seven others, he burned draft files with homemade napalm in Catonsville, Maryland. "Our apologies, good friends," Dan wrote in the Catonsville Nine statement, "for the fracture of good order, the burning of paper instead of children, the angering of the orderlies in the front parlor of the charnel house. We could not, so help us God, do otherwise."[2] After an explosive three-day trial in October, the nine were found guilty.

Catonsville was a turning point for Dan and many others. As Dan would write later,

> Catonsville was like a firebreak, a small fire lit, to contain and conquer a greater. The time, the place, were weirdly right. They spoke for passion, symbol, reprisal. Catonsville seemed to light up the dark places of the heart, where courage and risk and hope were awaiting a signal, a dawn. For the remainder of our lives, the fires would burn and burn, in hearts and minds, in draft boards, in prisons and courts. A new fire, new as a Pentecost, flared up in eyes deadened and hopeless, the noble powers of soul given over to the "powers of the upper air." "Nothing can be done!" How often we had heard that gasp: the last of the human, of soul, of freedom. Indeed, something could be done, and was. And would be.[3]

The Catonsville Nine offered dramatic nonviolent resistance to the war and caught the attention of the nation. Most were shocked and outraged, including and especially Catholics. Many were profoundly changed and suddenly found themselves emboldened to take similar risks because of the noble poet and his peacemaking brother and friends.

Dan traveled the country speaking out against the war and wrote passionate essays urging similar nonviolent actions for peace. "We have assumed the name of peacemakers, but we have been, by and large, unwilling to pay any significant price," Dan wrote shortly after Catonsville. "And because we want the peace with half a heart and half a life and will, the war, of course, continues, because the waging of war, by its nature, is total—but the waging of peace, by our own cowardice, is partial. . . . There is no peace because there are no peacemakers. There are no makers of peace because the making of peace is at least as costly as the making of war—at least as exigent, at least as disruptive, at least as liable to bring disgrace and prison and death in its wake."[4] Years later, he wrote, "The question for me, as peacemaking came to be a question, was one of soul, of center. The soul of peacemaking was simply the will to give one's life."[5]

With the war raging on, instead of surrendering to prison in April 1970, as the government demanded, Dan went underground. For over four months, he traveled the Northeast, speaking to the media, writing articles against the war, and occasionally appearing in public. On August 2, 1970, he preached at a Sunday worship service in Germantown, Pennsylvania. "We have chosen to be powerless criminals in a time of criminal power," he reflected. "We have chosen to be branded as peace criminals by war criminals."[6] Days later, on August 11, 1970, the FBI arrested him at the home of theologian William Stringfellow on Block Island, off the coast of Rhode Island. He was brought to the Danbury, Connecticut, Federal Prison where he spent eighteen long months. On June 9, 1971, while having his teeth examined, he suffered a massive allergic reaction to a misfired novocaine injection and nearly died. Finally, on February 24, 1972, he was released.

Dan wrote from prison:

My brother and I did not come to prison in order to reform the prison or to correct the injustices of the Federal Parole Board. We came to prison as an act of resistance against the war. And the government was acute enough to take us seriously. First, it sent us to prison for a number of years. And when we continued to resist in prison, when we refused to become cheerful robots or housebroken "model inmates," the government responded in two ways. First, it named my brother in yet one more tawdry and absurd indictment. Secondly, it refused parole to both of us. We could hardly have been paid a greater compliment. For indeed we are dangerous—dangerous to the warmaking state, dangerous in our unbroken will, dangerous in our nonviolence."[7]

After the 1972 indictments and mistrial in Harrisburg, aimed especially against Dan's brother Philip and Elizabeth McAlister, Dan joined his family and friends in a new examination of the culture's violence and the biblical requirements of nonviolence. They looked long and hard at U.S. militarism and saw that underneath the Pentagon's war in Southeast Asia lay plans for the destruction of the planet. With Phil and Liz's newly formed Jonah House community, Dan embarked on resistance as a way of life. Throughout the 1970s, 1980s, and 1990s, group members were arrested repeatedly at the White House, the Pentagon, and elsewhere for acts of nonviolent civil disobedience against U.S. nuclear policies.

"Our real shrines are nuclear installations and the Pentagon and the war research laboratories," Dan explains. "This is where we worship, allowing ourselves to hear the obscene command that we kill and be killed—a command which, it seems to me, is anti-Christ, anti-God. The mainline churches have joined this effort to make killing acceptable and normal—at least by silence."[8] The commands of Christ, on the other hand, could not be clearer: "No killing, no war, which is to say, above all, no nuclear weapons. And thence the imperative: Resist those who research, deploy or justify, on whatever grounds, such weaponry."[9]

On September 9, 1980, with Philip and six friends, Dan walked in to the General Electric plant in King of Prussia, Pennsylvania, and hammered on unarmed nuclear weapon nosecones. They were arrested, tried, convicted and faced up to ten years in prison. Their Plowshares action opened a new chapter in the history of nonviolent resistance. It stepped beyond Catonsville to the question of nuclear disarmament. More, it enfleshed the biblical command of Isaiah: "They shall beat their swords into plowshares and their spears into pruning hooks; one nation shall not raise the sword against another, nor shall they train for war again" (Isaiah 2:4). "All great moments are finally simple," Dan wrote of the action years later. "Why not, we asked our souls; why not us, our hands, our hammers? And if not us, who? So we took our small courage and our small household hammers in hand. It was, I need not add, a watershed hour for our lives—and who knows, perhaps also for the lives of others."[10]

On the stand, Dan testified to the truth before us, the imperative of nonviolence, the biblical command to disarm:

> The only message I have to the world is: We are not allowed to kill innocent people. We are not allowed to be complicit in murder. We are not allowed to be silent while preparations for mass murder proceed in our name, with our money, secretly. . . . It's terrible for me to live in a time where I have nothing to say to human beings except, "Stop killing." There are other beautiful things that I would love to be saying to people. There are other projects I could be very helpful at. And I can't do them. I cannot. Because everything is endangered. Everything is up for grabs. Ours is a kind of primitive situation, even though we would call ourselves sophisticated. Our plight is very primitive from a Christian point of view. We are back where we started. Thou shalt not kill; we are not allowed to kill. Everything today comes down to that—everything.[11]

Since that first hammer fell, over fifty Plowshares actions have occurred around the world. Dan continues regularly to break the laws which legalize mass murder. His life of nonviolent resistance finds him in and out of handcuffs, police vans, courts, and jails. He enters into this risky witness with his friends and does so as an act of prayer.

Dan has learned what St. Paul and the apostles learned—that following Jesus means peacefully, prayerfully, lovingly resisting the forces of death. Followers of Jesus, he tells us, resist the principalities and powers of death, the structures and forces which normalize war and "the metaphors of death." "We resist because we believe and we believe because we keep resisting," Dan writes.[12] As long as the United

States continues to maintain weapons of mass destruction and practices systemic violence against humanity, Dan keeps on following the biblical admonition to resist. For Dan, resistance is intrinsic to Christianity. It is a way to be human in inhuman times.

STANDING FAST IN TRUTH:
THE PEN IS MIGHTIER THAN THE SWORD—INDEED

Like St. Paul, Gandhi, Dorothy Day, and other resisters, Dan is a writer. To date, he has published some forty books of poetry, prose, and drama. He writes about truth and how we must act out the truth simply because it is truthful. We do the good simply because it is right to do it, he explains. Let go of results; get beyond success and efficiency; stand fast in the truth and leave the outcome in God's hands. Tell the truth and say your prayers, he suggests.

In his search for truth, Dan the poet and writer employs a new vocabulary. He speaks of "the abattoir," "anomie," and "acedia." He reflects on grace and fecundity as "lagniappe." As a writer, Dan is never, "so to speak," bromidic, or worse, mawkish. His many books make a lively "pastiche." His first book, *Time Without Number*, won the 1957 Lamont Poetry Award and was nominated for the National Book Award. His early works include *The Bride: Essays in the Church*; *Encounters*; *The Bow in the Clouds*; *The World for Wedding Ring*; *No One Walks Waters*; *They Call Us Dead Men*; *Love, Love at the End*; and *False Gods, Real Men*. His 1967 book, *Consequences: Truth and...*, chronicles his journeys to Selma, South Africa and Latin America. His diary, *Night Flight to Hanoi*, records his journey to North Vietnam.

After Catonsville, Dan's writing takes on a new urgency. His passion urges others to resist war. *No Bars to Manhood* tells his own story and includes fiery essays on the scriptures, "the times," Gandhi, and the need for civil disobedience. His play, *The Trial of the Catonsville Nine*, perhaps Dan's most widely known work, brings the testimony of resistance to audiences around the world. His stunning work *The Dark Night of Resistance*, written during Dan's months underground, offers St. John of the Cross's *Dark Night of the Soul* imagery as a guide for resisters. With Robert Coles, he published *The Geography of Faith*, "conversations while underground." *America Is Hard to Find* gathers together his letters and articles from the underground and prison, while *Trial Poems, Prison Poems*, and *Jesus Christ* offer his visionary hopes for prisoners and for peace. *Lights on in the House of the Dead*, his journal from Danbury prison, records his day-to-day prison struggles and reflections. *Selected and New Poems*, published in 1973, collects the best of his poetry up until then. *Absurd Convic-*

tions, Modest Hopes, a collection of interviews with Lee Lockwood, recounts the story of Dan's life underground, on trial, and in prison.

After he emerged from prison, Dan's writing deepened and matured as he explored the roots of faith and resistance. His book with Thich Nhat Hanh, *The Raft Is Not the Shore,* records their conversations on peacemaking from Christian and Buddhist perspectives. *A Book of Parables* retells familiar biblical tales from new angles. Chapters include "The Prison Letters of Cain"; "The Patience of Job in Detroit"; "A Brief Press Conference with God on the Fate of a Favorite Son"; and "Jeremiah or God Is a Downer." In *Uncommon Prayer,* Dan interprets the poetry of the Psalms from within our nuclear madness as pleas for disarmament and liberation. In *Beside the Sea of Glass* and *The Nightmare of God,* Dan unpacks the book of Revelation as a manifesto for radical discipleship to the nonviolent Christ for those living in empires. In *The Words Our Savior Gave Us,* he meditates on the Lord's Prayer. In *Whereon to Stand: The Acts of the Apostles and Ourselves,* he reflects about the early church as a community of resisters, models for our own active nonviolence. *The Discipline of the Mountain* delves poetically into Dante's *Purgatorio* as a metaphor of the world on the brink of nuclear destruction. *Homage to Gerard Manley Hopkins,* a book-length poem, offers not only Dan's gratitude to the great Jesuit poet but Dan's own poetic appeal to faith. *Jubilee* and *May All Creatures Live* celebrate Dan's poetic vision of Jesus and Dan's own gospel adventures. *Isaiah* probes the text of the prophet for application to our own turbulent times, while *Minor Prophets, Major Themes,* written during the Gulf War massacre, offers the biblical texts as sources for strength for the work of truth-telling.

In the last twenty years, Dan has published many journals and accounts of his life works. *We Die Before We Live* chronicles his experiences among the dying at St. Rose's home in New York City. *Sorrow Built a Bridge* shares his ministry and friendships with AIDS patients. *Steadfastness of the Saints* recounts his 1984 pilgrimage to El Salvador and Nicaragua. *The Mission* records his 1985 experience as an advisor on the set of the motion picture about the Jesuit Reductions in South America. *Portraits* profiles his friends and mentors, including Thomas Merton and Dorothy Day. *Stations* offers stark verse meditations on the modern-day stations of the cross lived out by Christ in the homeless poor. *Block Island* gathers poems written at William Stringfellow's island hermitage. *Ten Commandments for the Long Haul* muses on the years after his release from prison, calls Christians to radical discipleship, and presents Dan's biblical lesson plan for the long-term witness. His autobiography, *To Dwell in Peace,* published in 1988, chronicles the story of his life and remains, to my mind, a classic of resistance literature.

CLOTHED WITH JUSTICE, SHOD WITH THE GOSPEL OF PEACE—
OR HOW YOU TOO CAN MAKE A DIFFERENCE

"If you want to follow Jesus," Dan once said, "you better look good on wood." Dan's life of resistance spans the whole spectrum of justice and peace. He sees the struggle as one, a seamless garment of nonviolence. Throughout the years, as Dan taught, wrote, and spoke out for justice and peace, he has done so in defense of the poor and marginalized. Over the years, he has marched in Selma for civil rights; walked with Dorothy Day and the homeless; accompanied those dying of cancer and AIDS; stood with the oppressed in South Africa, Central America, Eastern Europe, Russia, the Middle East, and Ireland; supported dignity for gays and equality for women; and guarded the unborn and those on death row. Everywhere he goes he offers a consistent no to death, and a gentle yes to life.

Throughout his public journey, Dan has suffered for these stands, as his friends know. Church leaders, Jesuits, reporters, politicians, the FBI, and all sorts of people have attacked him for his witness. Nonetheless, Dan persists with his quiet, modest witness for justice and peace, in season and out. Whether attracting national media coverage or ignored by everyone, Dan keeps on keeping on. Like his great friends Thomas Merton, Dorothy Day, and William Stringfellow, he takes a faithful stand for life. His long-haul steadfastness may be his greatest gift. As so many reflect in this book, Dan remains faithful. For the faithful, fidelity—not results, not success, not power—is all that matters.

A message he wrote for Catonsville sums up his struggle, and the challenge before us all today:

We say killing is disorder, life and gentleness and community and unselfishness is the only order we recognize. For the sake of that order, we risk our liberty, our good name. The time is past when good people can remain silent, when obedience can segregate people from public risk, when the poor can die without defense. We ask our fellow Christians to consider in their hearts a question which has tortured us night and day. How many must die before our voices are heard, how many must be tortured, dislocated, starved, maddened? How long must the world's resources be raped in the service of legalized murder? When, at what point, will you say no to this war? We have chosen to say, with the gift of our liberty, if necessary our lives: the violence stops here, the death stops here, the suppression of the truth stops here, this war stops here.

Redeem the times! The times are inexpressibly evil. Christians pay conscious, indeed religious tribute, to Caesar and Mars: by the approval of overkill tactics, by brinkmanship, by nuclear liturgies, by racism, by support of genocide. They embrace their society with all their heart, and abandon the cross. They pay lip service to Christ and military service to the powers of death.

And yet, and yet, the times are inexhaustibly good, solaced by the courage and hope of many. The truth rules; Christ is not forsaken. In a time of death, some—the resisters, those who work hardily for social change, those who preach and embrace the unpalatable truth—such overcome death, their lives are bathed in the light of the resurrection, the truth has set them free. In the jaws of death, of contumely, of good and ill report, they proclaim their love of humanity.

We think of such women and men in the world, in the churches; and the stone in our breast is dissolved. We take heart once more.[13]

HOLDING THE SHIELD OF FAITH, THE HELMET OF SALVATION, AND THE SWORD OF THE WORD OF GOD

Fidelity, Dan quietly insists, requires taking Jesus at his word. "Blessed are the peacemakers. Love your enemies. Love one another. Put down your sword. Be compassionate like God." Jesus stands at the center of Dan's life. Over and over again, Dan keeps pointing us back to Jesus:

Once there was a dead man, a criminal, a subject of capital punishment. And lo! he refused to stay dead. He stood up. As the authorities shortly came to sense, this was an earthquake in nature; in the nature of law and order, in the nature of death, the nature of war. For in the nature of things, as defined by the nation state (a great one for deciding what the nature of things is)—dead people stay dead. The word from Big Brother, the word that gives him clout, inspires fear, is—A criminal, once disposed of, stays disposed! Not at all; along come these crazies shouting in public, "Our man's not dead; He's risen!" Now I submit you can't have such a word going around, and still run the state properly. The first nonviolent revolution was, of course, the Resurrection. The event had to include death as its first act. And also the command to Peter, "Put up your sword." So that it might be clear, once and for all, that Christians suffer death rather than inflict it.[14]

While underground, Dan wrote an open letter to the Weathermen, an underground group of violent antiwar rebels. "The death of a single human is too heavy a price to pay for the vindication of any principle, however sacred," Dan observes.[15] His message was taken to heart; they renounced their violence. In an open letter to Ernesto Cardenal of the Solentiname community in Nicaragua, he again respectfully lays out the biblical mandate of nonviolence: "Alas, I have never seen anyone morally improved by killing; neither the one who aimed the bullet, nor the one who received it in his or her flesh."[16] Unfortunately, this invitation, like others, went unanswered.

Once, while traveling in Europe, an internationally known moral theologian announced: "The Berrigans are off base; they are talking about the Sermon on the Mount as though it were realizable now. What we really need is an ethic of the interim." Dan commented later:

An ethic of the interim, as I understand it, would allow us to fill the gap between today and tomorrow with the bodies of all who must die, before we accept the word of Christ. On the contrary, I think the Sermon on the Mount concerns us here and now, or concerns us never. In whatever modest and clumsy way, we are called to honor the preference of Christ for suffering rather than inflicting suffering, for dying rather than killing; in that sense, all "interim ethics" have been cast aside. The time to obey is now.[17]

All this is to say that Dan takes God at God's word: Thou shalt not kill; put away your sword and love your enemies. These are the unpopular but cornerstone commandments of the scriptures, and Dan has spent his life obeying them, fulfilling them, and teaching them. He loves the Word and teaching that Word to others. Dan is a born teacher. In classrooms across the country, from LeMoyne College to Cornell University, to the Graduate Theological Union at the University of California at Berkeley and Union Theological Seminary, to DePaul University and Loyola University–New Orleans, Dan has been sharing his wit and wisdom. Over the years, he has taught "New Testament Theology," "Faith and Nonviolence" and "The Poetry and Literature of Prisoners." More than one class has been offered the opportunity for nonviolent civil disobedience to nearby war preparations. Throughout his journey, he has deepened his love of the Bible and its application to the struggle for justice and peace. In recent years, he has studied the book of Isaiah, the Psalms, the apocalyptic writings of Daniel, the minor prophets, the Gospel According to Mark, the Acts of the Apostles, and the book of Revelation. In countless retreats across the country, Dan shares his insights and reveals the wisdom of the scriptures to thousands of people. Nearly every weekend, Dan can be found at some podium quietly reflecting on the Word of God.

As a writer, speaker, and teacher, as a Christian, Dan epitomizes the best of our religious order, the Society of Jesus. Dan entered the Jesuits intrigued by their revolutionary history and remains just as intrigued today, fifty-seven years later, despite many ups and downs. When Thomas Merton first met Dan at the Abbey of Gethsemani in the early 1960s, Merton wrote in his journal (subsequently published as *Conjectures of a Guilty Bystander*) that Dan is "an altogether winning and warm intelligence and a man who, I think, has more than anyone I have ever met the true wide-ranging and simple heart of the Jesuit: zeal, compassion, understanding, and uninhibited religious freedom. Just seeing him restores one's hope in the church."[18] In a letter to a friend (on September 20, 1962), Merton wrote: "Daniel Berrigan . . . is a man full of fire, the right kind, and a real Jesuit, of which there are not too many, perhaps. . . . He is alive and full of spirit and truth. I think he will do much for the church in America and so will his brother Phil, the only priest so far to have gone on a Freedom Ride. They will have a hard time, though, and will have to pay for every step forward with their blood."[19] How right Merton was!

Over a lifetime in the Jesuits, Dan has been ostracized, exiled, ignored, accepted, embraced, and loved. To me and to our friends, Dan represents the best of the Jesuit ideal—a broad vision for humanity; a desire for God's greater glory, for the nonviolent coming of God's reign here and now; a dedication to the universal good; a passion for justice and peace; a discerning eye; a love for prayer, solitude, scripture, Eucharist, and friends; a willingness to sacrifice; a spirit of detachment; a sense of mission; and a contemplative, heartfelt devotion to Jesus. When the Central American Jesuits called upon North American Jesuits to stand in solidarity with them as they faced opposition for their denunciation of injustice, Dan responded and journeyed to Nicaragua and El Salvador to learn and listen to the suffering peoples and our noble Jesuit brothers. Five years later, on November 16, 1989, when Ignacio Ellacuría and the Jesuits of El Salvador, along with Elba and Celina Ramos, were assassinated, Dan was shocked and outraged by their martyrdom but equally proud and challenged by the witness of their blood. Teaching at Loyola University in New Orleans at the time, he joined people of faith to protest U.S. military aid to El Salvador. With two other Jesuits and many other friends, he staged a sit-in in the elevators of the fifteen-story Federal Building. As people blocked entrances to Federal Buildings around the country, Dan's witness sent a clear message: "Not one more dime for death squad governments. We won't stand for it!"

Since the early 1970s, Dan has lived at the West Side Jesuit Community in New York City. His apartment walls are covered with bright artworks, ikons, and pictures of "the cloud of witnesses" he has known during his life. We, his brothers, enjoy his gourmet cooking, his humor, his undying interest in others, and his caring service to community members, especially those who are ill. Most of all, we love him and his company. Dan makes living in community a blessing. Dan is the best of friends.

PRAYING IN THE SPIRIT, KEEPING WATCH:
A CONTEMPLATIVE SENTRY AT A WILDERNESS POST

A resister to state-sanctioned violence and a dedicated advocate of justice, Dan remains a true contemplative. He can be a peacemaker because he takes private time with the God of peace. He tends the roots of his spiritual life. He offers the Eucharist and spends time in silence and solitude. This grounding in contemplative prayer gives Dan the strength to stand publicly for peace. It enables him to take risky action for justice and peace. It makes him hopeful, generous, forgiving, and joyful. In prayer, Dan fulfills his vocation not only to resist institutionalized violence but to keep watch for the nonviolent coming of God in our midst.

In 1991, shortly after the Persian Gulf war, hundreds of us gathered in the Nevada desert to pray together, reflect on the days ahead for peacemakers, and cross the line in opposition to nuclear weapons testing. During the opening evening prayer, Dan sat on my left and Jim Wallis of *Sojourners* magazine sat on my right. After our prayer time, the organizers asked that we turn to those around us and discuss what we might do to oppose militarism. Dan and Jim turned and looked at me. So I spoke first. "We need to reorganize the peace movement," I declared. "We need to mobilize people around the country to come forward by the thousands, eventually by the millions, to demand disarmament and justice. We need to wake people up to the realities of war and its destructive consequences for our nation." After going on at length in this fashion, I finally concluded (much to their relief). There was a long pause. Dan turned to me and said quietly, "I just think we need to unleash the contemplative springs within."

I fell silent before the beauty and simplicity of Dan's dream. Dan's answer not only sums up the peacemaking task before us, but his life work as well. His effort to unleash the contemplative springs within his own soul and within others continues to bear fruit. As a resister, poet, writer, and Jesuit, Dan keeps the focus, rightly, on the God of peace.

THE PEACEMAKER'S HOPE: RESURRECTION OF THE HEART

"All we have to do is close our eyes and then open them," Dan once said to me. "I mean, close our eyes to our culture and open them to our friends. We've got enough to go on. We don't have a right to the luxury of despair."[20] Dan's message is a word of profound hope in a culture of entrenched violence and deep despair. Because Dan believes in God, prays to God, resists evil, and seeks truth, Dan's witness for peace inspires hope, hope not only in the nonviolent social change that is happening all around us, but hope in the God of compassion and peace, who is transforming us all, leading us into a new nonviolent world of life and joy, where every tear, every fear, and every trace of death will be wiped away. Jesus reverses Dante, Dan once commented, and proclaims to us all, "Take on hope all ye who enter here."

I think that Dan is filled with hope because he believes in the resurrection of Christ. He does not stop at the cross; he looks beyond to the beckoning Risen One. Speaking about the apostles, Dan notes that " 'witness of the resurrection' was the self-conferred title of honor of the early twelve. It meant they stood by life, to the point of undergoing death, as well as death's analogous punishments: floggings, scorn, jail. Their understanding was: where there could be no debate, there could be no combat. This is our glory, from Peter and Paul to Martin King and Romero. We know how to live and how to die."[21] In this journey of suffering and resisting death, Dan confesses that he and his friends have "tasted the resurrection of new life." In a world brimming with death, he proclaims resurrection.

"Peacemaking goes nowhere and yet it must be done," Dan once said. "That is the message of my life." Dan is a true apostle of peace.

In celebration then of seventy-five faith-filled years, a life of resistance and contemplation, saying yes and saying no, standing somewhere and sitting somewhere, walking forward despite the rocky road, sowing seeds of nonviolence and hope in a land of violence and despair, from a wide circle of friends, companions and admirers—this word of gratitude for your peacemaking life. Happy birthday, brother Dan. Let the celebrations begin!

NOTES

1. Daniel Berrigan, *Night Flight to Hanoi* (New York: Macmillan Co., 1968), 7.

2. Ibid., xvi.

3. Daniel Berrigan, *To Dwell in Peace* (San Francisco: Harper & Row, 1987), 220-21.

4. Daniel Berrigan, *No Bars to Manhood* (New York: Bantam Books, 1970), 48-49.

5. Berrigan, *To Dwell in Peace*, 163-65.

6. Daniel Berrigan, "Sermon from the Underground," in Stephen Halpert and Tom Murray, eds., *Witness of the Berrigans* (New York: Doubleday, 1972), 142.

7. Daniel Berrigan, "A Letter from Jail," in Ed Guinan, ed., *Peace and Nonviolence* (New York: Paulist Press, 1973), 13.

8. John Deedy, "Apologies, Good Friends": An Interim Biography of Daniel Berrigan, S.J. (Chicago: Fides/Claretian, 1981), 128-29.

9. Daniel Berrigan, "Swords into Plowshares," in Michael True, ed., *Daniel Berrigan: Poetry, Drama, Prose* (Maryknoll, N.Y.: Orbis Books, 1988), 182.

10. Daniel Berrigan, "Christian Peacemakers in the Warmaking State," in Leroy S. Rouner, ed., *Celebrating Peace* (Notre Dame, Ind.: University of Notre Dame Press, 1990), 182-83.

11. Daniel Berrigan, "The Push of Conscience," in Jim Wallis and Joyce Hollyday, eds., *Cloud of Witnesses* (Maryknoll, N.Y.: Orbis Books, 1991), 227.

12. Daniel Berrigan, "The Peacemaker," in Patrick Hart, ed., *Thomas Merton / Monk* (Kalamazoo, Mich.: Cistercian Publications, 1983), 226.

13. Berrigan, *Night Flight to Hanoi*, xviii-xix.

14. Daniel Berrigan, "The Box Within a Box: A Tale of Chastened Expectations," in Dedria Bryfonski, ed., *Contemporary Authors: Autobiography Series*, vol. 1 (Detroit: Gale Research Co., 1984), 58.

15. Daniel Berrigan, *America Is Hard to Find* (New York: Doubleday, 1972), 95.

16. True, *Daniel Berrigan: Poetry, Drama, Prose*, 170.

17. Hart, *Thomas Merton / Monk*, 226.

18. Thomas Merton, *Conjectures of a Guilty Bystander* (New York: Image Books, 1968), 251.

19. Robert Daggy, ed., *The Road to Joy: The Letters of Thomas Merton* (New York: Farrar, Straus, Giroux, 1989), 241.

20. "All We Have to Do Is Close Our Eyes and Open Them: A Conversation with Daniel Berrigan," *Pax Christi* (March 1986), 15.

21. Quoted in *The National Jesuit News* (October 1982).

THE PROPHET

Troublesome Image, Hopeful Sign

JOAN CHITTISTER, O.S.B.

Scripture gives us images we think we'll never see in life. We strain to understand them. We struggle to explain them. We hesitate to use them. We shy away from talking about them. We act as if they are not real, could never be real, are somehow or other beyond real. Yet, down deep, we are moved by them to depths beyond depth. This age has had such a one. His name is Berrigan, and the scripture he brings to life before our eyes has broken open the heart of the modern church.

Four images cry for recognition if we are to be able to find and follow the pathfinders present to every age but too often obscured by the clamor and conflict of the times in which they live. The lion of Judah, the lamb of God, David and Goliath, and the Holy One of Israel are signposts of the prophetic call. Every great period of history spawns all four. We should know; we have seen the lion roar, watched the lamb struggle, seen the little ones confront the powerful, and felt the presence of holiness in our midst.

To those who are really holy, of course, holiness is an embarrassment. Dorothy Day abhorred it. Thomas Merton laughed at it. Oscar Romero denied it. Martin Luther King despised the burden of it. Dan Berrigan, therefore, will not like this piece. But this piece is not for Dan Berrigan to like or to dislike; it is for the rest of us to pause before in wonder. And admiration. And challenge.

A span as wide and impassible as eternity lies between the trappings of holiness and the substance of it. Berrigan brings us face to face with its substance. Dan Berrigan's gift to the church has been to remind all of us, one more time, of lions and sheep, of slingshots and holiness.

Berrigan brought to the church a mighty roar at a time when the American church was just becoming comfortable with the role of loyal citizen. A Catholic presidency had taken the sting out of papism. The Catholic war dead of World War II gave proof of Catholic patriotism.

Catholic quietism in a time of moral confusion gave hope of Catholic integration in the civil religion. While Vietnamese villages burned and American youth moved over the border out of the reach of military conscription, the Catholic hierarchy stood by passively, said nothing, rocked no boats. Then Berrigan broke the Catholic spell and shook the Catholic establishment itself.

Berrigan castigated the church that teaches peace for its lack of peacemaking. He held up to it a mirror filled with its own hypocrisy, its own truth. While bishops said nothing about the planned nuclear destruction of the world and nuns taught catechism without a conscious nod to the sins of society and priests preached platitudes but not a word about the need for present day prophets and the laity made money on the war machines of the Christian world, Dan Berrigan roared in the faces of both church and state the gospel's classic cry: "Put away your sword," "Love one another," "Turn the other cheek," "Jerusalem, Jerusalem. . . ."

No one liked it, but everyone listened to the sound of draft cards burning and found their own lives changed as well. Berrigan simply stood in place while the rest of us squirmed. He forced us to take a reluctant stand against the forces of death and destruction that throttled all the values of Americanism in the name of "defense."

By not moving at all, he moved the glacier of our hearts. It is not that a prophet converts us. The function of the prophet is simply to force us to choose. Prophets make sure that we do not die from complacency and lack of conviction. They force us instead to die of harder things, of sterner stuff, of more pressing pain than painlessness.

In the presence of the prophet, lukewarmness is a sin. In the presence of the prophet, we can only be hot or cold. Berrigan taught us the temperature of our souls.

Dan Berrigan exposed the church to itself and each of us with it. His mighty roar penetrated the walls of my convent and hundreds of others like ours and gave us a chance to be real religious instead of plastic statues of a misplaced piety. Dan blared and bellowed and howled at us until the prayers we prayed became the life we lived. Dan Berrigan brought truth to piety, the sword to what had turned to saccharine, the gospel to the church. Berrigan was embarrassing and troublesome and terrible. He was the discomfort of us all, the conscience of a church too long comatose.

More than raging lion, though, Dan stood in our midst, gray and wan and thin and quiet as a lamb led to slaughter as well. They hunted him down, as systems always do to those who most unmask them, and bowing to its power, Berrigan emasculated it by refusing to become what he hated. They jailed him, but they could not silence him. His docile defiance took them down. Where it was hard, he was soft. Where it was predator, he was sheep. The fact is that it is not true that sheep go docile to slaughter. On the contrary, sheep squirm and squeal and run and resist the butchering sword with all their might. The only difference between the sheep and other animals in danger is that when cornered, though sheep scuffle, they do not bite. They do not attack what attacks them. They do not hate the hunter. They do not kill the killer. Berrigan smiled at jailers and prayed for prosecutors and tipped his head to judges. Berrigan brought the peace he proclaimed to the struggle he led. In him we saw resistance without reprisal, opposition without vengeance. It was the sight of defenselessness, of Berrigan the poet-priest, oppressed in our midst, that brought us to see the real face of the evil that called itself good, the militarism that called itself freedom, the destructiveness that called itself defense. From his jail cell, he led a mighty revolution of ideas. He was himself proof of the point: the system that jails its sheep bears watching.

Was he right to oppose the state through civil disobedience? Was he right to burn draft cards, to hide from the FBI, to lecture the state in its own courtrooms, to push the theology of the church to its outside limits by insisting that the "Peace be with you" of the Christian liturgy really demanded "Peace be to you" in the Christian's life? He took the symbols of religion and made them real. For the first time in modern history, being a Christian became a choice of values rather than a set of denominational niceties.

More than that, Berrigan persisted in his peace-mongering, his goading, his debunking of heroic myth, long after the crisis of trumped-up dangers had turned into the calm of ordinary, insidious, systemic evils. Berrigan, a David figure, took on the military Goliath of society long after most saw it as dangerous anymore. With the wars over, he kept calling the attention of the public to the warmakers who lurked under every piece of legislation, every item in the national budget. He attacked weapons of massive destruction with carpenter's tools. He broke into the most private of military sites to prove their public presence, their pathetic and ever-present malevolence. He made a fool of himself for the most foolish of reasons—the gospel—just when the church had finally been able to assert its political passivity and win, thereby, the most questionable of political approval. He did not win, of course—the powerless seldom do—but he did provide a triumph of conscience for all of us to see.

Even now, the establishment goes on budgeting for human destruction rather than human development. The states goes on imposing its military will. But the poet Berrigan, the jailbird Berrigan, the priest Berrigan, the prophet Berrigan stands as sign to the rest of us that the only thing that makes it possible is ourselves.

Berrigan brought to the church another kind of witness as well. Berrigan brought the presence of the kind of priest who cares for more than the vessels of the altar and the plastic respect of the Christian community and the symbols of sacraments seldom made real. He forgave the country's enemies and refused to maintain them. He made community out of the world. He chose the gospel over the institution. He confronted the legislation and resisted the lawgivers who cared for no law above the law. He made holiness an everyday affair instead of an exercise in private pieties. He took the priesthood from the pulpit to the streets and so gave it a pulpit heard round the world. He treated the streets of the United States like the roads of Galilee and led ragtag groups of determined disciples ransacking through the mansions of propriety that kept us more spiritually catatonic than authentically Christian.

Dan Berrigan is a troublesome soul, an irritating presence, an unforgettable memory, an immovable embarrassment for a people who prefer public approval to public contention of conscience. He challenges the church and defies the state. He contests with the mighty and gives hope to the weak. He makes the rest of us think.

Who is Dan Berrigan to the church? He is roaring lion and harmless sheep, slinger of stones against a mountain of dynamite, and prophetic priest in a church full of clerical professionals. He is the human voice of the gospel, the scourge of a domesticated church. He is Christian run amuck. He is the Jesus question let loose upon the land where once only the institution had been.

After Berrigan, the church spoke out, the nuns spoke out, the youth spoke out, the bishops spoke out. It costs him his entire life, of course. It costs us our complacency.

For myself, I mourn that complacency. Since Dan Berrigan the draftcard burner, the missile smasher, the government gadfly, the poet of practice walked through my life, I have had to confront every issue, ask every question of myself, put the scripture before the symbols, become a more real person than a plaster statue of a religion gone sour. It is no game plan for winning popularity contests but, down deep now, of one thing I am sure: the spiritual life is no excuse for Christian cowardice, no place for the weak and wimpish. And one more thing is equally certain: as long as the Berrigans of the world bring to life for the rest of us scriptural images that make the prophets plain, the world with all its dangers will be forever safe and someday, perhaps, full of lions and sheep, slingshots and holy ones.

An Easy Essay for a Post-Modern Ezekiel

(In Honor of Daniel Berrigan on His 75th Birthday)

RICHARD ROHR, O.F.M.

Surely many have said this before, or seen it.
Surely Yahweh would give this errant age its own:
A visionary priest who loves the Law, but too
    much.

"The Lord Yahweh says this, 'Whether they listen
    or not,
this set of rebels shall know there has been a
    prophet among them.'" (Ezekiel 2:5)

"There are thorns all around you and scorpions
    beneath you, but
do not be afraid of their words or their looks,
for they are a set of rebels." (2:6)

We tire of your mimes and charades:
Toy soldiers, war games, gashing and
cutting of hair,
Packing your baggage and leaving the imperial
    city,
Guerrilla theater of the absurd!
Prophet against the court prophets,
Poor Gog and Magog are just following their
    script.

Who will rid us of this troublesome priest?
"Siege and exile, Siege and exile" is all he knows of.
Is there no comfort, no consolation?

"We want a love song beautifully sung to music . . .
They throng toward you, they sit down in front of
  you
and listen to your words, but they do not act on them.
They cannot discern the truth." (33:31)

The nation indulges you; fellow priests avert their
  gaze,

Even the fashionable and enlightened are busy and
  embarrassed,
at these untimely words from a member of the
  Society.
Why not be a member of society?!

Or perhaps Daniels always like dens.
Ezekiels get lost in their bizarre visions.
Patronize the old fellow!

Surely, we are not "dry bones"?
It's Egypt that is the crocodile
"snorting through its nostrils, churning the water
  with its feet,
muddying our streams." (32:2)

We have the temple, the capital city.
Surely Jerusalem is forever and chosen.

But there you go with your mimes again
Insulting an intelligent populace:

"The people of this country have taken to extortion
  and banditry;
they have oppressed the poor and needy and ill
  treated the settler, for no reason" (22:29)
as he "lies on his *Left side*" in the public square.
Even scripture asserts it: 4:4 (Surely a later gloss).
Ye gads!
Whose God does he speak of?

The scroll that he displays is written on front and
  back:
"lamentations, wailings, mournings." (2:10)

But he eats it and asks us to eat!
"Satisfying . . . and as sweet as honey." (3:3)

This sentry of God signs us with the Tau. (9:4)
(Even sons of Francis take notice!)
"Remember, be covered with good shame, and in
    your confusion
be reduced to silence:
I have pardoned all that you have done,
It is the Lord Yahweh who speaks." (16:63)

Transported in vision, it seems
A different world he cares about
Where "a river flows through and from the temple . . .
And flowing into the sea it makes its waters
    wholesome . . .
Fish will be very plentiful . . .
On either bank, fruit trees with leaves that will not
    wither,
and fruit that never fails . . . good to eat and
    medicinal" (47:9-12)
And chariots take him there!

But he returns.
With awe before the Mysteries:

Speaking of shepherd more than king,
Grace *before* conversion,
"New hearts and new Spirit."

Perhaps?

But these footnotes, this small print he writes large:
His Holy God "stunts tall trees and makes the low
    ones grow,"
His loins of fire "wither green trees and makes the
    withered green." (17:24)
This is Apocalypse—now.
Who needs it?
What we need is the line-item veto, as King Ronald
    told us.

Seer, see no visions, if this is the outcome,
Syracuse might still have need of you.

"Can you explain the meaning these actions have
    for us?" (24:20)
None, we think
Business is good at the shipyards and young men
    went to prophet school
Until you began your antics—and we our agonies.

New Ezekiel does not stay in Syracuse,
or even in proper residence.

He shouts in word and street and city jail
Because of the insistent vision:
"You will speak and not be dumb anymore;
you are to be a sign for them,
and they will learn that I am Yahweh." (24:27)

There is only one message, prophet, only one
(From "the eternal solitudes" it comes):

The temple is not in Jerusalem.
The temple is not in Samaria or Rome.
The temple is not in London or by the river
    Moskva.
The temple is not in Washington or Hollywood.
The temple is not a Pentagon or a Street of Walls.
The temple is not in any temple.

So do not believe them when they say, "Lo, here!"
    or "Lo, there!"

The One signed by the Tau has told us,
The temple is *in you forever.* (37:28)
"The name of the future city is clear: Yahweh is
    here." (48:35)

God's sentry,
You have protected and guarded,
an open secret:
The Divine image in all that is matter.

Prophet and Pastor

RICHARD DEATS

Rabbi Abraham Joshua Heschel, long-time friend of Dan Berrigan, wrote in his book *The Prophets*:

The world is a proud place, full of beauty, but the prophets are scandalized, and rave as if the whole world were a slum. . . . To us, a single act of injustice—cheating in business, exploitation of the poor—is slight; to the prophets, a disaster. To us, injustice is injurious to the welfare of the people; to the prophets, a death-blow to existence; to us, an episode; to them, a catastrophe, a threat to the world. . . .

The prophet is a person who feels fiercely. God has thrust a burden upon his soul, and he is bowed and stunned before humanity's fierce greed. Frightful is the agony of humankind; no human voice can convey its full terror. Prophecy is the voice that God has lent to silent agony, a voice to the plundered poor, to the profaned riches of the world.

The prophets of ancient Israel recoiled at the injustice inflicted upon the powerless by the rich and powerful and at the complicity of the religious establishment in profaning the claims of a righteous God. Brooding in the hills of Tekoa, Amos thundered, "Let justice roll down like waters, and righteousness like an everflowing stream" (Amos 5:24). Isaiah shocked his hearers by saying that God is repulsed by the shallow religious practices that are no more than vain offerings, of incense that is an abomination. Speaking in the name of God, he says:

> Even though you make many prayers, I will not
>   listen;
> your hands are full of blood.
> Wash yourselves; make yourselves clean;
> remove the evil of your doings

> from before my eyes;
> cease to do evil,
> learn to do good;
> seek justice,
> correct oppression;
> defend the parentless,
> plead for the widow. (Isaiah 1:15-17)

Micah, too, cries out at the injustice and greed, even as he lifts up a vision of a time that is coming:

> They shall beat their swords into plowshares,
> and their spears into pruning hooks;
> nation shall not lift up sword against nation,
> neither shall they train for war any more;
> but they shall sit every one of them under
> their vine and fig tree,
> and none shall be afraid. (Micah 4:3-4)

Dan Berrigan stands in this prophetic tradition, which is immersed in the world and yet discerns what is happening with the eyes of faith, breaking through idolatry, complacency, and indifference to call men and women to accountability to the demands of the God's righteousness.

Dan grew up in a home where *The Catholic Worker* was read, where faith was expected to have significant consequences. The radical implications of the gospel were not forgotten in the Berrigan household. Thus when Dan was ordained into the priesthood in the early fifties, it is not surprising that he brought his students to the Lower East Side of New York City for exposure to the poor and to those who were ministering to them in Christ's name. Over the years, Dorothy Day helped him see the strong connection between the needs of the poor and the warfare state that brutalizes conscience and devours inordinate resources to produce the machinery of death.

The burgeoning civil rights movement exposed the deep sin of racism in American society. Dan threw himself into that struggle, and in 1965 he joined in the march in Selma. But in those Cold War years, with the nuclear arms race pointing to Armageddon and U.S. foreign policy moving into third-world societies, Dan more and more became a leading advocate of the anti-war movement. With fellow pacifists in the Catholic Peace Fellowship (which he helped found) and the Fellowship of Reconciliation, Dan—through his writing and preaching and activism—appealed to the U.S. religious conscience to turn from the way of war to the gospel of peace.

His first arrest came in 1967 in Washington, D.C. at a protest against the Vietnam war. He had no intention of getting arrested, but when he saw how those arrested, mainly students, were being treated, he joined them for a week's stay in jail.

The next year, he and his brother Phil joined seven others using homemade napalm to burn draft files in a parking lot next to the Selective Service Board in Catonsville, Maryland. A nation that had sat before TV sets watching villages, children, women, and men in Southeast Asia burn down with napalm was outraged that government property—about three hundred draft files—was burned. Just as a century earlier, William Lloyd Garrison burned the U.S. Constitution to protest slavery, the Catonsville Nine burned pieces of paper to scorch the conscience of America.

After the trial, sentencing, and appeal, Dan went underground for four months, staying with thirty-seven families in ten Eastern and Midwestern cities, all the while eluding the FBI even as he surfaced from time to time to preach and to be interviewed on radio and TV. At the First United Methodist Church in Germantown, Pennsylvania, he preached on faithfulness to the gospel: "For my brother and myself, the choice is already made. We have chosen to be powerless criminals in a time of criminal power. We have chosen to be branded as peace criminals by war criminals." He spoke of "a hundred ways of nonviolent resistance up to now untried or half-tried, or badly tried, but the peace will not be won without such serious and constant and sacrificial and courageous actions on the part of a large number of good men and women. The peace will not be won without the moral equivalent of the loss and suffering and separation that the war itself is exacting."

With a mixture of courage, whimsy, and good humor, Dan saw his going underground as a "modest way" to "summon even Caesar for an accounting." He finally was captured on Block Island off the shore of Rhode Island by grim-faced FBI agents disguised as bird watchers! With open hands and a smile, the dove gave himself up.

His subsequent two years at Danbury Prison in Connecticut proved very severe to his often frail health, but incarceration did not deter him from continuing to challenge the imperial state or from taking the consequences of choosing "to obey God rather than man." This led eventually to the Plowshares Eight action at the General Electric plant in King of Prussia, Pennsylvania, in 1980, in which two nuclear nosecones were destroyed—the first nuclear disarmament since Hiroshima.

On behalf of the Plowshares Eight, Dan wrote to USSR Chairman Leonid Brezhnev challenging him to announce to the world the dismantling of three Russian nuclear weapons and at the same time to invite President Reagan to destroy four U.S. nuclear weapons, after which the Soviets would up the ante and thereby escalate the pace of nuclear disarmament.

Such imminent good sense, of course, appealed to neither world leader, and the doctrine of Mutual Assured Destruction continued to lock the two superpowers in their deadly embrace. And Dan has continued his witness—at the Pentagon, at the Riverside Research Institute, at places where the machinery of death reigns. Even the end of the Cold War did not dislodge the place of a permanently bloated military establishment, so the difficult yet inescapable resistance continues.

In Nicaragua, in 1984, Dan praised many of the accomplishments of the Sandinista revolution even while warning against those who identified the revolution with the Kingdom of God and raising objections to those who placed justice before the gospel mandate of nonviolence and peace. His observations scandalized many, as did his scathing criticism of Israel in 1973. While many charged he had revealed an anti-semitic bias (a charge that would have been mitigated somewhat if the press had printed more than snippets of his remarks), his critique included the Arab states as well and was consistent with his fierce opposition to war and killing as the way to resolve problems. As he said in his speech, "I am sick of war; of wars hot and cold; and all their approximations and metaphors and deceits and ideological ruses. I am sick of the betrayal of the mind and the failure of compassion and the neglect of the poor. I am sick of foreign ministers and all their works and pomps. I am sick of torture and secret police and the apparatus of fascists and the rhetoric of leftists."

It is essential to remember that Dan Berrigan the prophet is also a gentle pastor, easily approachable, loving and considerate. For years, he has served the dying at St. Rose's Home and at St. Vincent's Hospital. In the beginning his work was mostly with cancer patients, then, increasingly, with persons with AIDS. He sees this work with the terminally ill as a very concrete and immediate expression of "this whole business of reconciling" so needed to counter the homophobia and indifference to AIDS by the religious establishment. Besides serving the ill and dying, he leads retreats and biblical reflections to help others deepen their understanding of the scriptures.

While Dan has felt called to say a bold "NO!" to the insanity of our time, he sees it as coming from a more basic "YES!"—a yes "to life, to the God of life, to God's living people, to the life of the mind, the life of the heart."

May his no and his yes continue to call us back to our senses, to embolden us anew, and to heal our broken and timid spirits.

Courage in Abundance

BISHOP THOMAS GUMBLETON

The first time I had direct contact with Dan Berrigan, it was like coming face-to-face with an Old Testament prophet.

Of course, I had heard of him when he had first begun to protest the massive bombing of North Vietnam ordered by President Johnson in 1965. I followed with some interest his difficulties with Cardinal Spellman and the Archdiocese of New York—and his re-assignment to Latin America.

But Dan was not gone long. And he came back with convictions about the war as deeply grounded as ever. Only now his protests began to catch even more attention. He not only spoke at rallies and joined in protest marches, but he also began planning actions of civil disobedience. Then came Catonsville. Dan was arrested with a small group of anti-war protesters. But he did not stop at just being arrested. There were trials and convictions. Then Dan was "on the run."

People all over the country kept up with his flight from the FBI. His spirit of playfulness and creativity served him well as he managed to make the FBI and the whole U.S. government look foolish as he found ways to show up at rallies, make a powerful call to end the killing and bring peace to Vietnam, and then slip away before federal agents could capture him.

Of course, not everyone who heard about Dan Berrigan's activities applauded what he was doing. Many people became angry. Dan was "un-American," or in the eyes of others a genuine traitor to the United States and all it stood for. Within the church his religious superiors and his fellow Jesuits had mixed reactions to him. He generated great controversy.

When he was finally captured and jailed, I confess that I was disappointed. Dan had forced me to do some serious thinking about the war and U.S. involvement in it. This was the effect he had on many people. But for most Catholics, there was a lot of discomfort with his activities against the war. Rallies and marches were bad enough, but getting arrested and jailed really upset people.

In my own life I was struggling to determine what my response to the war should be. It took a while, but I came to see clearly how wrong it was for us to be waging war in Vietnam. Yet I was still uncomfortable with public protests and even more with civil disobedience, especially by priests and religious. It took a long time for me to understand how such actions could be justified.

In 1968 I was ordained a bishop and began to bring the question of the war's morality before the National Conference of Catholic Bishops. And I was satisfied that we were making progress. In 1967 the NCCB had issued a statement that supported U.S. involvement in Vietnam as necessary action to stop the advance of communism. The next year I was glad to be part of a group of bishops that managed to raise serious questions about the justification for the war in the pastoral letter we promulgated in November 1968, *Human Life in Our Day*. The bishops were a long way from a clear cut condemnation of the war, but at least they were asking some of the right questions.

As my own convictions became more deeply rooted, I talked and wrote about the evil of the war. I began to be attacked as a communist and a traitor to the United States. And yet the more I got involved, the more it became clear the war was not justified. I kept working within the framework of the NCCB to achieve a clear judgment by the bishops that from the perspective of Catholic teaching, the war in Vietnam must be condemned.

Finally, in November of 1971, a resolution against the war was passed by the U.S. bishops. Since the resolution was developed from an intervention I had submitted, I felt some sense of accomplishment. It seemed to me that such a resolution from the Catholic bishops could have an important impact on U.S. policy and, even more, have an influence on Catholics who continued to be strongly in support of the war.

While this was going on, I was also engaged in national and international meetings to stop the war. And at the same time I found myself called upon by many young men who needed letters of support in order to obtain conscientious objector status.

In light of all of these efforts and this much involvement, I was stunned and hurt when I got a handwritten letter from Dan Berrigan in which he expressed anger and frustration that I had not joined in any actions of civil disobedience.

Dan was very blunt and, I thought, quite unfair in suggesting that I needed to be more outspoken than I had been, especially by risking arrest and jail as a way to protest very clearly U.S. policy.

By the time I received his letter I had become more involved not only against the Vietnam war, but also in the effort to end the nuclear arms race, which was accelerating rapidly during the 1970s. More and more I was feeling somewhat out of line with the majority of U.S. bishops, and Dan's letter seemed to be particularly insensitive. When I got it, I just set it aside without making any attempt to respond to it.

Slowly, however, I began to reflect on what he had written. It was not what I wanted to hear. Over a period of a few months, I was able to deal with his anger, and I came to realize that it was out of his deep convictions and his regard for me that he would even bother to write, and to write so honestly. I came to realize that his letter was in fact a real grace to which I was being invited to respond.

In some ways I was hesitant to write about this incident of Dan's letter and my reaction to it. But I have come to realize that this reveals something about Dan that could be overlooked.

Above all, he is totally honest. As he comes to know the truth, he is compelled to proclaim it and act upon it. His actions are completely consistent with his beliefs. He is unsparing of himself. He doesn't count the cost when he knows he has an obligation to speak and act against evil—especially the massive evil of war against the poor in Vietnam and the corruption of our own young by compelling them to be killers in an unjust war.

And Dan is just as honest in his willingness to confront others in our nation and especially within the church. Too many people, it seems, are unwilling to be confrontational, and evil is left unchallenged. Dan reminds me of Jesus, who, as a dinner guest at a leading Pharisee's house, was willing to rebuke his host publicly when he saw hypocrisy and sinfulness in the man. Dan has always acted on what Jesus meant when He declared, "I have come not to bring peace, but the sword."

It takes real courage to act in this way of Jesus. Dan has that courage in abundance—for which I am very grateful. And I have been grateful to Dan ever since. Over the years, as I have collaborated with him in various ways, he has continued to be a blessing in my life. He has shown me what it means to have unrelenting respect for human life by being opposed to violence across the whole spectrum—from abortion to nuclear war. He has become a friend with whom I have been honored to be arrested; a friend who was willing to be a keynote speaker at one of our Pax Christi national assemblies; and a friend for whom I testified when he was on trial for breaking the law at an abortion protest.

When I joined with hundreds of friends whose lives he has profoundly touched to celebrate his seventieth birthday, I wondered how many had come to know in a personal way the Dan Berrigan who could speak the truth to a friend with the passion of an Old Testament prophet. I now know, better than ever, the gentle and deeply caring Dan Berrigan who can minister to the terminally ill, who loves family and friends with extraordinary intensity. But I will always especially cherish Dan Berrigan the prophet, who speaks the truth to his friends.

Dan the Messenger

ROBERT COLES

I always will remember the time when I got to know Dan Berrigan; it was in June and July of 1970. Our youngest son, Michael, was born on July 7, 1970, while Dan was staying with us in our house in Concord, Massachusetts. How did he come to be our guest—for several weeks, actually? I have described in detail the circumstances of our meeting in *The Geography of Faith*, which offers a record of a series of conversations the two of us had while he was "underground"— being pursued by the FBI, even as his brother Phil was in a federal prison located in Pennsylvania. These two priest brothers had dared challenge our nation's commitment to a war in Southeast Asia, had dared "desecrate" federal property, the files of a draft board whose job it was, obviously, to sort out would-be conscripts for military service. Dan had chosen to go "on the lam," and while in such flight from the clutches of federal authorities was speaking to audiences here and there, now and then—a vigorous and unnerving confrontation with Washington's high and mighty folks, who for months were not able to lay a hand on him.

Friends of ours were friends of his, and they asked my wife, Jane, and me whether we'd be willing to have Dan as a guest for a while. Yes, Jane said instantly, no matter that she was pregnant, and the mother, then, of two boys, Bobby and Danny, ages six and four. I was more hesitant. I had been very much involved in the civil rights movement, had worked with SNCC (the Student Nonviolent Coordinating Committee) in the South, worked with the Mississippi Freedom Summer of 1964, and studied school desegregation throughout the South— but had had no involvement in the so-called anti–Vietnam War movement. At the time, my elderly parents, rather conservative politically, lived nearby. I had no job and was supported by a small foundation grant that enabled me to write about the work I had done in the South and to initiate a new effort meant to learn how the children of migrant farm workers grow up and come to terms with their quite special and arduous lives. It was Jane who had prompted me to do all that work—I fear that without her strong encouragement I'd have been quite willing to work with children in a Boston hospital as a child psychiatrist, a job I'd have been fortunate, indeed, to have. She prevailed not out of any animus, I hasten to add, for the kind of psychiatric and psychoanalytic practice I was trained to pursue, but out of a social idealism I only slowly learned to live with, an idealism, by the way, Dan Berrigan certainly brought with him to our house (to the point that, frankly, at times I felt a bit overwhelmed—the conventional burgher, the practical-minded realist, cornered, trapped: his wife on one side, his guest on the other!).

How well I remember, still, that time with Dan; and too, his time with my young family. He was ever gracious, generous, and kind. He loved being with, playing with our children, and was a great help, it turned out, to Jane, always ready to work with her in the kitchen, to ask her whether he might do this, do that, around the house. He was a first-rate cook, we discovered, not pretentiously so, simply out of an earnest and humble desire to do justice to the dignity of a meal—a reminder to us that the root, Latin meaning of *companionship* translates as "with bread."

When Jane went to the hospital to deliver Michael, Dan took care of our younger sons and prepared a memorable celebratory meal for us upon my return home. Meanwhile, he was very much the determined citizen-activist. He did not "take refuge" in our home; rather, he joined it as a small community and very much left it as a worker daily does: trips to visit colleagues, compatriots in the struggle he was waging, and visits to address others. A public "outlaw," he really took the world by surprise, this priest who suddenly appeared out of nowhere and soon enough vanished. Meanwhile Mr. Hoover's vaunted agency was daily being humiliated because it couldn't quickly lay its hands on him, and because it was in pursuit of such a person—a Jesuit, a poet, a teacher, a man who in standing up vigorously and non-violently to his government was, ironically, doing what those who founded this country had done in the eighteenth century.

All through his stay with us Dan and I had conversations, many of them taped, about the course of action he had taken, about the kind of life he was living, about his beliefs and values and responsibilities—and yes, about his sense of what ought matter to the rest of us, whose lives as members of the twentieth-century American secular bourgeoisie were so different from his own. We did not by any means always agree. Dan was far more willing, obviously, to challenge the prevailing "principalities and powers" than I, and a certain conservatism in me (especially with regard to so-called social or family issues) had me, ironically, defending the Catholic church's traditional views, as against his capacity to be open-minded, even skeptical. I was especially struck by his candor and, of course, the enormous flexibility of mind and manner that enabled him to keep on the move, to accommodate himself to the life, essentially, of an outsider who was being (to be blunt) hunted down by the law. He was never in danger of losing his sense of humor, and he was able at all times, it seemed, to take that long, historical view of things (and of himself, his life) that eludes so many of us.

In that last regard, I will never forget a moment in our talks—it was about nine o'clock and I was tiring. Our children got us up early, and anyway, I'm by nature (by childhood indoctrination!) an early riser (whereas Dan, I discovered, was a night person). I had become both angry and sad on his behalf. What was the point of all this—the actual war abroad, and as well, the lopsided struggle at home: unarmed, pacifist priests turned into enemies of the state by a powerful federal agency itself all too wildly lawless (as we would soon enough learn, when the various truths about Mr. J. Edgar Hoover and some of his henchmen would come to light). But Dan was of good cheer, even light-hearted. We'd finished our recorded talks and started sipping a bit of bourbon, a nightly routine. Dan suddenly embarked upon a spirited and wry consideration of his present life, his relationship to his religion, his church, his fellow Jesuits. The longer he talked, the more I began to realize that he wasn't really all that interested in the institutional church, his membership in it notwithstanding. He was, at that moment, of course, quite a remove from his Jesuit brothers— but also, I began to realize, from all the rest of us who had chosen to stay within the confines of the law, so to speak. This aloneness (not loneliness) connected him to—well, naturally, Jesus of Nazareth, whose life (let us remember) was not lived within the comfortable, reassuring domain of civil and religious authority.

Jesus was one of history's resolute (and persecuted) outcasts. Jesus lived a vulnerable, marginal life—"despised and scorned" by the high and mighty of church and state alike. The life Jesus lived was for Dan a signpost, a large moral reminder rather than a mere piece of information. Put differently, Dan was very much connected, mind, heart, and soul (I was beginning to realize as he talked) with the historical Jesus, whose life seemed so unpromising, so lowly, by the standards of the society to which he belonged. This Jesus, his travail, nourished Dan, gave him the succor he needed as he lived the jeopardy of a "wanted man." This Jesus was exemplary to him in other ways, too. He resonated with the humble communitarianism of the early church, before hierarchical structure and power had become consolidated— with the attendant dangers of arrogance, not to mention an all too profitable accommodation to the world of politics and commerce.

The more Dan talked, the more I harkened back to Ignazio Silone, to his exile, his embattled career that at a certain point made life hard, even dangerous for him; and especially to his novel *Bread and Wine*, with all its evocations of church and state in great moral and spiritual agony. In that novel, Silone has an idealistic, political revolutionary go underground disguised as a priest (wearing the garb, he lives out the feigned role more fully than many of those who wear that garb as a matter of daily course). Here, in contrast to Silone's story, was a priest sitting before me in civilian clothes, disguised as a visiting friend, an academic colleague of mine, so our neighbors thought. "Who is that man staying with you?" my oldest son Bobby, then six, had been asked by one of his playmates. Bobby's reply: "He's a friend of my parents." The playmate pressed further, as children, ever curious, are wont to do. Bobby could only add that he thought maybe this man was, like his dad, a doctor. But my son had also volunteered this, as an afterthought: "He's worried about the world."

Apparently that morsel of information stopped all further inquiry—psychology the great silencer! But as I heard my son tell his mother of that exchange, I began to see very much the difference between Dan and me—his insistence on worrying about so much in a way that challenged his very life, the manner in which it was lived, as against my kind of worrying: a furrowed brow, maybe, on a bad day with *The New York Times*. I thought of Bobby, and what he'd told us that evening as I heard Dan laugh, say that he found it a "privilege" to be doing what he was doing; say that he quite understood that he'd eventually be caught; and say that he looked ahead with a certain interest and even pleasure to his confinement—he'd have a chance to rest, even to meet some people who might well teach him a lot, even to write some poetry (he hoped).

Dan did, indeed, end up in prison, the federal one at Danbury, Connecticut. I visited him there, and we talked about our hopes and fears for an America with the Vietnam war eating away relentlessly at its moral and political life. I had, months earlier, driven him down from our Massachusetts home to another part of Connecticut; he was on his way to his friend William Stringfellow's home on Block Island, where he would finally be caught. I had been not a little anxious as we approached those tollbooths, even as I had been apprehensive in my hometown as we took our walks or went to get a restaurant lunch. But Dan correctly anticipated that he'd be apprehended because of some chicanery, rather than out of someone's recognition, and that is what happened. He also knew that prison, while no picnic, would not undo him, as I so often feared it would. When such matters came up, usually at his behest, he tactfully reminded me that he was "free" in certain ways not available to me—he wasn't a husband, a father. Still, I never settled for that distinction as so important. Rather, I believe Dan was (is, will ever be) more bound, not more free than I—utterly tied to certain principles, which thoroughly inform his life, his everyday being, to the extent that he simply can't shake them off. Hence their hold on what he does and why he does what he does.

Dan does, indeed, live up to this religious order's name; he is a follower of Jesus, not only by oath and training and church imprimatur, but out of the spirit of his very being. He is a soulful romantic who at the same time is dead serious in his prophetic ministry on behalf of this world's war-ravaged and impoverished millions. He is a man of letters, of great gentleness, who is also fiercely determined to yield not an inch to the various "merchants of hate" of whom I used to hear him speak. He is a thoughtful, constantly ready witness who won't hesitate at all to throw himself (no matter the cost to his daily life) into the thick of tough adversarial politics. He is, most of all, I have long believed, one of the Lord's messengers, sent to give us some hints about how it went for him when he went among us, took the various unpopular stands he did, and soon enough paid the exceedingly stiff price he did.

One of the Great Truth-Tellers

ROSEMARY RADFORD RUETHER

For more than thirty years I have been both inspired and challenged by the writings and witness of Daniel Berrigan. Our lives have run somewhat parallel to each other, crossing paths at some crucial moments, but more often engaged in the same struggles in ways that have been in implicit conversation. There are some ways that he has chosen to position his witness that have differed from my choices and understandings of issues, although in a context of common commitments to truth, justice, and peace.

I first heard Daniel Berrigan speak at the Commonweal Club in Los Angeles some time around 1963. I was beginning to become involved in the Civil Rights movement, and he was speaking about racism and the sufferings of black Americans. I remember that he ended his talk with a powerful invocation of the experience of blacks in America as a crucifixion. Blacks were presented as a collective Christ figure who had been hung on the cross of white American sins. I remember being deeply moved by this image, couched in the powerful poetic passion of Daniel's verbal genius.

As we drove home to Claremont, where my husband and I were completing doctoral degrees, I began to have doubts about this portrayal of black Americans. "I think blacks are going to get tired of hanging on the cross for our sins," I said. Soon after that experience, the Black Power movement began, in explicit revolt against the more pacifist Civil Rights movement. I became more deeply involved in civil rights at that point and spent the summer of 1965 in Mississippi working for the Delta Ministry. I traveled in rural Mississippi, visiting Head Start programs in black churches and canvassing voters to pass the Civil Rights Act that summer.

Although nonviolence was still the dominant method of our struggle for racial justice, the impatience of young blacks with what they saw as compliance with white "liberal" leadership in the movement was at

41

the boiling point. They wanted a more radical critique of American racism as a historical system than whites were willing to offer and also a movement more completely organized around black self-empowerment. Generally I agreed with them.

The break with the older phase of the Civil Rights movement was dramatically illustrated as our group drove from Los Angeles to Mississippi to spend the summer working for civil rights. As we crossed the border into this Southern state, Los Angeles was in flames in an outbreak of rage. Our group of white and some black pilgrims from California felt a little foolish. Obviously we were a bit like missionary do-gooders trying to help out with more distant problems, oblivious to the endemic conflicts in our own neighborhood back in Los Angeles. Later that year, after our return to California, Minnette Lall, a black woman from Los Angeles who had also been on the Mississippi summer project, and I got involved in some work in Watts in Los Angeles. But the question remained. Where should we have been and what should we have been doing in the summer of 1965?

In 1966, my husband and I and our growing family of three children moved to Washington, D.C. I taught at the School of Religion of Howard University for the next ten years. Teaching at a black theological school in a major black university allowed me to continue my commitment to civil rights and the black community. Black theology was just beginning to develop as a reflection on the Black Power movement from a religious context. The Peace movement, with its protest against the Vietnam war, was rising, and I would join with many others in Washington, D.C., in endless protest marches and short stays in jail for protest actions against the war.

Daniel Berrigan and his brother Philip were major leaders in the Catholic anti-war movement. Again our lives crossed in many ways and moments during this period. We became friends with Mary Moylan, a nurse who had been a missionary in Africa. She lived in the next block from us in a large house that was owned by an African missionary order. Groups concerned with civil rights, peace, and justice often gathered there for discussions and house Masses. The Second Vatican Council had sparked the beginnings of a small faith communities movement, in which lay people took charge of creating liturgy meaningful to themselves.

One day Mary told us that she was in touch with Daniel and Philip Berrigan and had decided to join the action they were planning: to destroy draft files in Catonsville, Maryland. After the action, as she awaited trial, she discussed with us Daniel's decision to resist imprisonment and to go "underground." She was angry at the clericalism that focused all the attention on the two priests. She decided that she would go underground also.

While Daniel's time in the underground got dramatic press coverage and became a major public event, Mary Moylan quietly disappeared from sight. More than ten years passed and still the forces of American "justice" failed to discover her whereabouts. Finally, she decided to surface and to turn herself in. She was given a fairly stiff prison sentence of several years, more than twice what others received who went to prison right away. We tried to contact her at that time, but to no avail. Friends told us that she didn't want to talk to former associates. I am sorry she decided she needed to compete with Dan's protest. What for him turned into a public drama, for her became simply a prolonged but largely unnoticed "house arrest," followed by a stay in prison that drew little attention.

Perhaps the most intense time in which my family and I crossed paths with the witness of Daniel and Philip Berrigan was during the infamous "conspiracy" trial in which the American government attempted to silence their voices by accusing them of a plot to blow up steam tunnels under Washington, D.C. I helped organize an all-night vigil at the FBI headquarters in Washington to protest this fallacious indictment. Our whole family became involved in the Berrigan defense committee and traveled to Harrisburg, Pennsylvania, during the trial.

I still have a little photo album put together by my then-six-year-old daughter, Mimi. Our caravan on its way to Harrisburg was followed by FBI agents. At stops along the way, she used her first camera to take pictures of these agents. Later I discovered she had put these photos in her album. Several photos showed men standing by cars, while one was of an agent leaning into our car. She had carefully labeled these photos, "FBI Agents." Her political education had begun. Today Mimi is a lawyer working for the city of Chicago. What conclusions did she draw about the American justice system from seeing FBI agents making outlaws of those who protested unjust wars and phony indictments?

During the late sixties I was beginning my first theological writing. I sent my first book, *The Church Against Itself*, to Thomas Merton. A lively correspondence ensued in which Merton struggled with ways to define his monastic vocation, and I questioned him about the relation of this vocation to the conflicts going on in society. Dan Berrigan was also a part of the circle of Merton's friends and correspondents. At one point Merton asked me to pick up a group of watercolor "Zen" paintings he had done. These paintings had been framed and were exhibited in a gallery in Washington, but Merton was uncomfortable with what he saw as the possible exploitation of his name.

When Merton died unexpectedly during his trip to Asia, where he was engaged in inter-monastic dialogue, I found myself left with these paintings. What would Merton want them used for, I wondered? I

decided he would like to have them used for the Berrigan Defense
Fund. So we held an auction of the paintings in St. Stephen and the
Incarnation Church and gave the proceeds to the Defense Fund. I still
have one painting. I don't know now who has the others. It never
occurred to me to keep a record of those who bought them. I don't
know if Dan and Phil know that Merton's paintings were auctioned
to help them defend themselves against the American government.

In the early seventies I began to research a book on Christian anti-
semitism. This had long been a concern of mine. My favorite uncle,
David Sandow, was Jewish, and the images of the death camps flashed
across newsreels in my neighborhood movie house in 1945 burned in
my mind. I researched this book during a summer fellowship at
Collegeville, Minnesota, in 1972 and taught this material in a seminar
at Harvard Divinity School that fall. I became intensely aware of the
ways in which Christian faith in Christ was constructed in such a way
as to make the Jews scapegoats.

Daniel Berrigan, through his friendship with Eqbal Ahmad, a Paki-
stani political philosopher, was becoming aware of the injustices to
the Palestinians in Israel, after many years of association with Jews in
the Civil Rights and Peace movements. He met with Yasir Arafat and
other Palestinian leaders and gave some talks and wrote articles raising questions about the construction of Jewish identity in Israel as
militant and violent, in contrast to their historic stance as sufferers in
protest of injustice. The American Jewish community exploded in rage
against him and accused him of being a representative of historic Catholic anti-semitism.

At that time I knew something about the Christian myth of the
Wandering Jew and the terrible toll that had taken on Jewish life in
Europe. But I didn't know anything about Palestinians. In 1980, having been asked many times to speak on Christian anti-semitism in
Jewish or Jewish-Christian venues, I traveled to Israel and got my first
taste of the treatment of Palestinians in Israel. I began to question that
injustice and eventually wrote, with my husband, Herman Ruether, a
book on it titled *The Wrath of Jonah: The Crisis of Religious Nationalism in the Israeli-Palestinian Conflict*. Like Dan Berrigan, I discovered how quickly and vehemently one falls from favor with the American Jewish community when one takes the side of Palestinian rights.

I haven't seen Daniel in some years. He lives in New York and
continues his witness against injustice. I have taught at a theological
school in the Chicago area since 1976. I network with liberation theologians and third-world women's struggles in places like Nicaragua,
Zimbabwe, and the Philippines. I think of Daniel Berrigan and me as
having similar basic values but different methods, and perhaps different spiritualities. I see him making the prophetic stance against the
outrage of violence and systems of destruction and their hypocritical

justifications. Such evil systems represent the power of the demonic, which can never be converted. The Christian doesn't expect to change such systems so much as to position himself or herself against them. I agree with that in part. But I also think we have to build some practical political bridges for change. One has to work for lesser evils in many cases, while the fuller good eludes us. Concretely, the relative and partial good or the lesser evil is often the measure of survival for those who live on the margins. As one of my friends who survived near starvation in Hungary during the Second World War once said, "The difference between a haircut and a decapitation is only relative, but it is also the difference between life and death when it is your head." I don't see these two spiritualities of prophetic protest and struggle for relative practical changes as opposed. They seem to me to be complementary within a larger process.

I deeply appreciate Daniel Berrigan's witness. He has been one of the great truth-tellers in American society and in the Catholic church.

THE RESISTER

Peacemaking Is Hard

JIM DOUGLASS

For years, peacemakers have felt the sting of a particular insight by Dan Berrigan. Whether in regard to resistance to the Vietnam war, preparations for nuclear omnicide, or the slaughter in Iraq, Dan's insight has been a perpetual sting to peacemakers because of the radical question of commitment it posed. Friends recently sent Shelley a beautifully scripted poster of Dan's challenge to peacemakers. His words now hang in a frame over the mantle of Mary's House, our Birmingham Catholic Worker house for homeless families:

> We have assumed the name of peacemakers
> but we have been unwilling to pay any significant
>   price for peace
>
> We want peace
> with half a heart   and half a life   and half a will
>
> the war continues
> because the waging of war is total
> but the waging of peace is partial.

In the Vietnam-era text from which these enduring lines were drawn, Dan went on to say:

But what of the price of peace? I think of the good, decent, peace-loving people I have known by the thousands and I wonder. How many of them are so afflicted with the wasting disease of normalcy that, even as they declare for the peace, their hands reach out with an instinctive spasm in the direction of their loved ones, in the direction of their comforts, their homes, their security, their incomes, their futures, their plans—that five-year plan of studies, that ten-year plan of professional status, that twenty-year plan of family growth and unity, that fifty-year plan of decent life and honorable natural demise. "Of course, let us have the peace," we cry, "but at the same time let us have normalcy, let us lose nothing, let our lives stand intact, let us know neither prison nor ill repute nor disruption of ties." And because we must encompass this and protect that and because at all costs—at all costs—our hopes must march on schedule, and because it is unheard of that in the name of peace a sword should fall, disjoining that fine and cunning web that our lives have woven, because it is unheard of that good men and women should suffer injustice or families be sundered or good repute be lost—because of this we cry peace and cry peace, and there is no peace. There is no peace because there are no peacemakers (*No Bars to Manhood*).

But where there are peacemakers, namely those who accept the price of peace, then there is no peace in the routines of war—as in the draft board of Catonsville, Maryland, whose peace of war was shattered at 12:30 P.M., May 17, 1968, by nine men and women, including Dan and Phil Berrigan. In front of the astonished office staff, the nine proceeded to stuff draft files into wire baskets. They then walked out to a parking lot, doused the files with homemade napalm, and burned the draft records of several hundred young men. While the flames rose from the wire baskets, the Catonsville Nine joined hands and prayed.

I was shocked to read the good news of Catonsville on the morning after it happened, standing beside a newspaper vendor at a corner of the University of Hawaii campus. How to believe—to enter into—the reality of liberation described on the front page in terms of peacemakers, good friends among them, openly destroying with napalm the deadly paper of Selective Service files? How to believe in the good news of these friends willing to offer years of their lives in jail as the price of peace?

In a commentary on this parable in action, Dan Berrigan "apologized" for raising such disturbing questions:

Our apologies, good friends, for the fracture of good order, the burning of paper instead of children, the angering of the orderlies in the front parlor of the charnel house. We could not, so help us God, do otherwise. For we are sick at heart, our hearts give us no rest for thinking of the Land of Burning Children. . . . We have chosen to say, with the gift of our liberty, if necessary of our lives, the violence stops here, the death stops here, the suppression of the truth stops here, the war stops here.

In the almost three decades since that "burning of paper instead of children," Dan Berrigan has had the grace and bad manners, in one struggle after another, to keep raising the question of cost: What of the price of peace? Can there be peacemakers where there is no acceptance of the price of peace?

Following the same accept-the-cost logic, Dan recently hypothesized through his dialogue with an angel a scenario of peacemakers confronting collectively one of our world's ongoing wars.

> "Suppose," the angel says, "[ten thousand war resisters] came unarmed to the border of a war zone, fasted there, prayed, marched right in. In sum, risked their lives, with one thing in mind: to bring sanity, an alternative, to a mad impasse. Suppose they hung in, refused to go away, eventually sat down with those bristling, untrusting leaders."
>
> [At this point in the dialogue, a doubtful Dan Berrigan—no doubt representing many more doubtful than he—interjects] "Wait a minute. Suppose they failed. Suppose they were gunned down."
>
> The angel responds by breaking into song, "Everybody want to go to heaven, nobody want to die." ("A Chancy Encounter with an Angel," *Sojourners*, April 1993)

To his Christian brothers and sisters, Dan's willingness to die again and again has made ever more visible and present our center of faith: the cross of Jesus.

The one who accepts the cross shocks us with the truth that the price of peace is simply the peace we enjoy now. Those willing to lose that peace for the sake of real peace return us to the transforming peace of the cross.

"Living Christ is a living cross," Gandhi said. "Without it, life is a living death."

Or as Dan Berrigan once said softly in a poem: "Peacemaking is hard, hard almost as war."

We Are Filled with Hope

Beating Swords into Plowshares with Daniel

MOLLY RUSH

The prophets Isaiah and Micah summon us to beat swords into plowshares. Therefore, eight of us come to the King of Prussia G.E. (Re-entry Division) plant to expose the criminality of nuclear weaponry and corporate piracy. We represent resistance communities along the East Coast. We commit civil disobedience at G.E. because this genocidal entity is the fifth leading producer of weaponry in the U.S. To maintain this position, G.E. drains $3 million a day from the public treasury, an enormous larceny against the poor. We wish also to challenge the lethal lie spun by G.E. through its motto: "We bring good things to life." As manufacturer of the Mark 12A re-entry vehicle, G.E. actually prepares to bring good things to death. Through the Mark 12A, threat of First-Strike nuclear war grows more imminent. Thus, G.E. advances the possible destruction of millions of innocent lives. In confronting G.E., we choose to obey God's law of life, rather than a corporate summons to death. Our beating of swords into plowshares today is a way to enflesh this biblical call. In our action, we draw on a deeply rooted faith in Christ, who changed the course of history through his willingness to suffer rather than to kill. We are filled with hope for our world and for our children as we join this act of resistance.

—The Plowshares Eight, September 9, 1980

We added our names to this statement, composed during a weekend retreat with friends at a Quaker meeting house near Philadelphia, just before our action. We had planned and rehearsed a number of possible scenarios for gaining entry to the rather nondescript G.E.

plant where the warhead casings for the Mark 12A missile were produced. At one point, someone proposed that we send someone in a
floral delivery truck to try to get beyond the rear entry door. I thought,
"These are the experienced resisters? What am I getting into?" Fortu-
nately, we soon put that idea aside and prepared several plans of action. If we could not get inside the back door, we would kneel and
pray. If we got inside and were stopped, we'd kneel and pray. If we got
to a locked door inside, we'd kneel and pray. Etc. Finally, Philip Berrigan
said, "We are going to get inside the building and find those nuclear
weapons, hammer on them and pour blood on them and then circle
and pray together." This was clearly a statement of faith and from
then on, we were ready.

On September 9, 1980, just before work was due to begin, having
concealed hammers and baby bottles of donated blood in our clothing,
we walked through the back door of the King of Prussia, Pennsylvania,
plant. Fr. Carl Kabat, O.M.I., and Sister Anne Montgomery, R.S.C.J.,
engaged the attention of the lone guard at the desk while Daniel and
Philip Berrigan, Dean Hammer, Elmer Maas, John Schuchardt, and I
walked inside, down a hall past another security guard, and into what
we later learned was the "Non-Destructive Test Area."

We used our household hammers on two of the Mark 12A missile
cones, one a fine spun gold-colored aluminum, the other coated with
a black carbon substance so that it could re-enter the atmosphere un-
harmed and its 350 kilotons of nuclear explosives could do their dam-
age. (The bomb that leveled Hiroshima contained 12 kilotons.) I was
astounded to see that weapons I had imagined to be invulnerable to
our little household hammers showed the marks from our blows. We
also poured blood over plans left sitting out nearby. Then we circled,
held hands, and prayed together until we were arrested.

For several years, members of the Brandywine Peace Community
from Media, Pennsylvania, had kept vigil and protested at the site. On
the reverse side of our statement they stated their support for our
action, the first of over fifty similar Plowshares actions that followed
all over the United States and in Germany and England.

It was Daniel Berrigan who had helped bring me, a rather unlikely
candidate for what I expected would be a long prison term, to this
day. His example, coupled with the fear that my own children and
future generations would not make it to the twenty-first century under the escalating threat of nuclear war, propelled me to take those
steps. He encouraged my faith and experience, which led me to believe that nonviolence was the only means to reach the blocked con-
sciences of those who would produce such weapons out of fear or for
profit.

As I try to reconstruct what brought me to this place, a few things
come to mind, such as a movie newsreel I saw in 1945. I was ten, but

I remember clearly the images on the screen of piles of skeletal corpses and smiles on the faces of near-dead prisoners just rescued by our troops. I remember reading Anne Frank's diary a few years later and trying to understand how people of my mother's ancestry could have engaged in such horrors.

The experience of our family—I am the eldest of eight—having to go on welfare and my mother's cooperation in sending my dad to jail for non-support (the one act of her life she said she regretted) helped bring me to this place. My father, Dave Moore, an opera-loving Irishman who loved to read, do crossword puzzles, laugh, and tell stories, was able to fix anything except his addiction to drink. My mother, Mary, is key to my journey. Her patience and deep faith kept us going. After I was grown and Dad had died, she wore a plastic trinket with a lemon which read, "When life gives you lemons, make lemonade." On the back she'd pasted a small snapshot of Dad.

A year out of high school, I married Bill, a gung-ho ex-Marine, and followed the example of my mother, having four children in six years. That same year, 1954, Dan Berrigan was two years into the priesthood and serving a short term in Germany as an auxiliary chaplain to U.S. troops, done "thoughtlessly and with a naive acceptance," he later wrote. We were still products of our time. "At the time, I enjoyed those months," Dan wrote. So did I.

For Dan, as well as for me, 1963 was a watershed year. He was headed for Europe. I was immersed in child-rearing, but I was looking around, too. Inspired by the earlier Montgomery bus boycott and the young people sitting-in at lunch counters with ketchup poured over their heads because they dared to challenge segregation, I hesitatingly joined the Pittsburgh Catholic Interracial Council. Soon I was marching with the United Negro Protest Committee as it fought to open up jobs to blacks at department stores, in the construction unions, and in other bastions of segregation. There I met priests, sisters, and lay people who were beginning to look at racism within church institutions as well.

The Second Vatican Council, which opened the windows of the tradition-encrusted Catholic church, and Pope John XXIII's great encyclical *Pacem in Terris*, brought the issues of the day right into the center of Catholic theology. A great pair, Martin Luther King, Jr., a Baptist preacher, and for Catholics, Pope John, were central to the total rethinking of our faith. I was moving from an emphasis on personal salvation to a broader and more inclusive view of the Beloved Community (as King called it) here on earth. These ideas brought me closer to the gospel of Jesus Christ, whose embracing love I had experienced on a personal level in my mother's faith. Now this love included everyone, including black people who were systematically excluded from society, even by the church.

In 1963, Daniel Berrigan headed off to Eastern Europe. The next year, he went to the Soviet Union, where he discovered "peaceable communities of faith, surviving and even thriving in the most difficult circumstances." At the same time, he was learning more about the war in Vietnam. He and others began to forge methods of protest—fasting, marching, picketing, and sitting-in. This was in a time when, as he put it, American Catholics "were doubly patriotic because they were Catholic."

By 1967, Daniel was arrested at the Pentagon in an anti-war demonstration, but he was challenged by the action of his brother Philip and three others when they poured blood on draft files in Baltimore. In early 1968, Dan traveled to Hanoi to bring back the first American fliers held in what was then North Vietnam. Then came the assassination of Dr. King. In May, Dan joined Philip and seven others in burning draft records in Catonsville.

In Pittsburgh, just a month later, I was about to give birth to my sixth child. I remember that summer, wishing I were able to join the protests at the Democratic convention in Chicago. The violent deaths of Dr. King and Robert Kennedy had left a pall of foreboding on me. The action at Catonsville, while appalling to many, offered a gift of hope to me and others shaken by King's assassination and the unending war. The news of King's death came during the intermission of my six-year-old son Dan's Catholic school play. The first remark I heard was from behind me: "Good. It's about time." Catonsville, just weeks later, came to me as a lifeline.

A few years later my older children accompanied my husband, Bill, and me to Harrisburg, where the Berrigans and their friends were on trial for conspiracy. We slept on the floor in an African American woman's apartment. We were there to demonstrate support, but I didn't think I could risk arrest at that time. I remember telling a friend, Marcia Snowden, a Mercy sister from Pittsburgh (who did spend a week in jail in Harrisburg), that the Vietnam war wouldn't end until ordinary people like myself, and not just priests and nuns, were willing to face arrest.

For some time, I'd been attending Sunday mass at St. Joseph's, a parish in a black neighborhood of Pittsburgh. I'd left my suburban church behind after a number of unhappy incidents, including the time the pastor called the police when members of Clergy and Laity Concerned About Vietnam had shown up with leaflets opposing the war. They ended up in my dining room drinking coffee and eating rolls as they described how they'd been forced to leave.

On the wall behind the altar at St. Joe's hung Daniel's words from his trial for the Catonsville action:

> We have chosen to say with the gift of our liberty
> if necessary our lives:

> the violence stops here
> the death stops here
> the suppression of the truth stops here
> this war stops here.
> Redeem the times!

Dan's words haunted me: "Our apologies, good friends, for the fracture of good order, the burning of paper instead of children." I'd anguished as my oldest son, Gary, neared draft age. The terrible war and Daniel's and Philip's bold actions moved a whole generation of Catholics who had grown up in the era of unquestioned assumptions that justified war.

In 1972, I joined with others in founding a ministry for justice and peace in Pittsburgh. We named it the Thomas Merton Center. Merton, the Trappist monk known for his writings on spirituality, was also a prominent critic of the war. The Berrigans and others in the Catholic Peace movement were close to Merton, even participating in a famous retreat at Gethsemani. I had never met either Thomas Merton or Daniel Berrigan, but both men, along with Dorothy Day, were heroes of mine. Eventually, I heard Daniel speak in Harrisburg and Pittsburgh.

Finally, in 1979, I met Daniel. We had been invited to join a retreat for peace activists outside of Cleveland. I was a last minute replacement for a sister from Pax Christi and was not feeling quite up to the task. Although I had been on the staff of the Thomas Merton Center, I'd never led a retreat. I'd engaged in many protests, beginning with the civil rights movement sixteen years earlier, but most of my time and energy had been reserved for my six children. Bob and Greg, then thirteen and eleven, came with me to the retreat.

Now I found myself telling Daniel of my concerns about the nuclear arms race, then widely accepted as both inevitable and too frightening to think about. My work at the Thomas Merton Center had educated me and pushed me toward thoughts of civil disobedience, but I was concerned about my two youngest boys. "What about my children if I go to jail?" I asked him. He told me of having the same conversation with a woman in apartheid South Africa, and his response, "What about your children if you don't?"

He said it quietly, gently. I remember the compassion in his dark, intense eyes as he spoke. A month later, I was held overnight in the Washington, D.C., jail for a protest organized by the Sojourners community outside an arms bazaar held at a Washington hotel, my first arrest. A year later, our small group was meeting to discuss the possibility of carrying out what would be the first direct action against nuclear weapons.

The question of nonviolence was a central one. Could we hammer on weapons and still consider ourselves nonviolent? In a way, the question was absurd. Would any act of dismantling weapons that are capable of killing millions of people be considered violent? This would be considered illegal—not the result of international negotiations. But aren't the weapons themselves being built in violation of international law and treaties that prohibit weapons of mass destruction?

Does the use of a hammer in itself constitute violence? I'd hung curtain rods using a hammer. In no case would I threaten or harm anyone. If challenged, we agreed we would put down our hammers rather than use them. Later, in court, Daniel was asked whether using a hammer upon an object is violent. "Oh," said Dan, ."not such an object [as the Mark 12A]. See, if these things contained buttermilk or ping pong balls, I'd leave them alone."

During our weekend gathering, just before our Plowshares action, Dan was clearly not feeling well. His back was giving him excruciating pain due to a deteriorating, arthritic condition. I did not see how he could go ahead, facing prison without access to decent medical care. We put off going to G.E. for a day. On the morning of the ninth, Dan was ready. So was I. I had spent the weekend dealing with my husband's pleas to come home. Eventually, he gave in, saying he would support me.

Soon we were all under arrest, with $150,000 required as bond. Four days later, Montgomery County Judge Vincent Cirillo refused to lower an ailing Dan's bail below $50,000, despite Dan's promise that he would not go underground (as he had in 1970) if released from jail. The judge said he was aware that the priest believed that a higher authority took precedence over his commitment to civil authority. Both the judge and the Jesuits had learned something from Dan. The Jesuits put up the $50,000.

During our trial, we tried to argue that we had acted out of necessity and in conformity with international law and treaties in which the weapons of mass destruction manufactured by G.E. "posed a grave and imminent danger to all people," in the words of Ramsey Clark, one of our attorneys.

In his opening statement, Daniel told the jury. "You have heard talk of hammers and blood. These things," he said, pointing to Mark 12As on display, "are the hammers of hell. These things are the hammers of the end of the world. These things are the hammers that will break the world to bits. . . . They confront you as well as us with this necessity of thoughtfulness, of conscience, of responding. . . . Dear friends, we would like you and ourselves to ponder together what befits us, what will make the next generation possible."

Later in his testimony, he spelled it out to the jury on behalf of the eight of us. "We come from churches. We come from America. We come from neighborhoods. We come from years of work. We come from earning a living. And we have come to this. And the judgment of our conscience that we would like to present to you is something like this. We could not *not* do this. We were pushed to this by all our lives."

"With every cowardly bone in my body," Dan continued, "I wished I hadn't had to do it. That has been true every time I have been arrested. My stomach turns over. I feel sick. I feel afraid. I hate jail. I don't do well there physically. But I have read that we must not kill. I have read that children, above all, are threatened by this. I have read that Christ our Lord underwent death rather than inflict it. And I'm supposed to be a disciple. The push of conscience is a terrible thing."

"We believe," he went on, "according to the laws of this state, that we were justified in saying we cannot live with that, saying it publicly, saying it with blood and hammers, because that thing [gesturing to the Mark 12A] being produced in our country every day [is] the greatest evil conceivable to this earth. There is no evil to compare with it. Multiply murder. Multiply desolation. Multiply."

He ended, "The only message I have is: we are not allowed to kill innocent people. We are not allowed to be complicit in the killing of innocent people. We are not allowed to be silent while preparations for mass murder are proceeding in our name, with our money, secretly."

We were not permitted by the trial judge, Samuel W. Salus II, to present a defense based on international law or necessity. We were not allowed to present expert testimony from witnesses such as Richard Falk, professor of international law at Princeton, who planned to discuss Nuremberg and other precedents. "Irrelevant," said the judge.

Later, in my closing statement, I talked about how I had accepted the bomb as "an unpleasant necessity, something for national defense, national security. It's taken a long time to get to the point of letting go of those illusions. . . . What I've come to see is that under the bomb, we are all vulnerable. The judge, the G.E. executives, the government officials, and my newborn grandson: we are all in the same boat. This ultimate instrument of power strips all of us bare of illusions that power maintained by force is effective or useful or wins. It never did win."

"If we really look," I continued, "we can see its true face, the face of the death of all of us and all of life. That is the final lie of those who would keep faith in the use of force. We swallow it. We believe it, as the Nazi death camp victims and victimizers did. This is the lie: that all of us are helpless in the face of the bomb, that people can do nothing, that we must accept the death of the world for ourselves and for our children and for our grandchildren. That is the big lie that's being perpetrated. So for my sake and for the sake of my children, I reject that lie. I believe in a God who is the spirit of truth and love. I am happy to go to jail if it means keeping that spirit alive on this planet."

After two weeks of trial, we were found guilty. At our sentencing, the Berrigans, Elmer Maas, and John Schuchardt were given three to ten years. Anne Montgomery and Dean Hammer received one-and-a-half to five years; I got a two-to-five year sentence. Eleven years of appeals followed. The result: the convictions were upheld, but we were to be re-sentenced before a new judge, James E. Buckingham, a World War II and Korean War veteran. At the sentencing hearing, he allowed each defendant to make a statement, and afterward, changed his mind about the sentences.

He noted that the crimes for which we were convicted were not violent crimes. "The defendants have made statements about their deep-felt convictions. I agree with many of these convictions. Nuclear arms and the nuclear industry are frightening subjects to all of us." He asked if we would agree not to repeat our action. None of us could make such a promise. Then the judge pronounced his sentence: time served.

For me and for many, Daniel Berrigan is one for whom word becomes flesh, faith becomes hope. A paralyzing cynicism about the organized violence of our time continually whispers to us: "Be real. What can anyone do?" Daniel provides a reply to the voices of despair and violence out of his pithy, fey wisdom: a consistent, poetic, brave, and faithful "No."

Just as the call to love one another may yet break through our hardened hearts, Dan's life inspires us to go and do likewise. No small feat. Thank you, Daniel.

The Heart's Beat, the Children Born, the Risen Bread

ANNE MONTGOMERY, R.S.C.J.

Some stood and stood and stood.
They were taken for dummies
they were taken for fools
they were taken for being taken in.

Some walked and walked and walked.
They walked the earth
they walked the waters
they walked the air.

Why do you stand?
they were asked, and
why do you walk?

Because of the children, they said, and
because of the heart, and
because of the bread.
                    —Daniel Berrigan

"Stand fast" (Eph 6:14). The word as spoken to and by Dan has become almost a mantra we can repeat to ourselves in moments of disillusion and discouragement: "Don't just do something; stand there." Such standing is countercultural, a new definition of effectiveness, a resistance to "winning" by the standards of our culture. Dan tells us that scripture was written by losers—those who call us to the margins. Sometimes we go from our places of worship, strengthened by word and eucharist, to speak truth to military death-factories. But we must also journey from the "deserts" in our cities, the dumping grounds

60

of the destitute and dying, to bring their message to the centers of spiritual death. In their name, Dan has repeatedly stood, a repeat "offender," before the closed doors of national security to say that, gifted with the friendship of the so-called useless hidden in our hospitals and prisons, we know "the world functions less badly when Christians are marginal to it, in resistance against it."

The principle dear to Gandhi that the means contains the end demands tough fidelity in the face of political facts. Dan points to the image of a wheel, winners on top, losers on the bottom. Behold: a vote won or a ruler overthrown, and the wheel turns, winners and losers change places. The prison doors open and close, and new prisoners write their anguish on the walls. But the one who stands in a different space, centered in compassion, can break through that cycle, rejecting the win-lose game of power and violence. How can one who trusts in a crucified Loser, lose?

Paul speaks of warfare against the Principalities and Powers. Dan's deep understanding of the nature of this conflict has enabled him to resist the temptations of compromise, whether with the strategies of the powerful or the seductions of the media. Poetry is the literary expression of the paradox of nonviolence, truth-force and symbolic action its enfleshment, the kind of prayer that opens the way for God's intervention. Walter Wink describes the steadfastness of another Daniel, facing the oppressive powers of imperial Persia, his prayers insistent enough to inaugurate "war in heaven" against the spiritual forces that are behind every ancient and modern military system and are perpetuated within the institutions of the national security state.

I remember how hard it was to bring a hammer down upon a modern idol, the Mark 12A warhead, as though the hardened nosecone was less resistant than fifty-four years of inculturation in the spirit of law-abiding citizenship. But behind me, on September 9, 1980, Dan was calmly drenching the blueprints for mass destruction in the blood symbolic of its victims. And then we stood in a circle of prayer, strengthened by community and trusting in God to do the real work of disarming the hearts behind the hardware.

Those few moments summed up what Dan consistently lives and teaches. We are to resist the degradation of words, above all of the Word, by reclaiming their inner meaning, not just by definition and illustration, but above all by enfleshment in presence and action. In a culture of individualism hiding behind impersonal corporate structures, of the walls between insiders and "misfits," Dan stresses community: not only standing or sitting together before the doors of the Riverside Research Institute, or lying together in a die-in at the Intrepid war museum, but also celebrating together with the bread and wine of eucharist or the gourmet cooking of the Berrigan kitchen. Then one understands the angel's command to Elijah: "Get up and eat, else the journey will be too long for you." In Dan's persevering journey we also know that he has heard in moments of darkness, as in the light, the "tiny whispering sound" of the Spirit and has been able to answer in truth the question: "Why are you here?" (1 Kings 19:7-13).

> Because
> the cause
> is the heart's beat
> and the children born
> and the risen bread.

Peace Pilgrim to Vietnam

HOWARD ZINN

Shortly after Dan Berrigan and I returned home from our remarkable (I am restraining myself in my use of adjectives to describe it) trip to Vietnam in early 1968, I wrote the following essay as preface to his book, *Night Flight to Hanoi*.

It was after that trip that Dan and the others of the Catonsville Nine carried out their historic act of civil disobedience against the war in Vietnam—and initiated for me a series of court appearances for group after intrepid group, trying to persuade judge or jury that civil disobedience was a historically respectable and morally necessary reaction to war. It was in connection with that act that Dan wrote:

> Our apologies, good friends, for the fracture of good order, the burning of paper instead of children, the angering of the orderlies in the front parlor of the charnel house. We could not, so help us God, do otherwise. For we are sick at heart. Our hearts give us no rest for thinking of the Land of Burning Children.

Two years later, I was shepherding Dan—an impossible lamb—around Boston, from safe house to safe house, as he carried out his extraordinary "underground" activity, continuing to speak out against the war while the F.B.I. sweated to find him. At one point, he sat in the sun in our backyard while the photographer-writer Lee Lockwood made his film about Dan, *The Holy Outlaw*.

When he was finally apprehended and jailed, my wife Roslyn and I visited him and Phil in Danbury prison. I went again on that celebratory day when he was released. He was at it again, within days, and for years; they could not, however they tried, stop his resistance to war and preparations for war. Nor could they stop him from producing poems that moved and inspired us all.

So I offer this reminiscence in honor of Dan, his poetry, his life witness.

I met Father Daniel Berrigan for the first time in a Greenwich Village apartment in New York, on January 31, 1968, the morning of the day we were to travel together, halfway around the world, to Hanoi. He seemed to me a French worker-priest, with his dark turtleneck shirt, his black trousers, lean body, puckish, wise eyes, cropped hair. Both of us had responded to phone calls from Dave Dellinger, editor of *Liberation* magazine, who had received a telegram from the peace committee of North Vietnam: "In celebration of our New Year Tet holiday, we are preparing to release three captured American pilots to the American peace movement. Please send responsible representative for reception and discussion."

Dave then called Dan Berrigan, who was teaching courses in modern drama and the New Testament (a logical combination, for the likes of him) at Cornell University, and phoned me at Boston University, where I teach political science. One of us, he thought, might be willing to go. Both of us said yes, and so, with a bit of worry about how to pay the travel agency (eventually, for even radicals use the credit system) for two fat airline tickets, Dave decided it would be good if both went—immediately.

We three met the next day in New York, with Tom Hayden, who had made one of the first trips to Hanoi back in 1965, and who had recently been involved in the release of three American prisoners of the National Liberation Front in Cambodia. Meanwhile, the news was traveling fast about our impending trip; the press reported on the telegram to Dellinger, and two wives of imprisoned fliers flew into New York from North Carolina to give us letters to their husbands, as well as letters from other wives of prisoners. They showed only a slight tension at meeting objectors to a war their husbands were waging; it helped perhaps that one of the two emissaries was a Jesuit priest and the other a professor who had once been an Air Force bombardier.

The other preflight visit, just before we drove out to Kennedy Airport, was from a State Department man in Averill Harriman's office. He offered to validate our passports for travel to North Vietnam, an officially forbidden destination. Father Berrigan and I had agreed quickly before his arrival that we did not want to recognize the government's right to approve or disapprove travel to any part of the world, so we politely declined. The State Department man was concerned over how the fliers would be brought back to the States; he preferred military transport to civilian airlines. We agreed to leave it up to the pilots themselves. This was later to become a point of intense, absurd controversy, argued out with the American Ambassador to Laos in the confines of an old airplane that had just brought all five of us (Berrigan, me, the three fliers) out of Hanoi.

Father Berrigan and I boarded an SAS flight to Copenhagen that Wednesday evening, the first leg of a race to Vientiane, Laos, hoping to get there in time to catch the Friday afternoon International Control Commission flight to Hanoi. For thirty hours we read, ate, talked, changed planes, tried to sleep: from Copenhagen to Frankfurt to Rome to Teheran to Karachi to Calcutta to Bangkok to Vientiane. We arrived in time, only to learn that the Friday ICC Plane had not left Saigon that morning, owing to the fighting around Tan San Nhut airfield; it was the start of the NLF Tet offensive. We would have to wait until Tuesday, because the ICC plane flew only six times a month— every Friday and alternate Tuesdays—on a carefully marked-out route, in a carefully timed procedure, so that neither United States bombers nor North Vietnamese gunners would interfere with the flight.

Dan Berrigan and I spent the next sixteen days together, seven days in Laos, seven days in Hanoi, two days en route home. Our week in Vientiane was a frustrating, fascinating period of waiting; we visited embassies, walked through Buddhist temples, ate with Laotian villagers in their huts, talked to foreign journalists, to a Pathet Lao leader. We heard from young Americans working with the International Volunteer Service, who were bitterly critical of the American presence in Vietnam, and also of its aid program in Laos. We walked along the Mekong River, sat on the curb in the sun, were interviewed by American television crews. Finally, the following Friday, just before dusk, we boarded the thirty-year-old, squatting, four-engine Boeing bird, and flew to Hanoi.

In Vientiane and in Hanoi, at mysterious moments before bedtime which I never discovered, Dan Berrigan wrote poems. For two rather silent types, we talked a good deal. He had been raised on a farm in New York State, became a priest and a poet. He visited Africa, studied for two years in Paris, became a radical critic of war and sympathizer with revolutions.

At certain moments, the confrontation with conscience was close and painful; a young friend burned himself to death in protest against the war in Vietnam. Sent to Latin America to "cool off," Dan became more radical. There he saw poverty, rebellion, repression: 150,000 human beings burrowed like rats in the dumping grounds of Lima. In the Amazon valley of Brazil, he saw consciousness growing among the peasants ("they were turning from cactus into people") and then the Castello Branco regime rushed in to stifle that growth. Home again, he joined the antiwar march to the Pentagon in 1967, and went to jail.

I liked what Father Berrigan had to say: "When absolutes enter the human scene, we have obsession—and possibly murder." Another time: "If you can't make it on the personal level, then you are abstract, you don't belong—it's not even rational, it's not *embodied*." And: "If God chose to come to earth and join humanity, this should say something about life, humanity, flesh." And: "The last thing Christ wanted to do was start a church."

We laughed a lot together during those days. But as I write this now, Dan Berrigan is facing prison because he (and his brother Phil, and others) decided to protest the mass murder of the Vietnam War by destroying draft card files in Baltimore. Of course he violated the law. But he was right. And it is the mark of enlightened citizens in a democracy that they know the difference between law and justice, between what is legal and what is right. It is the mark of wise men and women to know what is important and what is unimportant. The flesh of Vietnamese men, women, children—the blood of young American soldiers—the anguish of parents grieving over lost children—that is important. The papers and paraphernalia of the system that selects people for war—these are unimportant.

Let us hope that our country will become wise. But until it does—indeed, in order that it should—we as its citizens must act in the wisdom of our own conscience. That, to me, is the ultimate meaning of what Father Daniel Berrigan, in prose and poetry, says and leaves unsaid.

Humanity and Humor

EARL CROW

I sit in my office looking at a photograph of Father Daniel Berrigan, S.J. He has a beatific countenance as he reverentially/sacramentally lifts a bowl of Ben & Jerry's smooth mocha fudge ice cream. I cannot resist a smile. But that's not unusual. During my more than twenty years of friendship with Dan, much of the time spent with him has been accompanied by laughter. The picture not only evokes a smile, it presents itself as a metaphor. A man of conscience, often cast into conflict with life's destructive forces, is nevertheless a man who has found the grace to affirm life with courage and consistency while maintaining two endearing qualities: his own humanity and a sense of humor.

I first met Dan Berrigan in 1973, following his two-year internment at Danbury. Having recently been appointed chair of the department of religion and philosophy at my college, I was approached by a local minister requesting that we co-sponsor a Berrigan visit. I agreed.

In preparation for his lectures, Dan's play, *The Trial of the Catonsville Nine*, was presented on campus; and, as one of the audience chosen to participate on the mock jury, I had voted him guilty. It seemed simple. He had, by his own admission, broken the law by destroying government files.

On the day of his arrival on campus, I waited at the student center, somewhat suspicious and unsympathetic, to meet this recently released revolutionary. A priest in a black turtleneck sweater . . . not very tall . . . thin . . . at first glance unimposing, yet with an immediate and almost alarming . . . still, charming and calming, presence, presented himself. We shook hands, and, as we did, I had an unsettling, uneasy feeling I had made a mistake. Reflecting on the scene some twenty years later, it seems strange; yet, I distinctly remember that I had a sense of having voted to convict an innocent man.

His message to the students was simple, yet profoundly provocative. He reminded us that:

> Jesus taught love
> Not for gain
> But for our enemies' sake.

He shattered our myths with facts concerning:

> Military-industrial collusions,
> Pentagon power gaining,
> Foreign policy terrorism, and
> Arms race madness.

He talked about our:

> Vocation of death,
> Human annihilation, and
> The first do-it-yourself extinction of a species.

He called for:

> A commitment to life.

That was it! The simplicity of the message was disarming.

The humanity of Dan is witnessed in his refusal to compromise or complicate the message. Several years ago, my daughter decided to write her undergraduate senior thesis on nonviolent civil disobedience, focusing on the life and thought of Fr. Berrigan. I arranged a telephone interview for her with Dan:

Susan: Father Berrigan, could you tell me something about the theological and philosophical tenets underlying your acts of civil disobedience and your commitment to nonviolence?

Dan: Ah . . . what's that, Susan?

Susan: Father Berrigan, could you tell me something about the theological and philosophical tenets underlying your acts of civil disobedience and your commitment to nonviolence?

Dan: Oh, I don't know, Susan. It just seems to me that Jesus said we should love one another.

Needless to say, Susan was a bit taken back since she was assigned to write a twenty-page paper; but the truth of the matter is that Dan's message is that simple. No sophistic philosophying. No theological profundities. Rather, a direct and categorical imperative: we are not allowed to do harm to others. We are, as Tolstoy wrote, confronted with alternative ways of living: the Law of Love or the Law of Violence. Christians are to live by the Law of Love. Or as Dan put it to a group of ministers at Duke University, "There are two ways: the way of the cross, and the way of putting others on the cross." The miracle of his message, beyond its power, is that it comes not from naivete but from a life-long commitment to a wide range of reading in the classics and from serious biblical scholarship lived out in acts of faithful obedience.

My students are often curious concerning the theology of a man who has been such a social activist. "What does he believe about this and that?" they ask. Most of the time, I must confess that I cannot answer their questions. Once, while riding the Staten Island ferry, I tried to engage Dan in a theological discussion, probing for insights. He was delightfully evasive, preferring to talk about the skyline, the sea, and such. I recall having asked Dan's friend and fellow Jesuit Bob Keck, what he and Dan talked about when together. Were their conversations profoundly philosophical? His reply was: "We talk about life." It's a part of the humanness of Dan Berrigan that he is more concerned with people than with polemics.

Another part of Dan's humanness is his ability to cut through the chaff to the things of greater importance, to roll with and even enjoy the ironies of life, and to respond to people at the point of their humanness.

On December 7, 1993, Philip Berrigan, John Dear, Lynn Fredriksson, and Bruce Friedrich participated in a Plowshares action, damaging an F-15E Strike Eagle jet bomber at the Seymour Johnson Air Force Base in North Carolina. They were arrested and brought to trial in the small, coastal town of Elizabeth City, John's hometown.

Dan flew down. I met him at the Norfolk, Virginia, airport, and we drove the forty miles to Elizabeth City, where we had accommodations at a bed-and-breakfast inn within walking distance of the court house. Our hostess was cordial. She showed us our rooms and casually inquired as to the purpose of our visit. Having heard our story, she soon revealed that both she and her husband were retired from the air force and that she had been a squadron commander during the Gulf War. One might wonder about the possibilities of tension or even conflict in such an ironic setting: an air force squadron commander hosting a pacifist priest who had come in support of the civil disobedience of his friends and brother in their act of damaging an air force fighter plane.

It is not clear exactly what took place that week. I do know that our hostess was curious about what motivated a man like Dan. I know that, in spirit of his overt opposition to the war in which she had played a part, there was no hint of his judging her. They met, each respecting the human struggle of the other. By mid-week, Ash Wednesday, she joined us in the living room of the inn. A strange gathering: Father Daniel Berrigan, actor Martin Sheen, myself a puzzled professor, and hostess Judy Smith, formerly of the air force, currently keeper of an inn. And she received the ashes from Dan.

Dan's humanness is perhaps most clearly manifested in his sense of humor. One of the more celebrated events in his career was the Catonsville selective service files burning. Following his conviction, Dan decided that to submit to punishment by a government guilty of such war atrocities was, tacitly, to recognize the authority of that government. He went underground but periodically popped up on college campuses and in churches denouncing the continuing carnage. Then, to the consternation of the FBI, he would disappear again. He was finally found and captured in August of 1970.

It's difficult to imagine much humor in such a situation: convicted of a felony, sentenced to years in prison, a fugitive hunted by Hoover, hiding, on the run. But Dan's telling of the tale elicits laughter.

He had retreated to one of his favorite places of refuge, Block Island, Rhode Island. On the day of his arrest, the island was under siege by a howling "nor'easter" rain squall. Dan was comfortably sipping coffee in the kitchen of a converted stable which served as his inn. As he gazed out the window at the storm, he saw an incredible sight. Crouching in the bushes were two FBI agents, inappropriately and maladroitly disguised, dressed in orange rain slickers, with binoculars, pretending to be bird watchers. No birds in sight, except Dan. After months of flight, the prey was captured, frisked, cuffed, and carted off to the Coast Guard station for transport to the mainland.

In spite of its seriousness, the scene was comic: two armed agents of the law, overpowering the pacifist priest. The boat lurching in the surging sea. The agents turning green . . . not with envy . . . leaning and pitching over the bow, while the captive sits calmly, riding the waves, wearing an impish grin, as if he were enjoying a bowl of smooth mocha fudge.

In 1980, the Plowshares Eight engaged in an act of civil disobedience at the General Electric plant in King of Prussia, Pennsylvania. The sentence for Dan could have been up to ten years imprisonment, but the next ten years were spent in appeals. In 1990, Dan and the others were re-sentenced in Norristown, Pennsylvania. Following his statement to the court, Dan was questioned by the judge, who inquired if Dan had been convicted of any other felonies since King of Prussia. Dan seemed perplexed, uncertain how to answer. He turned quizzically to former Attorney General Ramsey Clark, who was present to offer legal counsel and was seated directly behind Dan. Clark confessed that he did not know either. The prosecuting attorney spoke up, volunteering the answer that Dan had not been convicted of any felonies during the period in question. The judge seemed satisfied, but Dan interrupted declaring: "But your honor, that doesn't mean I don't have a criminal mind." There was a brief moment of silence before those in the court, the judge included, recognized Dan's humor and gave in to laughter.

Toward the end of the proceedings, the judge was pondering his decision. He revealed that although he could not sanction the Plowshares acts, having listened to them in court, he had a better understanding of their motives. He questioned Dan again:

Judge: Father Berrigan, regardless of the outcome of these hearings, will you promise the court that you will refrain from such acts in the future?

Dan: Your honor, it seems to me that you are asking the wrong question.

The judge was visibly surprised by Dan's reply but continued:

Judge: Okay, Father Berrigan, what do you think is the proper question?

Dan: Well, your honor, it appears to me that you should ask President Bush if he'll stop making missiles; and, if he'll stop making them, then I'll stop banging on them and you and I can go fishing.

I was fearful of the judge's reaction; but, to his credit, he was able to discern the humor and humanness of the man before him and to respond, as we all did, in laughter.

How Our Daniel Came to Face the Lions

RAMSEY CLARK

Dan Berrigan is not an easy read. The dust jacket is a classic. Extraordinary grace, devastating wit, a gentle, tender, loving saint. For those who stop with the cover, he is perfect and, as with all covers, nothing.

But the text runs deep. Clearly a life of learning and growing and giving and teaching. What then are his lessons? Who is he? Who are we? For a third of Dan's life, I've studied his case, and this is my tentative, timorous brief on a single aspect of Dan the man.

Dan was in his dark night of resistance and only recently captured alive and confined when we met in the federal penitentiary at Danbury. As a catholic lover, resistance and incarceration were painful for him.

Dan lives for the ideal. No resistance is needed there. Love prevails. And in that land, Dan fits perfectly.

But what does a perfect person do in a far from perfect world? Be a misfit? While most of us grope in our quiet desperation toward selfish ends, Dan seeks ways to help without hurting, to ease suffering without causing pain. This is the field on which he met resistance.

Except for this confrontation, Dan would spend his life spreading smaller joys and comforts—a poem, a loving heart and hand at a child's death bed, a rapturous tale from a great family past, a four-star gourmet meal from the simplest fare, a glass of good red wine.

In resistance, Dan took up his nonviolent sword to outface irrational things like nuclearism, nationalism, churchism, materialism, racism, and sexism. He seeks to honor and defend the poor, the homeless, the prisoners, the dying, the enemy, the hated. He struggles to vanquish AIDS, fear, force, hatred, injustice, intolerance, and violence.

A decade after we met, Dan would describe in courtroom testimony his physical reaction to resistance and incarceration following history's first act of nuclear disarmament in King of Prussia. "My stomach turns over," he said. "I feel sick. I feel afraid. I don't want to go

72

through this again. I hate jail. I don't do well there physically. But," he continued, "we could not not do this. We were pushed to this by all our lives. Do you see what I mean? All our lives."

As I write, on the fiftieth anniversary of the execution of Dietrich Bonhoeffer, I reflect how Dan has written about and pondered Bonhoeffer's life. Before returning to Germany in 1939, Bonhoeffer wrote Reinhold Niebuhr about the terrible choice before the Germans, the choice between victory or defeat for their own nation, on which destruction or survival of civilization depended. "I know which of these alternatives I must choose," Bonhoeffer wrote, "but I cannot make this choice in security." Then Bonhoeffer asked the old question, "Is my faith just something in my own house, my own room?" He chose at his peril to resist in his own nation.

Dan has resisted all his adult life, at times with his body, at times with his word. He is by nature a person of the word, but he has never spared his body. Where a "clown tumble" is called for, he tumbles. Dan has resisted church, that "Amazon of Order." He has resisted state. "The trouble with our state was civil obedience," he writes. In prisons, he turned the "lights on in the House of the Dead." He has spread his word of resistance through every village and town, in Catonsville, Harrisburg, Nuremberg, Norristown, Goldsboro, St. Vincent's in the Village, Belfast, the Pentagon, the Nevada Nuclear Test Site, the Riverside Research Institute, the Lawrence Livermore Laboratories, the Groton Trident Submarine shipyard, Vietnam, the Middle East, Eastern Europe, South Africa, Russia, El Salvador, and Nicaragua. And always with love.

Throughout, Dan has resisted his own fear of the pain of resistance. This is the resistance called courage. He is a poet, ever sentient, and that fear and pain never leave him. And they never deter him.

Dan has learned and taught that in this imperfect world we must resist every force that threatens the poor, the meek, the children, and the sick. We must struggle for the ideal of a world of love. To dwell in peace, it is required that we resist. It is the loving thing to do. And Dan Berrigan could not not do it.

THE KEEPER OF THE WORD

Dan Berrigan, Theologian

WALTER WINK

Dan Berrigan—theologian? Well, of course, as all of us are, sure, but—would he characterize himself thus? Can you imagine Dan introducing himself to a group, "Hi, I'm Dan, and I'm a theologian." Hard to conceive. Poet, yes. Disturber of the peace. Felon. Peace activist. Nudger of conscience. But theologian sounds too rarified, too abstract, too arcane.

To be sure, theology underlies everything Dan has ever done, or said, or written. One can find traces of outright theological utterance in his books, but only rarely. God is seldom named by the standard labels. Instead, Dan mints new designations for the reality that defies death.

> Those moments of grace! like an arrow of sunlight
>   along a mausoleum floor
> Something is happening, the door must be slightly
>   ajar
> I have a name for you; you are
>   the crack of light
>   under the door
>   of the city morgue.
>   —*Uncommon Prayer*

How does one hold fast to God in the presence of so much death? When humanity seems determined to write itself out of the book of life? When the nations and powers crush the small buds of decency and grind under heel the tender shoots of a genuinely new order? How can one believe in God when the prophets are jailed and the judges are freed? Dan offers little by way of comfort.

During his time "on the lam," he experienced the dark night of the soul, when even God seemed to shun him.

> To speak of God—I remember only an ache, a void, as though of
> a breath indrawn and held, until it hurt. God was absence. Not
> nothing, but Someone who had withdrawn for the duration,
> where, I knew not. I heard only the voice of a messenger, angel
> or tempter: "You're on your own" (*To Dwell in Peace*).

So much then for the idyllic fantasy of religious desperado underground, defying the Powers but atingle with grace. Even God turned a
cold shoulder.

But this, after all, had been the experience of others. Of Jesus.

> We could certainly nurture a far more bitter complaint against
> the hand of God had not God's son fallen under its blade. "Who
> did not spare His only son . . . " The truth steals our thunder, it
> puts God in our camp, that bloody slave camp into which the
> world seems bent on transforming itself. It puts God there, not
> as torturer or commissar, but as the first victim of all. The fate of
> God is crueler than the fate of most of us; an argument hard to
> answer, give up on God though we do, refuse to trust God though
> we do (*Uncommon Prayer*).

God as victim.

> I believe that God dies a little with every murder, every twist of
> cruelty, every lie, every concession offered to death. God dies in
> us, God dies in nature, God dies in innocent blood, God dies in
> a dying universe. God's voice is stifled, God's holy will mocked,
> God's tenderness set to naught. Vast armaments declare God im-
> potent, vast military budgets prove God insolvent. Pretentious,
> absurd, sinister beyond belief, modern dictators declare God's
> rule ended (*Uncommon Prayer*).

A clue: Dan comments that no one has been able to demonstrate
that Christian worship leads, in any large or direct sense, to Christian
conduct in the world. The same could be said for theology. My experience of seminary was thoroughly idealist; thoughts were regarded as
having more consequence, more substance, more reality, than actions.
Dan has set his whole life as a repudiation of this mentality. What is
uppermost in his value system seems to be doing the one thing needful.

In Nazi Germany, the one thing needful was resistance to Nazism.
Baptism, conversion, spirituality, prayer, works of charity, the teaching of tradition, values, morality—all of that, so necessary, so essential, was sheer blasphemy in the absence of the one thing needful.

I had rather a hundred times spend my life's energies working to heal the injustice around me, and never once speak of God . . . than spend life converting others to God, while I gave not a snap for prisoners, slave camps, wars, starving peoples, the sins of the mighty. To what God would I be converting others, in such a demented case? In what God would I believe? (*Uncommon Prayer*).

What God, indeed?

So we seem to have several gods, or perhaps scores of them, all dissembling as the one true God, all faithfully upholding tradition, Bible, creed, and church, all demanding total allegiance. Will the real God please stand up? They all spring to their feet. How will we discern these spirits? By their fruits, their capacity to lure us, despite our willing apostasies, to do the one thing needful.

The end of the Cold War, the relaxing of the nuclear crisis, and the emergence of the Pax Americana have done nothing to lessen the crisis we face. For the enemy never was the Soviet Union, or the United States. The enemy was, and is, and remains, the power of death. Where do we see that power most clearly manifested today?

I would say—in domination and its goon, violence. The churches have never yet decided that domination is wrong. So they continue to wobble between just-war theory and a kind of nonviolence in the breach—a nonviolence to be pursued until it proves ineffective, at which point one turns with alacrity to violence. A position that may be characterized, not as nonviolence, but as not-yet-violent.

Dan's legendary capacity to make the rest of us uncomfortable, leading us to suggest that he might be a bit too extremist, too self-righteous, too sure of his own rightness, comes from the clarity with which he sees our situation. It is not a matter simply of reforming the system, reducing the violence, spreading the goodies better. It is, in one of his most potent images, a matter of seating ourselves at a cannibal feast, the hideous banquet of war.

> The guests lean forward in silence; with gusto, with a good conscience, they tie their napkins about, balance knife and fork, await the entree. But faith is more tentative, shows more pain and less certainty. A faithful few refuse the menu and are, of course, punished for bad manners. . . . The faithful do not hang around the banquet, tempted here, nibbling there, hoping to reform the institution of eating humans. Not trying to formulate Nine or Ten Conditions for a Just Cannibalism. The banquet is not a good scene, such folk say stubbornly; they are intolerable spoilers, beyond converting. They keep saying things like, the

banquet cannot really be reformed. The plain trouble is human beings are the main course. And they shouldn't be. . . . But there you are, we're stuck with saying no to a question that should never have arisen in the first place: whether human beings ought to eat human beings (*Uncommon Prayer*).

There is in Dan's writings a vast storehouse of truth still awaiting recognition. And it is beautifully, breathtakingly written. The stunning poetry of his writing is itself a glimpse of a more beautiful order. It participates in God's domination-free order, which is coming. It is a paradox: the very beauty of the description of our rush to hell serves to awaken us, makes us hunger for love, the one thing needful.

The Way the Book Invites

CHED MYERS

[The Eagle] cries woe upon our world, before the event. Some call him a symbol of John, that soaring, indomitable spirit. He is also, if the expression can be pardoned, symbol of the United States Air Force. Indeed, symbol of the nation. As such, he flies high and mighty, wide and handsome over this world. Purely as symbol, he is ravenous, carnivorous, rockets in claw and preternatural skill at smelling out living creatures, falling on them with his clutch of thunder bolts. . . . All this is of course beside the point of a learned exegesis. To most scholars of the Bible, the crimes of the U.S. Air Force are forever beside the point. Thus does crime multiply and scholarship rot.
—Daniel Berrigan, *The Nightmare of God*

I wish to reflect on Daniel Berrigan's contribution to my understanding of how to reach and teach and live the Bible. If my appreciation seems like a eulogy, it is because I believe that good words about those we love are better spoken before they move on. And I am one of the many who love Dan and owe him a great deal.

I first encountered Dan's writing in 1976, which makes me a latecomer relative to most contributors in this volume. I was at that time a relatively new Christian who was just beginning to be radicalized by the insights of Clarence Jordan, Sojourners, and the Catholic Worker movement. Initially, I knew little about Berrigan's notoriety—Catonsville, Harrisburg, the underground. Instead, it was the power and vitality of his biblical reflections that attracted me.

My introduction was the essay "The Day the Empire Fell, and How, and Why," Dan's reading of Revelation 18, later published as a chapter in *The Nightmare of God*. I was mesmerized. It wasn't just the way in which Dan's poetic ingenuity brought the text alive. It was also the

81

way he read the text, without apology or qualification, as if it were addressed to our world.

America is Babylon. The suggestion seared me to a sweat. Yet Dan showed how the ancient metaphor, once reappropriated, could unmask the modern Denial. I sensed that this was not just another reading of the text. This was the text reading us.

Indeed it was. Dan's approach, I soon learned, was indebted to his close friend William Stringfellow. It was Stringfellow who put the matter concisely in the preface to *An Ethic for Christians and Other Aliens in a Strange Land*: "The task is to treat the nation within the tradition of biblical politics—to understand America biblically—not the other way around, not (to put it in an appropriately awkward way) to construe the Bible Americanly."

This was good, if also disturbing, news to me. Like so many Protestant evangelicals in the mid-1970s, I was at a kind of "hermeneutical impasse." I loved scripture and believed it had something to say not only to me but to the world as well. Neither the liberal nor the conservative traditions of biblical interpretation, however, seemed able (or, more likely, willing) to make concrete, compelling connections between the text and the world.

Liberal scholars were preoccupied with historical-critical methodologies that posited an impassable gulf between text and reader. This gulf in turn kept them demurring about the Bible's relevance to modern dilemmas. Conservatives, on the other hand, despite their invocations of the "authority of scripture," were highly selective about what guidance it might give us. Paul's admonitions to sexual fidelity were championed, the apostle's jail witness ignored; the Old Testament was instructive on war, but not the New Testament on nonviolence.

In short, neither liberals nor conservatives offered much biblical counsel on the personal and political challenges of racism, feminism, militarism, or economic justice. However much they claimed to be rivals, both seemed to be reading the Bible "Americanly." Which meant, as Dan put it, that "the crimes of the U.S. Air Force are forever beside the point."

I had suspected that something was indeed rotten with the biblical scholarship I was just beginning to learn, but I felt theologically orphaned. Dan's essay was like a switch being thrown, light for the road ahead. And it portended not just a new understanding; it invited me to practice.

I later had the good fortune to hear Dan teach Revelation in two contrasting venues. One was the weekly Sunday Bible study and liturgy at Jonah House in Baltimore, where Dan frequently visits and conspires with brother Phil, Liz McAlister, and others in the broader Atlantic Life Community. The other was at the Pacific School of Religion, in Berkeley, California, where Dan had been invited for a guest semester. The living room of a resistance community and the class-room of a mainline seminary could scarcely have represented more contrasting contexts. But Dan's handling of the text changed not at all—except that he slowly but surely created in the latter the atmosphere of the former. At the end of the PSR semester, he invited his students to participate with him in the "final exam": a protest against the University of California's participation in nuclear weapons research.

Unlike most Catholics of his generation, Dan is keenly literate in scripture. He can hold forth at will from the psalms, Hebrew prophets, or gospels, expecting his audience to keep up. His Jesuit training no doubt helped; his friendship with the likes of Abraham Heschel and Thomas Merton certainly did.

I am particularly fond of the way Dan breathes life into the psalms, deftly wielding paraphrase and poetic gloss. The parody of idols found in Psalm 115, for example, is transformed into a wry critique of militarism:

> They have idols, a pantheon of idols!
> basilisks, scorpions / satyrs, tri-headed dogs
> puppets wired for sound / yes and
> arrows and bows, tight strung / true in flight
> cannons ranting like mastadons
> tight lipped M-14s / those wooden sticks
> touch them—dry as dung / they speak to them—
>   ears of stone!
> put them to shoulder / they jerk awake
> they bark like dogs / they leap from the leash
> their sights zero in / their victim lies asprawl, throat
>   torn.
> then / Little Boy, Big Boy / squatting in bunkers
> dogs in caves / eyes half closed, jaws
> boiling with doomsday juices / their yawn, their
>   bark
> makes vincible dust / of the world's 7 fold wonders.
>   —"I Lift My Eyes Unto the Lord"
>   *The Catholic Worker* (December 1976)

Nor is Dan shy about moving beyond paraphrase to parables of his own making, as he did earlier in *Love, Love at the End,* and later in such pieces as "The Man Who Couldn't Say Yes or No" and "The Arms Race and the Hole in the Ground."

But it is the stories of scripture to which Dan keeps returning. He trusts them, commending them to us with the genuine heart of a pastor. The prophetic edge is the story's own, chosen carefully for its relevance to the topic at hand. His reading of 2 Samuel 24, for example, offers a portrait of King David as an "interesting imperialist," who is in turn "invariably and depressingly predictive of those in power." Similarly, a reflection on Isaiah 30 takes aim at the church's own apostasy:

> The word evidently is addressed to a group of so-called "believers" who have side interests involved, having nothing to do with the prior agreement that they have made with the Lord. . . . which had to do with their wheeling and dealing with the Power of this world, symbolized by the phrase "to go down to Egypt." Egypt being, of course, the perennial symbol of empire. I would submit as a strictly minority opinion that the first fact about American Christians is that they go down to Egypt rather than up to the Lord ("Living in the Shadow of Egypt," *Radix*, Fall 1977).

The gulf that seems so impassable to the scholastics Dan bridges by a deep grasp of the text's central subjects as archetypes, master metaphors that continually "speak to our condition" (as the Quakers would say) personally and politically.

Dan's best expository work can be seen, in my opinion, in *The Nightmare of God*, his "commentary" on the Apocalypse. As we might expect, he does not begin with the standard scholarly prolegomena and equivocation about the difficulties of interpreting such highly symbolic literature. Instead, Berrigan offers a meditation about the symbolic act of digging graves on the White House lawn, which has landed him in a D.C. jail, from where he will try to unravel the visions of another political prisoner, John of Patmos. A poem, "Zen Shovel," concludes:

> And the angel whispered / to my puzzled soul
> The further you dig / into origins
> the deeper deeper / origins get

The verse serves as a double entendre, suggesting that the task at hand is an archaeological excavation of the imperial unconscious.

Indeed, Dan approaches the Book of Revelation as a kind of dream text, a labyrinth of conflicting imperial and divine semiotics. His excavations are alternately dark and delightful. The reflections on the fall of Babylon that caught my attention almost twenty years ago still ignite my imagination:

> The "shipmasters and seafaring men, sailors and traders" form another chorus of mourners. The fast buck, so to speak, has slowed. . . . They saw many cities in their voyages; indeed, they

laced together the cities of the world, erasing boundaries, ignoring distances, weaving the great myth more cunningly and tightly—"intercivilizing" the violent, satiating the covetous, renewing the jaded, puffing the myth that the earth, in service to human appetite, is literally boundless in its promise, and its delivery, of paradise. And now, what their transfixed eyes behold is—hell. The city is burning.

Seeing Los Angeles in flames during the uprising of 1992—a hell that erupted inevitably from the disenfranchisement engineered by the managers of global capital—convinced me how truly Revelation 18 unmasks our sociopolitical reality. Yet among the commentaries, only Dan's dares to make the connection to our own imperial demise so explicitly.

America is Babylon. Dan is only revising the equation that the author of Revelation himself makes: Rome is Babylon. It is not, therefore, stooping to crude literalism or fundamentalism. Rather, Dan understands that John's symbolic discourse articulated a concrete (and costly) stand in a particular historical context, and that it may be recontextualized into another, analogous historical situation. This is of course exactly what liberation theologians did in reappropriating the Exodus (and later the Exile) motif for the situation of oppression of the third-world poor.

It is interesting to note that Berrigan the Jesuit is employing a hermeneutic not unlike that which James W. McClendon attributes to the "baptist vision," that is, to the theological legacy of the Radical Reformation:

> Scripture in this vision effects a link between the church of the apostles and our own. . . . This interpretation is not a rejection of biblical studies in favor of naive biblicism; rather, it is a justification for intense biblical study by every intelligible means, since the biblical story has present, not mere antiquarian, relevance. . . . The Bible is in this sense the church's book: we are the people of that book (*Ethics*, 32f.).

The relationship between the biblical communities and the church today, McClendon continues, is "neither developmental nor successionist, but mystical and immediate; it might be better understood by the artist and poet than by the metaphysician and dogmatist." Dan, the artist and poet, verifies the hypothesis.

Though Dan's own expository style eschews scholarly apparatus, he keeps a keen eye out for engaging and relevant studies produced within academia. He was one of the first to commend the liberation theology coming out of Latin America; I recall, for example, his enthusiastic promotion of Jose Miranda's *Marx and the Bible,* when North American seminaries were studiously ignoring its brilliant and polemical reading of Paul. Dan's collegial relationship with Nicaraguan priest Ernesto Cardenal similarly helped give wider exposure to the popular Bible study style of the *comunidades de base.*

Above all, however, Dan has kept vigil for signs of biblical literacy in the North American scene. He has exhorted many an activist to deeper study and many a student to action. In the last years of Bill Stringfellow's life, he and Dan dreamed of an "underground seminary" where biblical readings of America might be nurtured. Dan has kept that dream alive over the years, convening ad hoc sessions and encouraging those he felt had "made the connections" between word and world. Such a circle of critical reflection and action was, he confided to me once, what he hoped his own Jesuit order would one day become, again.

I know of Dan's quiet role as a mentor to many because he went out of his way to support and hearten my own work, offering his solidarity particularly through times of discouragement. He endorsed my commentary on Mark, even though my discipleship pales next to his own. And he continues to remind me how important the world of younger biblical expositors is to the movement.

On the rare occasions we see each other now (living loyally on opposite coasts as we do), Dan has been almost fatherly toward me, a gesture he no doubt intuits is all too lacking in radical Christian circles. This has been his greatest gift to me, more important than any degree or academic imprimatur could ever be. He understands from the biblical story that it is the blessings of elders that keep the movement going from generation to generation.

We miss the good news of scripture, Berrigan writes at the outset of *The Nightmare of God,* because we are "not free as yet to believe in the way the book invites." So he continues faithfully both to tell us and show us the Way of that freedom, of that belief, of that book.

Daniel, you have served us well. Pray now for us to do the same.

Taking the Book
with Life and Death Seriousness

BILL WYLIE-KELLERMANN

In 1972 I was a student at Union Seminary in New York City. The antiwar and civil rights movements had already left their impression on my young politics. I was to be sure a seminarian, but expected to merge some sort of community organizer with "a theological perspective." Frankly, much of what I believed was little more than sociology.

I recall at the time a course in the passion of Christ from an eminent scholar. We were treated, among other historically critical data, to the latest in archeological evidence for the method of crucifixion, how the ankles would be turned and the nails driven, the excruciating mechanics of death. The accuracy was impeccable, but the passion was at a safe remove: past tense and lukewarm.

As providence would have it (from my perspective like an intervention of the Word) Dan Berrigan just then walked out of Danbury Prison, where he'd done time in consequence of the 1968 Catonsville action, and into that Upper West Side academic fortress. With him came the scent of prison. The smells of the charnel house, of napalm and tiger cage tortures, were also in the wind. He stood before us and read the news with Jacques Ellul in one hand and the Revelation of John in the other. We recognized the passion. Present tense afire.

Never had I met anyone who took The Book with such life and death seriousness. Who thought in its own idiom. Who read it from the inside out. Who expected to find therein the powers of this world demythologized and exposed; and who took recourse to the scriptures in hopes of imagining the real world. Who thereby resisted the former and bet his life on the latter.

I got knocked off my horse. A tidy worldview crumbled. I do not exaggerate: I was struck dumb and wandered the seminary for a time more than a little lost. Berrigan noticed and one day called my name down a long basement hallway. Would I come up for Irish coffee? By and by: did I pray? Or read the Bible for any reason but a paper assigned? Had I ever seen these books: Merton on the Desert Fathers or Dorothy Day on the Long Loneliness? What signposts in the landscape did I follow? I took up the questions, like signposts in the landscape, and made them my own.

I have seen him do this with others since, some virtually in the grip of despair or death. Don't die, he would say. Come along, we need you. Don't be a conscious integer in the empire's spiritual body count. He made it seem as if resurrection and discipleship were synonyms.

And lo and behold: among us at Union a community of faith and resistance arose and followed at the edge of the fortress wall. Berrigan was to us as the angel to John in Revelation who hands on the little scroll with the urgent admonition: "Take it and eat; it will be bitter to your stomach, but sweet as honey in your mouth" (Rev. 10:9). In the fortress cafeteria, where sippers and samplers might taste, where scripture was easy on the tongue, he urged us eat the book. Swallow it whole; let it rumble with history in your guts.

It strikes me that this is always the character and consequence of his biblical scholarship. Moreover it may be the very reason his gifts of biblical interpretation are sometimes unaccounted. With barely an exception, he was viewed askance or completely ignored by the eminents at Union. I note that even Michael True's excellent compendium of Dan's work, *Daniel Berrigan: Poetry, Prose, Drama*, runs thin on this as a category of writing. There his book on the Psalms is represented, but bring on the commentaries and extended meditations on Isaiah, Daniel, or Jeremiah, the life and prayer of Jesus, on Paul in chains, or the Acts of the Apostles, the vision of John the Divine, and his most recent book, *Minor Prophets, Major Themes*.

It may serve to consider this new one at some length, to glimpse, as it were, the Berrigan method. To begin with, the book has a context: Yet another war is in the air with its ever perfected mechanics of death: now cruise missiles, fuel air bombs, laser guided etceteras. Their shadows cross the pages. Their victims cry out.

The liberation theologians contend there is no theology without a context. Berrigan suggests precisely the same of scripture study.

This is to say, the drumbeat of war is not merely contextual background noise, it is virtually the occasion of recourse. Who would have thought that meditating on Haggai or Zechariah during the Persian Gulf War could preserve one's moral sanity? Indeed prove the very act of sanity? That is Berrigan's claim.

His commentary ought to be required reading in Old Testament seminars, though one suspects in some it would need to be "snuck in the door." For one, it's more than a commentary in the conventional sense. It jumps the track of passionless objectivity and moves readily across time, deftly implicating our lives and history. (It would implicate even the seminar.)

This is not to suggest that conventional scholarship is pre-empted. The academics are, in fact, attended to and given their due. Berrigan defers to them and lets them speak, setting off their quotations to shade in background or a historical skyline, to provide a subtle insight, or even to serve as an ironic foil that may typify ourselves and our culture-bound imaginations and judgments.

But then. The commentary cracks and breaks open the genre. More than a new hermeneutic is commended: it partakes the prophetic method.

Even the style betrays an intuitive act of mimicry. These reflections are laid out on the page almost in fragments, with breaks or breaths or seams between. We are reminded how the prophetic utterances were gathered up (by the prophets themselves or mayhap their disciples) and stitched together—by their best lights and inspirations—into more or less coherent books. The scholars, in their turn, never tire of reversing the process, sifting and separating the isolated "pericopes," even rearranging material according to their own lights. In any event, the seams are there to be recognized. You can feel them in the fits and leaps of reading. And in between, in the gaps and the cracks there is— what? sighs too deep for words? a silent agony? the wrestling with God or doubt or death? the movement of history? All of these and more.

In reflecting on their words, Berrigan echoes the rhythm of this biblical style. And in those seemly breaks on his page, what? silence and tears, the lunge of empire, more and the same.

Minor Prophets has its own pre-history. One hears portions offered and refined in retreats where this or that prophet was commended for common consideration. One imagines passages circulated hand to hand in jail cells, where prisoners of conscience abide and take heart. Certain fragments were surely commended among those preparing for public witness action at, let us guess, a faith and resistance gathering. These are reflections hammered out in common decision.

One recalls the Plowshares movement (now flourishing fifteen years or more) and wonders: Was Micah 4 virtually the breaking and entry point for this book? Was it the way in, the door opening for Berrigan upon the whole ragtag crew of the minor prophets?

A small irony: the minors were almost exclusively word prophets, but Berrigan's commentary is shot through with present-day deeds and symbolic actions—more after the fashion of Jeremiah's signs: crashing down the pots, donning the yoke of empire, burying the loincloth, or investing in the absurd real estate of return. The actions Berrigan invokes—at Pentagon and nuclear installations, laboratories and bunkers, in the streets and on the road of return with Salvadoran campesinos—are invariably to the point. Across time, by grounded imagination and faith, the words and the deed, the text and community, illuminate one another.

Dan's work is stunning in its ability to evoke the humanity of the prophets. Why should that seem such a rarity? From one theological extreme their canonization sanctifies them beyond reach or (another version of the same thing) renders them faceless and empty conduits for the word. From another, more sophisticated, they are reduced to cultural ciphers, instruments of the social forces which engage in the literary production of texts. In *Minor Prophets, Major Themes*, however, they are granted life, summoned in all their humanity. The word is their struggle with conscience, their burning tears, their prayer, and choice. In that sense, their humanity provokes our own.

And a conversation begins. Having heard them in their full humanness (with all the foibles and confusions, blind spots and shortfalls entailed) Berrigan claims a freedom to respond, to disagree and criticize, even to call these mentors to account before community and our God. Do they challenge our lives and hearts? Yes. But if we're truly in this thing together, then let us push back.

Their sexism comes to mind, with Hosea a flaming exemplar. Has he reduced his wife, Gomer, to a theological metaphor? Berrigan names this nothing less than abuse, and turns things back on the prophet by imagining a Book of Gomer, which gives the silent nobody a voice. Is Hosea thereby written off and out? By no means. But in his exposure we are all made the better.

Or take Obadiah. How, Berrigan goes so far as to ponder, did this small-minded, rancorous prophet full of vengeful bitterness even make it into the canon? He supplants Yahweh with Mars, and sits smugly in the book. And yet, his humanity is so like our own in this very regard, as are his confusions. "Let Obadiah remind us of a long and bitter history of bellicose folly." Even then the prophet has flashes of insight: if he's wrong about God, his take on empire is clear seeing and lucid.

Herewith another astonishment: that the prophets should be shown so unanimous, so univocal, so collectively relentless in their complaint against empire in its manifold forms, near and far. Does Berrigan inflate or inflict this on the texts, bringing along and imposing some politic of his own? Read the texts. They are uncompromising. Perhaps our amazement is evidence against us that the imperial spirit, near and far, has muted and suppressed these neglected voices too long from our hearing.

There is one thing Berrigan does bring unapologetically to such conversations and reflections: the commitment to nonviolence. It functions like the plumb line of Amos. He holds it out to us, out to the prophets. Its line goes straight to the heart of earth, straight to the heart of Christ. Of course, beside it empires are crooked and top-heavy walls shown ready to collapse. But prophets too may be bent; even their ideas of God might suffer a twist.

Another way of saying this is that the gospels are never far from the page. The One who is the fullness of humanity, a prophet mighty in deed, steps from the wings now and again—not so much to speak as to show his wounds, to look the prophets in the eye and love them.

Echoing Dorothy Day's derision of being called a saint, William Stringfellow used to inveigh against those who labeled Dan Berrigan a prophet (or a poet) in order to write him off, beyond the realm of ordinary people, ordinary responsibility, and normative and human action. I suppose it is not unlike the tactic of confining the word of God only to a sacred book—in order to banish it safely from our scene, as though it were not everywhere and always to be recognized in common history and our lives.

The fact of the matter is that Dan Berrigan is both prophet and poet. His biblical theology and interpretation verify those vocations all the more so. But let none of us thereby be off the hook of mere Christianity's demands, nor fear to recognize, and even partake, the bittersweet word of God wherever it may be found.

The Angel of Recidivism

MEGAN McKENNA

"Recidivism," according to the dictionary, is "a tendency to re-lapse into a previous condition or mode of behavior, especially relapse into criminal behavior." It is habitual criminal action. And so "the Angel of Recidivism," as Daniel Berrigan calls this angel, is the one who lures, the one who leads us into patterns that upset the social order and refuses to allow history to ignore the reality of truth according to the gospel.

The stories about this angel are found primarily in the Acts of the Apostles, chapters 5 and 12. First, Peter meets with the believers in Jerusalem in Solomon's Porch. People bring their sick there hoping that Peter's shadow might fall on them. The High Priest and his supporters, the party of the Sadducees, become jealous of the apostles and have them arrested and thrown in the public jail. "But an angel of the Lord opened the door of the prison during the night, brought them out, and said to them, 'Go and stand in the Temple court and give the people the message of life.' Accordingly, they entered the Temple at dawn and resumed their teaching."

This kind of behavior landed them in the clink in the first place.

The court convenes and the prisoners are sent for. The soldiers return and report: "We found the prison securely locked and the prison guards at their post outside the gate, but when we opened the gate, we found no one inside." Everyone is baffled. Word spreads quickly, and the Sanhedrin is informed that "those folk you arrested are back at their preaching." They are brought by the guards, this time without any show of force, back to court to face the music. The charge is clear: "We gave you strict orders not to preach such a Savior, but you have filled Jerusalem with your teaching and you intend charging us with the killing of this man." And the defense is crystal clear: "Better for us to obey God rather than men!" What ensues is bedlam. The authorities want to kill the prisoners, literally, but Gamaliel, a teacher of the

92

law, intervenes in their behalf and stills the murderers' intent for the time being. After Gamaliel's lengthy speech, the Council has the apostles whipped and orders them not to speak again of Jesus Savior. Then, it says, "they set them free." The result: "The apostles went out from the Council rejoicing that they were considered worthy to suffer disgrace for the sake of the Name. Day after day, both in the Temple and in the people's homes, they continued to teach and to proclaim that Jesus was the Messiah." Not very repentant criminals. Recidivists, no doubt about it.

Persecution sets in, in earnest. King Herod has James killed, and when he sees that it greatly pleases the Jews, he has Peter arrested also. On the night before the trial, the Angel of Recidivism comes again—a pesky bit of light intruding in the darkness:

> Peter was sleeping between two soldiers, bound by a double chain, while guards kept watch at the gate of the prison.
>
> Suddenly an angel of the Lord stood there and a light shone in the prison cell. The angel tapped Peter on the side and woke him saying: "Get up quickly!" At once the chains fell from Peter's wrists. The angel said, "Put on your belt and your sandals." Peter did so, and the angel added, "Now, put on your cloak and follow me." [Peter has heard these commands before!—see John 21:18ff.]
>
> Peter followed him out; yet he did not realize that what was happening to him with the angel was real; he thought he was seeing a vision. They passed the first guard and then the second and they came to the iron door leading out to the city, which opened of itself for them. They went out and made their way down a narrow alley, when suddenly the angel left him. [They have a disconcerting way of disappearing, like the One they serve.]
>
> Then Peter recovered his senses and said, "Now I know that the Lord has sent his angel and has rescued me from Herod's clutches and from all that the Jews had in store for me." Peter then found his bearings and came to the house of Mary, the mother of John also known as Mark, where many were gathered together and were praying (Acts 12:1-12).

What follows reads like a comedy. Mary is so excited that she leaves the door locked and goes to announce the good news of Peter's freedom—and leaves Peter standing outside. Then there is moving him to another place. At daybreak, there is commotion and the guards pay heavily for Herod's frustration: they are questioned and executed. The style of life is set: preach about the power of that Name publicly; accuse evildoers of killing and injustice; get arrested and jailed; go to court; escape by the skin of your teeth (often losing some skin in the process) and go back and do it again! The Angel of Recidivism is loose and hard to ignore.

This angel seems a guardian spirit to those who stand in the breach and go on about the presence and the power of that Name: that Name that cannot tolerate evil. Prophets are driven by the Angel of Recidivism. They know the hard realities, and they cannot abide easy avoidance of the issues. Not to describe insidiousness is to contribute to the anguish. Decay unchecked, despair encouraged, hate tolerated, unnecessary deaths forgotten, violence romanticized, pollution accommodated, spiritualities intent on desensitizing the individual to others' pain—these are the newer rings of hell.

So truth is served. We are reminded that pain is an open door to heaven, but mostly for the victims, the unesteemed, the crucified. It is time for penance, massive asceticism—the fresher form of nonviolent resistance to violence. God is repulsed by religious people seduced by self-knowledge and hearts turned resolutely aside from the incarnation in suffering people.

Evil—mundane, acceptable, ignored, devised, rationalized, excused, analyzed, exported, made profitable—calls for defiance. It demands accusation and judgment. We are often a people, a culture, a nation, a church that will be remembered for our abrogation of personal responsibility, our scapegoating, greed, vengeance, lying, and violence. We are mean, spiteful, divisive people, heartless, self-obsessed, inhuman.

Of course those who talk like that, write like that, pray like that, publicly and in people's homes, will be arrested and thrown into the public jail and taken to court. And, if such persons should, in the ancient traditions of the old prophets, symbolically enact the truth, even just by letting their shadow fall upon the sick, not to mention the structures of untruth, then they deserve to suffer the consequences of their spurious behaviors. The first time they can be labeled "overly enthusiastic." The second deserves calling them to the attention of the authorities and getting the point across that this will not be tolerated in a lawful society. And if it should be deliberately planned, secretly plotted a third time and forever thereafter, perhaps we should all chalk it up to obeying the Angel of Recidivism. Perhaps the way the angels scratch on our souls these days is the scraping around of sliding bars and prison doors, the shackles dragging and the long days and nights of incarceration due to "civil disobedience," known in more scriptural communities as "preaching that Name."

That Angel of Recidivism! There is a medieval legend that will perhaps throw some light on who this mysterious angel really is.

There was an archangel, Michael by name, charged by the Holy One with casting Lucifer forth from heaven, down to earth. There was war in heaven and some fell from the abiding presence of the Light. Then Michael was commissioned by God to defend the earth, to take charge of the garden where Yahweh God would place the first humans, Adam and Eve. He went, obeying immediately. It is believed that Yahweh God knew Satan's intent to upset the harmony and balance of the earth, to distort the plan of God to lift humans up from their lowly place below the angels to be God's friends. So God sent Michael to be on the lookout for Satan and to protect our ancestors from their choice and fate. But Michael failed. Michael was expecting a creature of light, the one he battled in the heavens. The angel once known as Lucifer had changed form into a crafty, sly, and devious serpent. And so it was that Michael let him slip by, unsuspecting, and Satan trapped Adam and Eve, and they too fell from glory and grace.

And so Adam and Eve were exiled from Eden, and Michael was stationed by God with a flaming revolving sword at the gate of the garden, charged to keep Adam and Eve from entering again. Again Michael obeyed. But Michael was crushed and broken-hearted that he had failed God's charge, and worse, that he had not been able to prevent Adam and Eve from sinning, that he had not protected the people of God from evil. He stood guard and yet, he had pity on Adam and Eve, who now had to toil and sweat, to work and suffer just to survive, and then to die. Yahweh God had made for them garments of skin and clothed them so that they did not go naked into the world. So Michael thought to give them a gift as well. In pity for the wretchedness of their lives, Michael took his flaming sword and transformed it into a plow, teaching Adam to till the fields and bring forth food from the land, easing their burden and his own sense of failing God.

They say that ever since then, Michael is the defender of the honor of God, and, like God, he cares for the poor and the lowliest of the earth, the ones who plow the fields and harvest the crops and provide food for others. Like God, he defends and guards all those who struggle face to face against evil, confronting it and seeking to stop its power in their flesh and lives. He is the special patron of the prophets of God.

They say too that Michael was the first to learn that one cannot fight evil on earth as one does in heaven, and that Michael was the first proponent of nonviolent resistance to evil. It is Michael's experience of Satan on earth that is remembered and echoed and given substance in all the visions, hopes, and promises of the prophets, especially the most ancient and heartening: "This God will rule over the nations and settle disputes for many peoples. They will beat their swords into plowshares and their spears into pruning hooks. Nation will not raise sword against nation; they will train for war no more" (Isaiah 2:4). The Angel of Recidivism, who keeps returning to spring the unruly and uncontrollable preachers of the Name, could be none other than Michael the Archangel, guardian of God's honor.

Those who know and obey that angel know that all mysteries of God are hard—hard as nails, hard as wood, hard as fire, hard as jail, hard as isolation, hard as death; but they know, too, that justice is that Holy One among us, that Criminal who nurtured the tendency to forgive and who stood in court saying: "For this I was born and for this I have come into the world, to bear witness to the truth. Everyone who is on the side of truth hears my voice" (John 18:37). Blessed be that Name!

Thank you, Daniel, for blessing that Name.

THE POET

Walking with Father Dan

THICH NHAT HANH

I like to go walking with Father Dan. We have walked together in Central Park in New York City, in the Parc of Sceaux near Paris, and a lot of times among the hills behind my hermitage in Fontvannes, situated in the area of the Forêt d'Othe, an hour and a half's drive southeast of Paris.

Father Dan walks faster than I do. I have gotten into the habit of walking slowly, coordinating my breath with my steps. It happens so often that during our walking together, he has to stop and wait for me. Then, we start again. We used to walk in silence.

In one of his visits, Father Dan stayed with us in Sceaux for more than a month. Of course, besides the walking, he shared with us the sitting and the tea drinking. As I write these lines, I see all his friends as my friends and all mine as his. Quite a lot of us are walking together, sitting together, and drinking tea together. And by doing so we try to give peace a chance.

Father Dan is a great poet. I also write poems. Many of them are about walking and sitting. I would like to share with him and his friends a few poems of mine that have to do with walking and sitting. I hope he likes them. I hope you all enjoy them.

Your cup of tea is steaming and hot, Father Dan.

Joyeuse anniversaire!

GOING IN CIRCLES

O you who are going in circles,
please stop.
What are you doing it for?

"I cannot *be* without going,

because I don't know where to go.
That's why I go in circles."

O you who are going in circles,
please stop.

"But if I stop going,
I will stop being."

O my friend who is going in circles,
you are not one with
this crazy business of going in circles.
You may enjoy going,
but not going in circles.

"Where can I go?"

Go where you can find your beloved,
where you can find yourself.

EARTH TOUCHING

Here is the foot of a tree.
Here is an empty, quiet place.
Here is a cushion.
Brother, why don't you sit down?

Sit upright.
Sit with solidity.
Sit in peace.
Don't let your thoughts lift you up into the air.
Sit so that your thighs touch the Earth.
Be one with her.
You may like to smile, brother.
Earth will transmit to you her solidity,
her peace, and her joy.
With your mindful breathing,
with your peaceful smile,
you sustain the mudra of Earth Touching.

There were times when you didn't do well.
Sitting on Earth, it was as if you were floating in
    the air,
you who used to go in circles in the triple world

and be drawn into the ocean of illusion.
But Earth is always patient
and one-hearted.
Earth is still waiting for you
because Earth has been waiting for you
during the last trillion lives.
That is why she can wait for you for any length of
    time.
She knows that finally you will come back to her
    one day.
She will welcome you
always fresh and green, exactly like the first time,
because love never says, "This is the last";
because Earth is a loving mother.
She will never stop waiting for you.
Do go back to her, brother.
You will be like that tree.
The leaves, the branches, and the flowers of your
    soul
will be fresh and green
once you enter the mudra of Earth Touching.

The empty path welcomes you, sister,
fragrant with grass and little flowers,
the path paved with paddy fields
still bearing the marks of your childhood
and the fragrance of mother's hand.
Walk leisurely, peacefully.
Your feet should deeply touch the Earth.
Don't let your thoughts lift you up into the air,
    sister.
Go back to the path every moment.
The path is your dearest friend.
She will transmit to you
her solidity,
her peace.

With your deep breathing,
you sustain the mudra of Earth Touching.
Walk as if you were kissing the Earth with your
    feet,
as if you were massaging the Earth.
The marks left by your feet
will be like the marks of an emperor's seal
calling for Now to go back to Here;

so that life will be present;
so that the blood will bring the color of love to
    your face;
so that the wonders of life will be manifested,
and all afflictions will be transformed into
peace and joy.

There are times when you did not succeed, sister.
Walking on the empty path, you were floating in
    the air,
because you used to get lost in samsara
and drawn into the world of illusion.
But the beautiful path is always patient.
It is always waiting for you to come back,
that path which is so familiar to you,
that path which is so faithful.
It knows deeply that you will come back one day.
It will be joyful to welcome you back.
It will be as fresh and as beautiful as the first time.
Love never says that this is the last time.

That path is you, most intimate sister.
That is why it will never be tired of waiting.
Whether it is covered now with red dust
or with Autumn leaves
or icy snow—
do go back to the path, sister,
because I know
you will be like that tree,
the leaves, the trunk, the branches,
and the blossoms of your soul
will be fresh and beautiful,
once you enter the mudra of Earth Touching.

Living What You Believe

DENISE LEVERTOV

Daniel Berrigan and I made a sort of joint debut together (along with Franklin Reeve) as "New Poets" in a series at the Poetry Center in New York, somewhere around 1959. We were each "introduced" by the late R. P. Blacknur, who retired to the greenroom (and the whiskey) during our successive readings. . . . In those pre-'60s days, we were all shy and reserved with one another and did little to become acquainted. In fact, I don't believe Dan and I exchanged a single word on that occasion.

Later on, the antiwar movement brought us into fairly frequent proximity, and we increasingly knew many of the same people, among them Thomas Merton, Dorothy Day (whom I met several times through Eileen Egan), and Michael True, who became a good friend of both Dan's and mine.

I would never have imagined that the shy, old-style, young Jesuit with whom I'd shared a stage in 1959 would have become the bold hero of the nonviolent movement I grew to admire so much. A trace of flamboyance seems to enable him actually to enjoy some of his strategies, which though undertaken in profoundest seriousness and commitment, have had about them a certain theatricality, a kind of boyish adventurousness. I love this quality. Among my memories of Dan is one of those occasions when, while in hiding on Block Island, he slipped into Cambridge to do a fund-raising evening at someone's house. All the guests were invited to meet an unnamed guest of honor, but I doubt if any of us was taken by surprise. Yet since he was subject to arrest, the event had a Scarlet Pimpernel thrill to it, and Dan himself had a kind of dash and twinkle thoroughly in keeping with the adventure.

Our paths have crossed few times in many years, except on paper. But my most recent experience of him is to me the most moving. A friend of mine in New York City, a young man who'd been my student, then my secretary, and then my continuing, dear friend, had AIDS, and I felt that—so many friends of his, including his partner, having died—he was much too isolated. I decided to ask Dan to put him in touch with some AIDS assistance services he might not know about. Steve was not a Catholic, but I felt sure he would be responsive to any practical suggestions Dan might offer, both because they would come through me and because he admired Dan's political commitment.

The very day he received my letter, Dan called him—much to Steve's astonishment and gratification. And not long after, when Steve was hospitalized, Dan visited him. Steve died almost the next day. I shall never forget the promptitude of Dan's actions in response to my request.

Dan is a man who really lives what he believes, without compromise or ambiguity—and yet gently. It's a privilege to join in honoring him.

A Poet for Difficult Times

ELIZABETH BARTELME

In my first summer as a fledgling editor at the Macmillan Company, I was asked by the editor-in-chief to speak gently but firmly to an author who had departed, with his former editor, to another publishing house. Reluctantly, I caught a train and made my way to Fordham University where Daniel Berrigan was teaching summer school. I had not met him previously and was charmed by this eager-looking young priest who was astonished to discover that he had violated the option clause in his contract. He didn't know he had an option clause. What did it mean? And so on.

After an hour of conversation, mostly about friends we had in common—Dorothy Day, Ned O'Gorman—it was clear that the Reverend Father Berrigan was not about to return to Macmillan. He was distressed, concerned, and immovable in his loyalty to his original editor. This was the first time I was to encounter this aspect of Daniel Berrigan, but by no means the last. I returned downtown to Manhattan, unsuccessful and sad to think we had lost our prize-winning poet, who also was obviously a special kind of person.

Sometime later it developed that all was not lost: things had not worked out with the other publisher. Could Daniel Berrigan come back to Macmillan? I was delighted to say yes, of course, and so began a long and unusual author/editor relationship. Dan's book *Time Without Number*, had won the coveted Lamont Award of the American Academy of Arts and Letters for a first book of poetry and been nominated for the National Book Award. He had then gone on to write two prose works and two more books of verse. Now the Jesuits had given him a sabbatical year, and he was off to Paris to work and study.

A new contract was prepared and Daniel departed to be heard from only occasionally in that year. The following spring I myself was in Paris, and Dan undertook to be my guide. Seeing Paris for the first time through the eyes of a poet was a revelatory experience. It was May, the chestnuts were in bloom—everything was as it was supposed to be (and probably rarely was) in enchanting Paris. Poems flowed naturally from its ambiance. *No One Walks Waters*, the book Dan was working on, contains his "Paris Suite," a paean to the loveliness of that place in that time.

When I next heard from Dan, he was back in New York, working as an associate editor on *Jesuit Mission*, an assignment not quite to his taste or worthy of his talents. However, in order to spruce up the magazine, he established an "advisory board" of several of his friends, who met from time to time to eat, drink, and hand out suggestions. It was useful and fun but it didn't last long. Dan's many run-ins with the authorities were about to begin. He has related these clashes at length in his autobiography, *To Dwell in Peace*, and as is well known, most of them were related to his resistance to the Vietnam war.

The first came about when he was accused of disobeying an order not to talk about the purported suicide of a young Catholic Worker. For this he was exiled to Latin America, and because of this exile, his friends protested at such length that after four months he was allowed to return, exhausted but considerably toughened. Meanwhile, the war protests had accelerated and huge crowds were beginning to gather to demand an end to that unjust conflict. Dan was teaching at Cornell, surrounded by student ferment, when he was asked to go to Hanoi to escort home three American pilots who were to be released in honor of the Tet festival.

The afternoon before his flight left he called me and asked me to come to the airport and bring as many copies of his books as I could carry, and particularly the more recent ones, which dealt with resistance to the war. I rounded up as many as I could find, got into a taxi, and rushed out to JFK. There Dan and Howard Zinn were being seen off by Dave Dellinger and Tom Hayden and a camera crew from CBS. I handed him the books, which were intended for the Vietnamese, said good-bye, and rode back to the city with the camera crew. In the end the pilots were brought back, not by the religious emissaries, but by an Air Force plane. Dan felt betrayed, and he poured out his story in *Night Flight to Hanoi*, a manuscript he delivered to me shortly after his return.

Always a prolific writer, Dan seized every opportunity to address his growing public about the problems that preoccupied him, the problems of peace, poverty, and racial justice. As he wrote very rapidly, he produced a steady stream of manuscripts. Sometimes there were so many that he needed more than one publisher. And as he wrote both his poetry and his prose took on a sharper edge, a more political tone.

These changes, of course, came about primarily because of Dan's opposition to the Vietnam war. Prior to the war years he had produced lyrical poetry and prose of a theological nature. Now his writing began to assume the prophetic tone and the call to resistance that has marked it to the present time. His poems became looser, less wedded to conventional form. What had once been a self-effacing style became straightforward and, at times, accusatory of those who supported the war.

He was not only writing against the war, however, but becoming involved in actions—the most serious of which was the burning of draft files at Catonsville. For this, along with his "co-conspirators," he was tried and sentenced to prison. Daniel decided not to turn himself in and eventually was arrested at the home of his friend William Stringfellow on Block Island.

Daniel was unable to publish while he was imprisoned, but he was not prevented from corresponding with those on his approved list. I had had submitted to me a group of paintings by two young artists, Gregory and Deborah Harris. I took them to Danbury and showed them to Dan, who was pleased and impressed by them. Soon I began to get letters inspired by these works, and from them it was possible to produce a coherent text. Thus the book, *Jesus Christ*, took shape, a modest offering to be sure, compared with some of his other works, but remarkable considering the handicap under which it was written and produced.

By this time I had moved to Doubleday, and Dan had moved with me. His flow of books continued with *No Bars to Manhood*, *The Dark Night of Resistance*, and *America Is Hard to Find*. For the latter title, he provided the jacket illustration, which bore his distinctive touch. When Dan appeared on the *Today* show, NBC blew up the cover of *Love, Love at the End* (which had been designed by his friend Corita Kent) into a huge poster and used it as a backdrop for the interview. What they could not show were the endpapers of the book that Dan himself had inscribed calligraphically with one of his poems, "Prayer from the Catbird Seat." Dan's sensitivity to all forms of art was splendidly employed in this merging of the visual with the written word. Further, a different art form, that of the drama, emerged in *The Trial of the Catonsville Nine*. During the actual trial, it was as if the proceedings were orchestrated by Daniel, and there were moments of almost liturgical ritual. When the trial was produced as a play in New York, with professional actors using Dan's words, it was again strong and moving. As both *auteur* and actor, Dan was incomparable.

Although from the time he became an active antiwar protester, Dan's writing reflected his passionate dedication to peace, his work was deeply rooted in his religious beliefs. Critical though he might be at times of the institutional church, he loved the person of Jesus in the gospels, in the eucharist. The New Testament was and is his life source; his poetry flows bounteously from it.

Despite the intense convictions of his prose work, the dramatic quality of his life, and the fervor of his peacemaking activities, it is for his poems that Daniel will be remembered—or so it seems to me. The poetry moves from lyrical to apocalyptic, from wonder at the beauty of the world to disgust at the ugliness human beings have made of it. The poems embrace the cries of children and the cries of refugees; the tenderness of his love for his mother and the frustration of uselessly trying to please his father; wedding feasts and the bitterness of prison. There is very little that this large-hearted Jesuit has not experienced, and he has written about all of it brilliantly. Which is to say, he is a poet for difficult times, for our time.

Just the other day, my doorbell rang and there was a package from Daniel—his most recent book of poetry, *May All Creatures Live*. I sat down with it and began to read. Poems of wonder, of hope, poems of the city, of prison. A new book from Dan. It was like old times.

Unka's Catfish Pizza, Cappuccino, and Poetry

FRIDA BERRIGAN

When I was young, my brother and I would sit with Uncle Dan (Unka) and talk about catfish pizza. We planned to open a restaurant and serve it—crust, tomato sauce, whole cloves of garlic, cheese, and big pieces of catfish—to all the customers, whether they wanted it or not. We laughed for hours about it, clapping our hands with delight.

When I was born, the first child spat from Jonah's whale, he wrote fourteen poems that my folks gave to me when I turned eight. Today is my twenty-first birthday, and I have just begun to read and understand and love those poems. In one he reminds me that—

> You are named for a dying woman
> weak as water, lucid as steel
> She takes death in stride
> She looks life in full face
> When you rest in her withered arms
> You will know, you will know.

I shared the earth with Grandma Frida only briefly and have no memory of her. She is built from photographs and the loving, rich words of my father and uncles. I never "knew" her, but I know her through Unka's poem. He wears her wedding band alongside a silver ring etched with the symbol of the fish. I am named for her, and I carry her with me, a fragile image and strong words. These lines took twenty-one years to reach my heart, but they lie there now, etched in the pulsing muscle—warming and strengthening, comforting and challenging.

Unka tells me stories of our family coming over to the United States as we sit sipping cappuccino in a cafe in New York City. He tells me how the immigrants had to carry their trunks up a huge flight of stairs and if they didn't make it, they were turned away. I will not forget that I stand on a rock of history, carrying the dreams of women "lucid as steel" inside of me.

His poems, recently discovered, also remind me of a past, present, and future struggle, and when I am full of fear and doubt, Unka's words from the stand in King of Prussia, "I could not not do what I did," reverberate in my mind, pulling me out into thoughtful action, up into joyous action. "You are a child of struggle," he tells me—

> You came from a Harrisburg pit
> You came of custom house blood
> You came from Catonsville fire
> You came from jail
> You came in spite of Judge Mace's death's head
> shaking NO in its socket.
> You came without regard to
> Writs, torts, barbed wire;
> You came up from the least known
> Phiz, China and beyond
> Down from Dante's crystalline
> paradise—a round eyed
> round trip freeloader.
> You came from a nun
> You came from a priest
> You came from a vow
> Yes and No and the Great Tao
> that creeps, a vine
> claiming like two arms
> the world's rack for its own
> dismembering and flowering.

Unka is a source of stories, jokes, laughter from deep in the belly, tumbling words, admired by the aspiring and gleamy-eyed, a teacher, a poet, one who reminds and is rewound to be listened to again and again. For these poems, for my grandmother, for his laughter, and for his catfish pizza, I love him deeply and sing lilting hurrays and gruff guffaws for him.

An Easy Essay from a Catholic Worker

CARMEN TROTTA

The little (Vietnamese) boy
his face breaded with rice
fathered   under the rain of fire
in your stigmatized (American) hands
somewhere   between
on the long trek homeward
this century's boneyard   and
the land of unknowing.
Heft of flesh .and bone
A Hiroshima child from hell.

Or was it she, the comely one
the one and only
lonely one
who made of house
that house
those grudging narrow windows
past mistress of a thousand ways
of coping with
poverty and children
                a home
her unobtrusive, hardscrabble faith
that bore all
poverty and children and yes, of course, you
And somehow gracefully
Impossibly.

Impossibly: Your Father.
Wild Irish riddle

riddled your youth with
his
idiot thrashing storms
fear and confusion.
Did you ever love him?
       Yes!
And it is he gave us
what others call distemper   madness
the best of his juice and brawn
unified tension to good purpose
That hammer having to fall.

And just as surly
Fathered alike, the other
of whom your loquacious self
Dwelling in Peace
speaks not the promised word
No   maladroit specimen he
but broad shouldered
and strong enough
to lift
the world   perhaps
and you   at least
like one of those Apostles
on Chartres stained glass
to see
an extra Gospel mile.

Or was it Dorothy?
Was it Merton?
Was it all of those?
You say who.
But you look pointedly beyond
to that
graceful grotesquerie
A man
standing on his nails
an ash like dew, a sweat
upon his face.
Thank him?
Do you think He is
really not Dead?

Well then
Thank You Christ Jesus

for hearing the prayers of
the faithful
and granting to America
(secular as hell)
so hard to find
what she so badly needs and needed
a priest of God Most High.

THE PEACEMAKER

A Great Lake of Beer

JIM FOREST

Written in large letters in Dan's black coat-hanger-like script on the wall above his refrigerator, a container always likely to have some beer inside if nothing else, was a quotation from the great Irish saint and abbess, Bridget:

> I should like a great lake of beer for the King of
>   Kings.
> I should like the angels of Heaven to be drinking it
>   through time eternal.
> I should like excellent meats of belief and pure
>   piety.
> I should like flails of penance at my house.
> I should like the people of Heaven at my house;
> I should like barrels of peace at their disposal;
> I should like vessels of charity for distribution;
> I should like for them cellars of mercy.
> I should like cheerfulness to be in their drinking.
> I should like Jesus to be there among them.
> I should like the three Marys of illustrious renown
>   to be with us.
> I should like the people of Heaven, the poor, to be
>   gathered around us from all parts.

I copied the text and treasured it, all the time wondering if it were really Bridget's words or Dan's, composed in her honor and in homage to the Irish love of beer and all the good talk that flows with it. I did in time discover the text was truly Bridget's own. Still, in my own mind the words are a kind of Berrigan gospel, for behind nearly everything I know about Dan is joy in hospitality and an overwhelming hope that sooner or later everyone will gather with the King of Kings around a great lake of beer, share barrels of peace, and be drenched themselves in flails of penance, celebration, and mourning folded together in cellars of mercy.

One of the penalties of living most of the past two decades in Europe is that I am not merely a lake but an ocean away from Dan. It's an age since I last had a beer from his refrigerator. I can't even be sure Bridget's words aren't long worded over with some newer revelation. Still, whatever is currently on the wall, till his dying day Dan will be trying to shepherd us all toward "excellent meats of belief and pure piety."

Though a poet, playwright, and teacher, Dan is best known for troubling state and church, and has indeed done much to torment both. Worse, it is all too obvious he has enjoyed his mischief. There has been a persistent playfulness about his disobedient actions, whether burning draft records, disturbing bomb makers, or tormenting religious superiors, a definite cat-fed-on-the-canary look whenever being led away by police or banished to ecclesiastical Siberias.

Perhaps because I was only twenty years old, this wasn't evident to me when I first met him in 1961. I had come along from the Catholic Worker community one evening with Dorothy Day to hear him read a paper. That night, at least, he looked as law-abiding as a secretary to Cardinal Spellman. In his finely-tailored black clericals, one would never have imagined this lean Jesuit would in a few years' time be a renowned dissident or a nonconformist of any kind. Were not Jesuits specialists in obedience? Nothing about Father Daniel Berrigan suggested otherwise.

It was in Paris that we next met, brought together by a Fellowship of Reconciliation project the centerpiece of which was participation in the Christian Peace Conference in Prague that July. In France on sabbatical, Dan was still wearing black, but now turtleneck and chinos plus a faded green windbreaker. A battered leather sack over his shoulder served functions that for other professional men his age would require an attache case. He had lost not only his clerical uniform but, more striking to me, the clerical demeanor that in those days kept laymen in their place.

If in 1964 he no longer looked like a Roman Catholic priest of the era, yet it became clear as we made our way to various parts of Europe (Basel, Rome, Prague) that nothing mattered more to him than his vocation as a priest. The trappings had changed but not what the traditional clothing was meant to imply: a person for whom sacramental life was central, whose main action was to celebrate the liturgy, who was eager to explain the gospel to anyone who was even vaguely interested, and ready at a moment's notice to be a channel of God's forgiveness. At the same time, in Dan's company, it was clear that following Christ was an adventure second to none. To be with Dan was to be with an explorer.

While in Prague that summer, several of us decided to start the Catholic Peace Fellowship. Though the war in Vietnam was still a minor skirmish that no one could imagine would soon tear America in half, still it was clear that a Catholic response to the Cold War and the militarization of society was urgently needed. As a consequence of my becoming the CPF's first secretary and Dan living nearby and being in effect ex-officio chaplain to the Catholic Peace Fellowship, we were to see each other nearly every week, sometimes several times a week, except those times when one or the other of us was traveling.

At the time Dan was an editor of *Jesuit Missions* and was living in a mid-Manhattan town house that had somehow made its way to the Jesuits after belonging to the New York socialite and arbiter of manners Emily Post. Dan had a top-floor room that, I can only guess, had once housed a maid. Here we would look over the incoming mail the Catholic Peace Fellowship was receiving and talk about what directions the CPF's work should take. The conversations gave shape to initiatives that resulted in a remarkably high rate of Catholic conscientious objection to the war in Vietnam.

But the main event at those quiet meetings was invariably the Mass, which Dan celebrated in his small room in the simplest possible manner, this at a time when such events rarely if ever happened outside church buildings. Dan's Mass was stripped of nearly everything but a few prayers, a few readings, short and often conversational reflection on the texts, consecration of the bread and wine (both emerged from a drawer in his file cabinet), and communion. This simple eucharist was at the heart of our lives for two or three years in the mid-sixties.

Dan had received several warnings from his superior that this was not an approved use of his room, but the same superior would have done as well to advise Caruso to give up singing on the balcony. I can vividly recall Tom Cornell and me coming up to Dan's room one bright day to find Dan deeply distressed as the advice not to say Mass in his room had now become an order. We did our best to get on with our meeting minus the Mass, not doing very well in the funeral parlor atmosphere. Then Dan, mid-sentence, got up, opened the drawer where the bread and wine were kept, put them on a small table, recited the prayer that leads up to consecration, then said not the usual words but instead, "Let the Lord make of these what he will."

I doubt we had many more meetings in his room that year, as it was soon after that Dan—his anti-war speeches and activities having greatly irritated Cardinal Spellman—was abruptly sent out of the country to Latin America. Perhaps the cardinal hoped it would be a one-way trip, but the public protest that Dan's expulsion from New York ignited (including a crowd of Catholics picketing the chancery office) had the effect of making it impossible for him to be kept from returning. As for punishing Dan with a journey to Latin America, one could only think of the story of B'rer Rabbit being thrown into the briar patch.

Dan sometimes mentioned that he had grown up with *The Catholic Worker* in his house. It had influenced him profoundly. While many people admired what Catholic Worker communities were doing by way of hospitality, Dan was one of those who shared fully Dorothy Day's conviction that killing, whether by war, abortion, or social neglect, had nothing at all to do with being a Christian. Such pacifism had become rare in most Christian societies since the time of Constantine, but was especially uncommon in the American Catholic Church prior to the war in Vietnam. I can't think of another Jesuit in the early '60s who held a similar view. One could far more easily find priests ready to approve the use of nuclear warfare in combating communism. *"Pro Deo et Patria"* was carved over the entrance of many an American Catholic school. The U.S. flag was often in the church sanctuary near the altar. There was no church more willing to rally around the flag than the Catholic church. Cardinal Spellman's irritation with Dan has to be seen in that context. What is surprising is that the cardinal backed down, and what is perhaps still more amazing is that the Jesuits did not decide to toss Dan overboard. There must have been many members of the order who thought of him as a traitor both to America and to the Society of Jesus.

Yet Dan, despite his difficulties obeying orders, was the most devoted of Jesuits. He took comfort in stories of more radical times in Jesuit history when members of the Society had sided with the victims of colonialism and gotten into trouble with imperial powers and with the Vatican itself. His idea of obedience in the Society of Jesus was that it had mainly to do with obeying Jesus.

But his loyalty wasn't simply to Jesuits of another, more radical era but to the actual Jesuits he lived with. He loved his community, even if there were borders of disagreement cutting through it. If Dan had one deep dread, it was that he would be forced to leave. Yet he often found himself unable to do those things which would have made his situation more secure. (Of course there remained a critical edge. Showing me the amazingly comfortable place the Jesuit Community on West 98th Street had set up for itself, Dan commented, "If this is poverty, bring on chastity.")

Most people have a hard time doing the right thing because of fear of consequences: punishment, lost friends, angry relatives, job dismissal, an uncertain future. Far from playing it safe, Dan's special gift has been to plunge his head into the lion's mouth. As he said at a small retreat we had with Thomas Merton at the Abbey of Gethsemani in November 1964: "The church's fearfulness is our confession of unconvertedness." Much of Dan's work as a priest, especially through acts of resistance to killing, has been a frontal assault on fear. If "the root of war is fear," as Merton had written, peacemaking requires fearlessness.

But fearlessness is just one more abstract word. One of Dan's oft-repeated phrases is "we have to make things concrete." His sensibility is deeply incarnational, the conviction that we have to live our spiritual lives in the flesh, not in the imagination. It isn't enough to pray for peace or speak out against events that cause the innocent to die. One must find gestures that in some way incarnate our words, such a gesture as burning draft files, denting bomb casings, pouring one's own blood on devices meant to cause bloodshed. In a society often baffled by the "merely" symbolic and uncomfortable with ritual, what Dan does has often been dismissed as a kind of sideshow, yet he and others acting in a similar vein have again and again touched nerves that were unmoved by anything else.

For all his politically engaged activity, it may come as a surprise to realize that there are few people less political than Dan. It used to be said in the press that he and his brother Phil were leaders of the "Catholic Left." Those who were truly of the Left must have found such a label exasperating. More than anything else, Dan is in the tradition of Jesuit missionaries. There is no single thing more important to him than unwrapping the gospel and making Christ's face visible. The only interesting question for Dan is how to do it, a question he has approached more as a dramatist than a theologian. Much as he loves to play with language, he knows conversion can't be brought about with words alone. It can't be done as if we were not living in a particular time and place, as if the gospel could be lived outside of history.

Dan also knows that one of the forms darkness takes is grim seriousness. "The worst thing," he has said more than once, "is an omnivorous solemnity." In the face of death, rather than maintain a polite silence, he talks back.

I think of Mel Hollander, a young man who in the early '70s signed up for a class Dan was teaching on pastoral care of the dying. Mel himself was dying of cancer, and his illness was easy to notice. During the period of silence with which Dan started each class, his eye fell on Mel and stayed there. At last Dan broke the quiet with a question to Mel, "What's the matter?" Mel said, "I'm dying." Dan, without batting an eye, replied, "That must be very exciting."

Mel told me afterward that no medicine he was taking, no book he had read had done so much good for him as those five words. They were a kind of lightning flash. In the light of that flash was the resurrection of Jesus, as real as the streets of New York. Mel knew at once that he was in the midst of the most remarkable experience of his life. Nose to nose with death, he had never felt more alive.

That moment of truth somehow pushed the cancer back. Mel, who had come into Dan's class expecting to die within a few months, lived another decade, finally dying in a fire. In what Mel called his "extra years," he devoted himself to work with Vietnamese refugees.

I'm not in a rush, but some day, at the edge of a great lake of beer, I hope to meet Mel again. Surely we will be talking about Dan Berrigan.

The World Will Be Saved by Beauty

MARY EVELYN JEGEN

Although I do not know Dan well, he has had a steady influence on my efforts to live as a Christian in a world full of violence, precisely because he never lets me forget that I share responsibility for it.

In 1979, a month before I took up my responsibilities as the first national coordinator of Pax Christi, I spent a month in a hermitage on the grounds of the Sisters of Loretto, near the Abbey of Gethsemani in Kentucky. I brought with me the Bible and only one other book, *The Words Our Savior Gave Us*, a small volume of Dan's meditations on the Lord's Prayer.

I really don't know why I chose that book as a kind of backup in case I needed more to read than the Bible during that month. I read Dan's small volume from time to time and remember clearly two lessons I carried away with me: one, that working for Big Causes, trying to rid the earth of nuclear weapons, for example, could easily be an escape unless there was a dimension of physical solidarity with suffering persons all around us. Dan wrote his book on the Lord's Prayer largely out of his experience as an orderly in a hospital for terminal cancer patients, where he worked regularly as a volunteer. For me, a neophyte in the peace movement, that combination of resistance and genuine pastoral presence spoke powerfully. It still does.

The other insight I gained from reading Dan's book was that we need to pray for the grace to seek forgiveness from those we have offended. I see more clearly than I did in 1979 that this is central to peacemaking. It is easier to forgive those who have offended me, in most cases, than to seek forgiveness from those I have offended. First of all, I am tempted to avoid or overlook those I may be offending. For example, there are banana pickers in Central America and elsewhere who provide my breakfast fruit at the expense of their health and that of their children, even at the expense of their very lives, shortened and brutalized by injustice. Seeking their forgiveness means finding some way to join in their struggle for justice. It means having a firm purpose of amendment. Another example: the Iraqis who are destroyed by sanctions imposed by the UN Security Council at the insistence of the United States. Until recently, there was not so much as a whimper of protest on my part. People keep reminding me that Saddam Hussein's behavior is reprehensible, and that therefore we should keep up the sanctions. This is specious reasoning, but it is all too easy to be silenced by it.

From Dan Berrigan, I began to learn that when we, or our country, are offended, the normal (which is not synonymous with the good) thing to do is to make a case that the other person deserves our retaliatory injury. It is so easy to blame the victim and to let ourselves off the hook by thoughtless or specious rationalization. This is a hard truth to face, and it needs to be learned over and over again.

A year after encountering Dan in one of his books, I telephoned him to invite him to be the keynote speaker at the Pax Christi National Assembly. The national council had offered the invitation, and as coordinator of our national section, I was to make the actual arrangements. I had never spoken to Fr. Berrigan before and was a bit nervous about my assignment. In the course of our conversation, I told him how I had been nourished by his actions and writings, adding, "I can't do the things you do for peace, like getting arrested and going to jail, but I want to thank you for what you do." I never forgot his reply. He said with unmistakable sincerity, "Sister, there are many things to do for peace besides going to jail." I have thought of that often as I have spent most of my peacework hours in some of those other ways.

At the same time, it has become clear to me that in the peace movement there must be a strong dimension of resistance. Dan Berrigan stands out as a leader in nonviolent resistance. The first step in resistance is to name the evil. Dan has done that for decades in the most clear and dramatic ways. I have lost count of the number of times I have been in discussions with critics of blood-pouring during antiwar actions and Plowshares actions. Many insist that pouring blood alienates people. I suggest that the very fact that pouring blood, or burning draft records, arouses such vehement criticism suggests that at some deep level people are brought face to face with the truth about war from the perspective of the victims. This is precisely what our militarized culture does not want us to do. Instead, we are told about "surgical strikes" and informed that the only casualties that matter are those on "our side." Dan doesn't let us off that easily, reminding us that the blood of our brothers and sisters cries to heaven with Abel's, and that heaven does not ask for national identity papers. When I find myself with critics of the blood drama of Plowshares and other actions, I offer the opinion that what is going on is genuine street poetry, akin to other forms of street art, a powerful form of social criticism.

I entertain the notion that there is a suppressed poet or other artist in each of us, waiting to be liberated and brought into the service of the peace movement. Dorothy Day was fond of quoting Dostoevsky: "The world will be saved by beauty." I am haunted by that line, and by another from a poem by W. H. Auden, written at the outbreak of World War II: "We must love one another or die." For me, Dan Berrigan's life corroborates those two trenchant lines.

Among the Finest Treasure
in the Church

TOM FOX

On our kitchen wall in our home in Roeland Park, Kansas, hangs what in Catholic parlance might be called a sacramental. It is to us a sacred object. Among the family photographs, one is a small color snapshot framed in wood and prominently displayed. I walk by it each morning as I leave the house on the way to work.

This photograph even has a name. My wife, Hoa, and I have titled it: "The Two Daniels." One of the Daniels is better known. In the photograph his face has a mustache and a bushy beard grows from his chin. He is wearing a short-sleeved shirt. He is standing, his hands gently clasped in front of him at his waist. He has a smile on his face. He appears content and happy.

The other Daniel, only two years old at the time, is held by my side. I am proudly looking at Hoa and she at me. Everyone is smiling—except the younger Daniel, who is sucking his right thumb.

It was 1975, and it was the first time the two Daniels had ever encountered each other. It was the first time the older Daniel met his namesake.

Daniel Berrigan had just completed a challenging speech in the gymnasium at Marymount College in Detroit. It was basic Berrigan. No rhetoric. Simple talk. Gospel-rooted talk. No notes. Compelling in honesty. He did not tell others what to do, only how and why he lived as he did.

This is by way of saying I am profoundly grateful to Daniel Berrigan. So much so that after my wife gave birth to our first child, a son, there was no question about the name. It would be Daniel. A strong, biblical name; our son would be named after a modern biblical prophet. We immediately informed Daniel Berrigan yet another child had taken his name. In the years since, we have encountered Daniels named after

Daniel Berrigan wherever we have traveled. Days after we notified Berrigan, he wrote back to thank us and to encourage us along the journey. I did not take the time then to explain to him just why we made the choice we did. Allow me then to explain.

Years ago, Daniel Berrigan became a distant soulmate at a time in my life when I most needed one. Without ever knowing it, he guided me, coaxed me, encouraged me, prodded me, challenged me, and held on to me with his far-reaching, embracing spirit. I would never forget.

It was in 1966. In an expression of idealism characteristic of the times, I traveled to Vietnam after graduating from college. Working for International Voluntary Services, I learned to speak Vietnamese and worked as a volunteer in the Dong Tac refugee camp in Central Vietnam. It was one way to protest the war. Tens of thousands of refugees lived marginal lives on the coastal shores; their villages had been destroyed by warfare, most often by U.S. bombs.

Those war years grew to be a time of great alienation from the United States and American life. I lost all interest in returning home. It was also a time in which I witnessed overwhelming Catholic complicity in the war effort. Those were the years the cardinal of New York blessed tanks headed to Vietnam and a future New York cardinal was in Vietnam, an admiral in the U.S. navy.

That both my country and my church pressed to win an unwinnable war, doing so much violence to so many, baptized me to the arrogance of power. Idealism came crashing down around me. This was the United States unveiled, the iron fist within the velvet glove. And the fist would be used—at whatever the cost—when required. This I would never forget. But it was a torturous lesson.

Certainly, I thought, the painfully clear distance that separated the gospels from U.S. policy would be too much for the church to patch over. U.S. planes had dropped 4.5 million tons of bombs on Vietnam by the time it was finished. And no Catholic outrage was to be heard.

Twenty-two years old at the time, still new to adulthood, I thought it unfathomable that the U.S. bishops could support such a war. Those were lonely years. My bishops not only kept silent, but when they spoke it was to encourage the conflict.

It was an utterly devastating and disillusioning time in my life. I preferred to live among the Vietnamese. At least they understood, and I could communicate with them. We shared a sense of powerlessness.

During those years, certainly the darkest but curiously also some of the most spiritually nourishing of my life, my thoughts often drifted back across the South China Sea and Pacific Ocean. Over there, back in America. I had lost almost all connection points. Most depressing was the deepening spiritual isolation. My beliefs were refugees, not unlike the impoverished and wasting-away peasants among whom I lived and whom I loved.

It was in a state of dark depression greater than I had ever known—or experienced since—that I began to read stories about the Berrigan brothers, Daniel and Philip. The May 1968 Catonsville draft file burnings, I realize years later, the deliberate, provocative actions of two Catholic priests, a Jesuit and a Josephite, did nothing less than help me find a God in heaven.

Since then, in my mind the name Berrigan has been synonymous with conviction, courage, and spiritual integrity. From Catonsville to King of Prussia, from federal prison to Faith and Resistance retreats, from Pentagon blood pouring to New York AIDS ministry, the Berrigan witnesses remain among the finest treasures found in the Catholic church.

Years have passed. My Vietnamese wife and I keep the photograph in front of us. It is a reminder that light can shine through darkness. Good can come out of evil. But it takes work. Each in his own way, the two Daniels continue to challenge us. They remind us to keep the faith, to hold on to convictions, to try to live in concert with those convictions, and never to give up hope.

Moreover, our "two Daniels" photograph, three generations of spiritual vision, sings out to us each day: "The Daniels are coming! The Daniels are coming. Christian witness lives." Namesakes all, they have been raised in Berrigan grace, they live in cities and towns throughout the globe. Once infants, they are now coming of age. These are specially blessed souls. They have grown up listening to their parents speak of nonviolence, of the prophet Isaiah, and of the work of the Beatitudes. At a young age, these children learned of the Catholic Worker movement and a woman named Dorothy Day. They attended court trials and visited prisons, finding interesting folks in both.

They have come to know the name Berrigan stands for compassion and peace. They carry their Daniel with pride.

Thank You for Converting Me

BISHOP WALTER SULLIVAN

I first heard the name Daniel Berrigan in 1968 when a group of activists, "the Catonsville Nine," broke into a Selective Service office in suburban Baltimore and poured blood on draft registration records. Newspapers and TV reporters typically took a hard line. The Nine, especially a Jesuit priest named Daniel Berrigan, were categorized as radicals, terrorists, un-American communist sympathizers. At the time, U.S. military activity in Vietnam was at its peak. I was just beginning to recognize the horror, the utter barbarity, and the futility of the conflict raging in Southeast Asia. I began to find the "body counts" released each day profoundly troubling. I rejected as obscene the jingoistic contention that victory was in sight because more Vietnamese than Americans were dying. It dawned on me that, from the very beginning, I had never understood U.S. intervention in Vietnam and that I could not continue to accord it support "by default."

The Catonsville action challenged my passivity and made me wonder if, in Merton's phrase, I was "a guilty bystander." In retrospect, I am convinced, the Nine initiated my personal involvement in the peace movement. I began by supporting individual draftees who were conscientious objectors. I also incurred the wrath of the IRS and Department of Justice by supporting a priest of the Catholic Diocese of Richmond who refused to pay a special tax on telephone service imposed to finance the Vietnam conflict. In that particular case, it took Washington two years and an expenditure of $15,000 to collect $15.20 in back taxes.

After I became a bishop in 1970 and traveled to all areas of our 37,000-square mile diocese, I discovered firsthand how hostile and unforgiving the majority of Richmond's Catholics were toward people who witnessed for peace by means of civil disobedience. Daniel Berrigan, I found, headed their lists of "disloyal troublemakers." "A priest should not be in politics," they insisted. "This Father Berrigan is a disgrace to our religion. Why don't the Jesuits do something about that wild man?"

Initially, I limited my public peacemaking activity to visiting incarcerated "peaceniks." From time to time, those arrested in demonstrations at the Pentagon were jailed in Richmond. I made it a point to visit them in prison. I visited anti-war activist John Shields (now deceased) in a prison in Washington, D.C. The Berrigan brothers were detained there, too, and I had a brief meeting with them which made a lasting impression on me. It laid to rest the image of Dan Berrigan that had been created in my imagination. He didn't seem to be wild after all. In fact, I left with a diametrically opposed impression. This out-of-control priest was calm and reserved! He spoke softly and manifested a remarkable serenity and composure in a tension-filled, inhuman environment. He set me thinking about Paul under house arrest in Rome, and Bonhoeffer in a Nazi prison, and Martin Luther King, Jr., in the Birmingham jail. Dan's calm, peaceful behavior contrasted starkly with and aroused my indignation at the heavy-handed approach of the Department of Justice. It was apparent that our government was interested not in correction but in vengeance. This first brief meeting with Dan Berrigan also confirmed my hidden fears. Peace advocates could anticipate not invitations to dialogue but rejection and denunciation.

I began to wonder what motivated Dan to accept imprisonment in pursuit of peace. While I never felt called to join Dan in acts of civil disobedience, his example led me to risk participating in peace marches and helped me summon the courage publicly to condemn nuclearism, the U.S. war-by-proxy in Central America, the arms race, the invasions of Grenada and Panama, and the Gulf War. The example of Dan Berrigan pointed me from Emmaus back toward Jerusalem. My eyes were opened and my heart changed. Dan's vision and faithful discipleship empowered me to devote what talents I have to peacemaking.

Dan Berrigan has earned a place among a very special group of women and men whom I particularly revere—Gandhi, Dorothy Day, Oscar Romero, and Ita Ford, for example—peace activists who refuse to bow down before the "gods of metal," who have the courage to expose the blasphemous illogic which argues that the saturation bombing of Dresden and the incineration of Hiroshima were "steps toward peace," and who refuse to remain silent when illegal, immoral "covert operations" are justified by the invocation of "our national interest."

I got to know Dan Berrigan as a person on the three occasions I was privileged to offer him hospitality when his ministry brought him to Richmond. Not everyone in the Richmond area, including some prominent Richmond Catholics, was thrilled to learn that Dan was staying at the Bishop's House. Some of them demonstrated their displeasure by refusing to contribute to the annual diocesan appeal for support of various charitable and missionary activities. Others, almost always under the cover of anonymity, denounced me for harboring a criminal, a communist, and an un-American traitor.

I am under no illusion, nor, I recognize, is Dan. Despite Dan's "subversive" presence in southern Virginia, the Commonwealth's massive stockpile of weapons and munitions isn't in the slightest danger of being converted into plowshares. His time in Richmond was, though, a grace for a modest-sized but growing network of Christian believers who are trying to become instruments of Christ's peace. We particularly valued the "evenings with Dan Berrigan" I hosted at my residence. Not the least of the fruits of these sessions was our discovery that this clear-sighted, intrepid prophet is a wonderfully humble, good-humored, peaceful man. I asked Dan how he continues to be hopeful. "By doing hopeful things," he replied.

I can still recall the first time I heard Dan preach. In the tradition of the Hebrew prophets and of the Baptist, he identified the pharaohs of our own times. He turned the spotlight on the idols, on the "abominations of desolation," that the world powers worship. Without hesitation or equivocation, he challenged the high and mighty powers-that-be. His language was poetic, his tone measured, the effect galvanizing. I kept thinking: What a paradox! How can this man be such a threat to the system: a quiet, loving person, a man of peace and nonviolence? Dan has re-enforced for me Jesus' guarantee: "The truth will make you free," free to speak the truth before princes, free to live the truth, free to discern what the "Spirit is saying to the churches."

In October 1994 I came to New York City to give the keynote address at the annual Pax Christi Metro New York Assembly. Dan housed me. As it always is, being with Dan was a graced experience for me. Dan not only proclaims peace; he lives it. I found this man— a priest, poet, and scholar, admired by some and demonized by others (one is never neutral about Dan)—spending large parts of his time visiting persons living with AIDS. He is never judgmental, never reluctant to visit, to touch, to eat and drink with those pushed to the margins of society.

It doesn't matter whether Dan Berrigan is beating swords into plowshares, spilling his blood on the Pentagon steps, or bathing those dying of cancer or AIDS; he keeps on witnessing to his trust, not in human might, but in the God who is our peace, revealed to us in Jesus the Christ. Others have known Dan Berrigan longer and have been more intimately associated with him than I have, but my experience of and with Dan has been a genuine kairos. He has effected my conversion and made me a peacemaker.

Dan, I thank you for converting me, for leading me to commit my life to seeking the peace of Christ. As you complete seventy-five years of faithful discipleship, may the Lord bless and guide you. May the Spirit dwelling in you make you an ever more efficacious instrument of the peace of Christ.

A Rebel for Peace

JEAN VANIER

The last time I met Daniel Berrigan was in Paris in April or May of 1964. We had lunch together in a little restaurant near Saint Sulpice church. I spoke to him about people with mental handicaps and about the community I was planning to start. He asked if I needed help and proposed to send us Louis Pretty, a young Canadian architect who wanted to take a year off in service to the poor. Louis came and became a good friend and an indispensable helper in those early days of the L'Arche community. And so it was that Dan was part of L'Arche as it began.

Dan was a good friend of Tony Walsh, who died in 1994, well over the age of ninety. Tony founded the Benedict Labre House in Montreal, welcoming homeless men off the streets, giving them food and shelter and much more—friendship and a listening ear. As a young Jesuit, Dan would go up from Syracuse, New York, to Benedict Labre House to visit Tony. Dan, as a companion of Jesus, saw in Tony the light of the gospel message and an answer to the question: Who and where is Jesus today? What is he doing? Tony saw Jesus as a lover and as a healer. With all his energy and inner fire, Dan felt burdened by the heaviness of the institutional church, which can hide the face of Jesus behind laws, ideas, and order, behind a comfortable and virtuous way of living that is far from the poor to whom Jesus came to bring the good news. Tony played his part in awakening and confirming the fire in the heart of this young Jesuit.

Tony and Benedict Labre House were a light shining in the darkness for me, too. It was this light which was the bond linking me to Dan. Yes, Dan is a rebel for peace, giving support and friendship to every person and initiative that can reveal the heart of God and the yearnings of the Spirit. Dan is a rebel for peace gently fighting against the weight of spiritual power that crushes people in the name of God. Dan is a true seeker of peace.

Peace brings into one body the rich and the poor, the inwardly broken and the outwardly broken. Jesus has a vision for our world: to bring to birth societies and communities that are not first of all a pyramid of power—with the rich, the privileged, and the powerful on the top, and the poor, the useless, and the powerless on the bottom—but a body, where the weak and the strong support each other, are there for each other, and give life to one another.

It is not easy, however, for the poor to rise up from the ruins of their existence to claim life and responsibility for themselves, to find hope and new laughter. It is not easy for the rich to allow themselves to be touched by the poor, to enter into communion with them, to let themselves be stripped of luxury and comfort. No, it is not easy for the rich and for the poor to sit down together at the same table.

And yet Jesus says to us:

When you give a lunch or a dinner, do not invite your friends or your relations or rich neighbors, in case they invite you back and repay you. No, when you have a party, invite the poor, the crippled, the lame, the blind; then you will be blessed (Luke 14:12-15).

To eat at the same table is to become friends. The vision of Jesus is to break down the dividing walls of hostility and prejudice that separate people and to bring them together in love. But the poor are wounded and angry, fearful and depressed. They disturb. Their anger disturbs. The rich too are wounded and fearful, hiding behind barriers of self-satisfaction and power. Communities of faith, of God's reign, bring together into oneness those who by culture and by education are far apart. This is the body of Christ. This is the church. The poor are evangelized. They discover they are loved. But even more, the poor evangelize. They possess a healing power that awakens and transforms the hearts of the rich.

There are now over a hundred L'Arche communities in the world, including forty in North America. Six years ago, in our community in France, we welcomed Antonio, a small man of twenty-six, who has a severe learning disability and is fragile in many ways. Constantly in need of oxygen, he cannot walk or speak or fend for himself. He lives in one of our homes with five other people with severe handicaps and five assistants. If you approach him and call him by his name, he responds with a big smile and shining eyes. There is no depression, no revolt, no anger in him. He is transparent with trust. Assistants living with him tell me often that Antonio has transformed their lives. He is leading them from a world of conflict, competition, and hierarchy into a world of tenderness, healing, and covenantal relationships.

The folly of the gospel is the folly of the Word who became flesh. He became a child, became weakness, in order to bring together in unity all God's children. The folly of the gospel is the presence of Jesus hidden in the weak and the powerless in order to open and heal the hearts of the powerful and the rich. Jesus says:

> Whoever welcomes one of these little ones in my name, welcomes me, and whoever welcomes me, welcomes the one who sent me (Matthew 12:5).

This remains one of the most mysterious and challenging promises of Jesus.

In community with the poor, everything is not simple and gentle. To respond to the cry and the needs of Antonio implies loss. Antonio heals, but at the same time, he disturbs because his needs are great. He disturbs also because living with Antonio, everything seems so useless, little, physical, and emotional. Nothing big, nothing great. Giving baths, cleaning, cooking, eating, laughing, getting angry, praying. For many assistants, it can be a good experience, an awakening, but it is not easy for them to put down roots with Antonio and others like him who have been crushed by sickness, weakness, and rejection. What is the meaning of all this?

We need peacemakers like Daniel Berrigan everywhere, every day, in our families and our cities and our churches, our places of work and our places of fun. We need peacemakers like Dan today in Bosnia and Rwanda, just as we needed Dan and others during the Vietnam war. We need people who love like Dan. To love is to reveal the hidden beauty in the hearts of all people, to trust them and to call them forth to greater trust. To love is a way of looking, of touching, of listening to all: taking time with them, especially with those who are broken, depressed, and insecure, revealing to them their importance. As we take time with them and enter into communion with them, they in turn reveal to us our beauty. Communion is a to-and-fro of love; we give and we receive mutually. We give our hearts bonded in gentle unity as words flow into silence and inner voice, as movement flows into quiet peace and inner rest. Life flows from one to another.

We are not all like Antonio, who seems to accept so beautifully his brokenness. A light of peace and the warmth of tenderness arise from all that is shattered and broken in him. Others cry out their pain, their revolt, and their anguish. This awakens the pain, the darkness, the fears, and the wounds in me and in others. They reveal not only the beauty but also the violence of my own heart, my capacity to hate and to kill. But this too can become a healing experience, if we accept it and find its fullest meaning.

When Paul sought to be relieved of the thorn in his flesh, he cried out to Jesus, who answered him: "My grace is sufficient for you; my power is manifested in your weakness." As we approach people in pain, they reveal to us our pain and brokenness. We are not an elite. We need help. We need the help of Jesus and of sisters and brothers in community; we need to talk to wise, listening, and compassionate hearts who can help us to assume all that is broken within us and to find wholeness. We become free when we accept ourselves as we are, cry out for help, and use wisely all that we are to build peace.

Dan is a peacemaker, not only during the Vietnam war, but today, by his desire to bring people together, to welcome into his heart the rejected and the dying, by walking with them, from near and afar, from Vietnam to St. Vincent's in New York City. Let us all discover, together with Dan, what it means to be wise and loving, what it means to be a peacemaker.

THE JESUIT

Life in Community with Dan

DON MOORE, S.J.

The request to contribute to this volume for Dan Berrigan came as both an honor and an onus. In almost every way I am an outsider in comparison to the many other distinguished contributors to this volume. I am neither a peace activist nor a poet; I am in no way a celebrity or a prominent church person. I have never spent a night in jail, and I would certainly never be asked to contribute my face to a Ben and Jerry's ad!

So why was this request directed to me? There is one area of life that I share with Dan which might set this contribution apart from all of the others. I live in a Jesuit community with Dan on West 98th Street in Manhattan; we call ourselves the West Side Jesuit Community. It has been Dan's home for some twenty-five years now, and my home for most of the last sixteen years. So this contribution of the outsider is, if I may be so bold as to say, a view from the inside, a view of Dan's private or interior life, or rather, a view of one aspect of that interior life, that aspect he shares in community with his Jesuit brothers.

And that underscores the onus of this effort. I am asked to write about Dan from the community's perspective, which would be a bold undertaking at any time for any community, but it is a particularly daring venture to write in the name of the West Side Jesuit Community. There are twenty other Jesuit voices that also should be heard; they clamor to be heard; they desire to be heard. To complicate matters, I am jotting down these lines in the holy city of Jerusalem, some five thousand miles from New York and from the community. In writing these comments, however, I am not deaf to community voices. I shall try earnestly to listen to them and to be faithful to them, but the final redaction is fully my own responsibility.

Dan has given fifty-seven years of his life to the Society of Jesus. What is it like to live in religious community with Dan? What is it like to share the Jesuit life with him? I would respond simply by saying that it is disturbing, demanding, and delightful.

Dan can be and is a constant disturber of community living—whether at community celebrations of the Eucharist, monthly community meetings, semi-annual weekends away, or our occasional week-long retreats together. Dan has the habit of re-phrasing simple questions, pointing out something we had overlooked, or suggesting other aspects of a problem that tend to shatter our accustomed and comfortable way of viewing our community life or of dealing with outside issues. We suddenly find ourselves treating the given agenda in a much different way. Who are we as Jesuits? What is our purpose as community? Why are we living together? Where are we in our living together? Where are we in our prayer together? What more can we be doing for one another, for our Jesuit province, for the Society, for the church, and, most important, for our world, our city, and our sisters and brothers who live in this neighborhood, a neighborhood where half the funerals are for victims of AIDS? Dan is constantly bringing us back to the fundamentals of our Jesuit and religious life.

Community is crucially important for Dan, and certainly there are many communities that give him welcome and support and encouragement, but in my estimation, the one community he most relies on for support and encouragement is that of the Jesuit brothers with whom he is living. If just one of us can be there for him—at a hearing or a trial or a demonstration or a poetry reading (we don't follow Dan, except in spirit, all over the country!)—it means more to him, I'm convinced, than most of us realize. And if we are not there, even though for very good reasons, then something of real importance is missing. Dan senses that keenly, and many of us do also. Dan's presence in our midst compels us to ask ourselves how we can be of greater support to Dan in his various endeavors, in the risks he undertakes for us all. How can we be more involved with him and for him? And the obvious corollary of such questioning: How can we manifest greater support and love and concern for one another? Dan is indeed a disturber of community life; he is a reminder of the enormous responsibility that comes with community living.

Martin Buber once wrote that, in the final analysis, it is only in community that the fullness of our responsibility as human beings is put to the test. Further, the real builder of community is not our relationships to one another, important as these might be, but rather our relationship to the Living Center, our relationship to God. Dan has made those words come alive. He doesn't allow us the luxury of viewing community simply as something we slide into as a matter of convenience; it is, after all, something we choose for our own sake, for the world's sake, for the sake of the greater glory of God. To live in community with Dan is to recognize the basic driving force of his life, as well as the basic driving force of the community's life. To be with him in any kind of faith sharing—at the Eucharist, speaking of our own experiences of prayer, or simply relating where we are in our Jesuit lives—is to recognize how much he strives to discern and to respond to the promptings of the Spirit in his own life. Dan's relationship to the Living Center of our community invites each of us to examine and deepen our own personal relationship to God.

Through all such "disturbances," Dan helps us to confront the demands that community life should be making upon each one of us. He consistently goads us to try to "bring back to the fold" those who tend to divorce themselves from the mainstream of community life or to confront someone whose lifestyle tends to be disruptive of community living. He will not let us keep private our disappointments or problems or discouragements. It is a failure of community, in Dan's mind, if someone is shouldering a burden alone, whether overwork; change of ministry; difficulties with religious or apostolic superiors; problems of loneliness, self-doubt, or discouragement; or, perhaps of greatest importance, being confronted with a terminal illness. These are problems that also concern community. Dan insists that we must be quite clear with one another. If someone is reluctant to speak out, perhaps the community is at fault. Perhaps the community has not manifested to one of its own a loving openness and acceptance. This demands that the community, or better, that each member of the community carefully nourishes with the others a spirit of concern, friendship, trust, and sense of presence.

It is difficult to cite specific instances of the above without betraying community confidence. One example, however, comes to mind that has been more or less publicly acknowledged: the community's response, led in many ways through Dan, to the terminal illness of Father Lew Cox, who died in 1986. Granted that Lew himself was strongly community-oriented and that Dan was one of Lew's closest friends, nevertheless, because of the understanding of community that Dan had so strongly helped to engender, it was clear from the first diagnosis of Lew's inoperable cancer that this was a community problem, a community concern, a community commitment. The community to a man, led in many ways by Dan, rallied around Lew; we would be with him to the very end.

Lew's diagnosis was made through an operation performed on Ash Wednesday, 1986. At the time I asked Lew if we could entrust his cause to the intercession of Franz Jaegerstaetter, the Austrian farmer and father of three young daughters who was beheaded by the Nazis on August 9, 1943, because, as Franz put it, "I cannot at the same time be a Catholic and serve in the army of the Third Reich." Lew was delighted at this suggestion. I should mention that Franz Jaegerstaetter is also a special patron of Dan's and of many others in the peace movement. I phoned Franziska Jaegerstaetter in Austria to ask for a relic. She sounded uncertain over the phone, but on Palm Sunday, one day after Lew was finally discharged from the hospital, there arrived in the community via a guest from Austria the relic of Franz plus two small loaves of bread baked by Franz's eldest daughter from grain grown on the Jaegerstaetter farm. Almost immediately Lew designated one of the loaves for our community celebration of the Lord's Supper. It was during this Holy Thursday liturgy that Lew announced to the community: "No matter what the outcome of this cancer, I want you all to know that the whole process of this illness has been and is a pilgrimage toward life." Rarely has the meaning of community been brought home to us so demonstrably and so beautifully, and it was clear to many of us that Franz's intercession was already manifest. In the remaining eight months that Lew was with us, Dan was continually a model of care, concern, and compassion; it almost seemed that the months and years he had spent in volunteer assistance to those dying of cancer and of AIDS was in reality a preparation for leading us in our care for Lew. These were days and weeks of intense and profound community living. In his homily at Lew's funeral, Dan talked about his last Eucharist with Lew less than forty-eight hours before his death. They had talked and prayed together over Mark's rendition of the storm at sea and the obvious parallels with the cancer that was slowly sapping Lew's many vital energies, providing a unique opportunity for faith and hope in God's saving power.

It is almost a matter of routine now within the community that each Jesuit's problems and predicaments are, to the extent that he wishes it, the community's problems and predicaments. This is as it should be; we are not alone, and we are all, in St. Paul's terms, ministers of reconciliation. This community attitude is due in no small way to Dan's persistence in urging us to meet the demands of our living together. I am convinced that every member of the West Side Jesuit Community is today a better Jesuit because of Dan's presence in our midst.

Finally, living with Dan in community is in so many ways sheer delight. Just as he can be disturbing and demanding, he can also abruptly relieve our tension. Many a long evening session has ended with one of his favorite interventions: "Enough of serious talk; we all deserve a drink!" And the ensuing hour or so of relaxation helps us all to grasp a bit more clearly and personally whatever the topics of our discussion have been.

Our lifestyle at 98th Street involves a prepared evening meal Monday to Friday evenings. Community guests are always welcome, and conversation often continues well past the last rack of dishes in our faithful but aging dishwasher. Invariably, one of the last to leave will be Dan, provided he has no other appointment that evening. The topics of conversation are endless, but rarely, if ever, trivial. The participants will differ from night to night because of differing responsibilities, but the impression I always take away from such sessions, an impression shared by the other Jesuits in the community and by so many of our community guests, is that here is a group of Jesuits who really enjoy one another's company. It isn't that Dan created or originated such community interaction, but clearly what he brings to community and what he demands of community tend to support, strengthen, and sustain the joy we experience through being in one another's company.

On weekends, our genial Dan turns into Daniel, our gourmet chef. I'm sure each Jesuit in the community has more than once received the message from Dan: "I'm having a few friends in for supper Sunday evening. Why not join us?" The "friends" may turn out to be other Jesuits in the community or anyone from Ramsey Clark to Martin Sheen to members of Pax Christi or the Catholic Worker to a neighbor dying of AIDS. On such evenings, we can always count on both gourmet cooking and gourmet conversation. Dan thoroughly enjoys preparing a meal and sharing it with friends. I look on the care and attention and "loving informality" given to the preparation and serving of the meal as Dan's way of saying to each one of us: "Hey, you are really significant in my life." It's important for us to know that and to understand that, just as it is important for Dan to know the significant role he plays in our own personal lives and in the life of the community. In the genial atmosphere of Dan's apartment, the conversation is almost always pleasant and purposeful. A spirit of genuine dialogue reigns over the gathering. I know it sounds trite, yet often at the close of such evenings, as I head back to my own apartment, those common scriptural comparisons would come to mind: "Wherever two or three are gathered in my name . . . ," or "And they recognized him in the breaking of the bread." The dinner and the dialogue again and again dissolve into prayer. Dan has so many ways of delightfully rooting us ever more profoundly in our Jesuit mission, our Jesuit pilgrimage.

I could go on and on detailing the impact of living in community with Dan. But there is not enough space to express the community's profound gratitude for all that Dan has brought to us individually and communally and to wish him in the name of his brother Jesuits more than just *ad multos annos*: Dan, may the years allotted to you continue to be richly rewarding, joyfully creative, and lovingly realized, not only for yourself personally, but for all of us and for our world *ad majorem Dei gloriam!*

Daniel and the Joseph Coat

WILLIAM HART McNICHOLS, S.J.

I first heard of Daniel Berrigan in 1968 in the Jesuit Novitiate at Florissant, Missouri. Our novice master, Father Vincent O'Flaherty, wanted us to be acquainted with as disparate a group of Jesuits as he could gather. And so he gave us some recent articles about Daniel Berrigan to read; it was clear that Father O'Flaherty admired him.

During the second summer of novitiate I read Jim Douglass's book *The Nonviolent Cross* with overwhelming relief and recognition. I knew with my whole being that this book was both rare and true. Yet I was only twenty years old, and I needed time to grow into the implications of this profound theology for my life.

But things were happening too fast. Other young men my age were being drafted and sent off to Vietnam. The whole country was in chaos, anger, and grief over the war. One of my fellow Jesuit scholastics gave me Daniel Berrigan's *No Bars to Manhood* and *The Trial of the Catonsville Nine* to read. It was with these two books that I became truly aware of Daniel Berrigan.

Artistically, the books were mature and beautiful. The voice inside was beautiful and unique. I will never forget the impact of this first encounter with that haunting, healing voice. I am sure anyone who loves reading, and searches for a new book as guide and friend knows the joy of discovering a great artist.

But it didn't stop there. This writing also had the mysterious effect of drawing me to pray, to think, to want to act and change. It was spiritual reading, meditation, contemplation . . . like reading the lives of the saints or the writing of the prophets. And this work of prayer, this reading, led almost immediately to involvement with anti-war activities. It also strongly influenced all my choices in philosophy studies and poured out everywhere in the work I was doing in art classes.

This is not to say I fully trusted the author, far from it. For though I admired his art, courage, and holy actions, I was too insecure and too much in awe and fear of his prophetic side to try and meet him; in fact, I decided not to meet him. But I taught *The Trial of the Catonsville Nine*, along with *Antigone* and *The Crucible*, during the following period of Jesuit High School teaching, and I read every new book of Dan's poetry and prose as it came out during the time of theological studies, and often measured myself by his witness.

I moved to Brooklyn in 1980 to get an MFA in painting from the Pratt Institute. Around 1981-1982, the sky fell. A mysterious disease called GRID or AIDS began to invade the whole New York area. In 1983, I was asked to celebrate a mass of healing and anointing for people with AIDS for Dignity, Manhattan. Dignity is an often-unacknowledged, grassroots gay and lesbian Catholic organization, and from this group came some of the original caregivers for people with AIDS; it was with these people that my ministry began.

Words still fail me when trying even to describe those early days of the devastation of this pandemic. Suspended in a limbo of shock and terror, I was continually on the subways, in and out of hospitals, homes, and apartments all over New York and New Jersey. Never had I seen so much suffering and vicious bigotry combined. It was at this time, and in such a state of disorientation, that I finally met Daniel Berrigan.

I was waiting for the uptown number one train at the 59th Street Station. The train arrived, the doors flew open, and there he was, directly in front of me, looking more like a homeless leprechaun than the fierce Amos or anguished Jeremiah I feared. I let myself be drawn toward him. Swaying on the center pole, I introduced myself, then sat down next to him, and there our friendship began. Later, he asked me why I hadn't ever called—it was not lost on him that I'd already lived in New York for three years. I simply told him the story of why I had made a conscious effort not to meet him. After that, each time I went to his apartment for a chat or a meal, I'd always bring flowers; this was my "drink of water for the prophet," and the only way I could think of to express my gratitude.

Dan was interested in working with the St. Vincent's AIDS Hospice, and I put him in contact with the compassionate leader and visionary, Sister Patrice Murphy, who was happy to have him come. He seemed absolutely at home with everyone and brought his great gifts of companionship and joyful affection to so many men and women with AIDS. At times, we'd go to visit these friends together. He would come to the healing mass I celebrated at Our Lady of Guadalupe Church on 14th Street, or he would gather together a small group of us for a home-cooked meal at his apartment. Once in a while we would be asked to conduct a funeral together. Whatever the situation, I was always glad he was there and felt very comfortable in his presence. And I learned so much that was natural about the ideal of Jesuit companionship and spiritual conversation. I'll never forget him referring in an off-handed but poignant way to St. Ignatius's "third degree of humility" when I told him of the first Jesuit to be hospitalized with AIDS.

Later, when I moved into the same Jesuit community on 98th Street, and we became even better friends, I discovered how much fun he could be. All my projected fears and categories just dissolved. Here was a real prophet and a man who could also be a great and loyal friend. I also saw, at times, some hostile people around him hurling their projections, sins of omission, and competition at this gentle man. The main reason, it seemed to me, was that he had been given the "Joseph coat." This ambiguous favor of father to son from the book of Genesis brought the original Joseph nothing but jealousy and separation. It wasn't enough that Daniel Berrigan was lauded as a great writer, poet, and theologian, but now he was a symbol, an archetype, a sometimes maligned and unwilling prophet. All this, to say the least, was and is a heavy coat for him to bear. It still seems to me that this obvious gift (even to his enemies) of the coat of many talents, a sign of the Father's love and promise, is what stirs up people the most. But Dan's life struggling with the scriptures, and then feeding others with what he finds, is food to him. This living prayer nurtures him, soothes the despair, and calls him to continue his many creative ways of peace-making under the benediction of the Savior: "How blessed are the peacemakers; they shall be recognized as the children of God."

> Daniel
> is the child
> who never learned
> to speak in lies,
> who suffered endless
> false fathers,
> brutal and misleading.
> His own gentle inner skin
> was scorched by prison
> and the blasphemies
> of a violent culture
> drunk on the blood
> of the Lamb.
> He brings the Son
> of the beatitudes
> to those beyond the pale
> of church and society.
> He cannot see what we
> who love him behold:
> the shower of light
> the hovering Spirit.

He cannot hear the
tender Father say
what we drink in
full mercy . . .
"This is again
my beloved,
hear him."

A Christ Figure

RICHARD McSORLEY, S.J.

Because of my years of experience in the civil rights struggle as a pastor of a church in southern Maryland, as soon as I heard of him and his work for civil rights, I saw Dan Berrigan as a Christ figure. I remember hearing about Dan and his brother Phil trying to get permission to join the Freedom Rides through the South, to integrate the bus stations. On those buses they would risk their lives and run into almost certain beatings from the crowds of white racists who didn't want them in the South.

Dan and Phil tried to join a Freedom Ride in 1963 to protest the segregation of bus terminals in Jackson, Mississippi. A mass sit-in was planned, and both of them wanted to be part of it. Dan asked his Jesuit provincial for permission to join the Freedom Ride, and his request was denied. Phil flew to Atlanta to join the Freedom Ride, but in the airport he was paged to a telephone and ordered back home by his Josephite superior. The bishop of Jackson had called and threatened to complain to Rome if Phil arrived in Mississippi. Phil returned home, but the incident made headlines around the country.

In Dan, I saw a Jesuit whom I knew was willing to risk his life to show that racial segregation was wrong. I had enough experience with racial segregation during my years as pastor to St. James' Church in St. Mary's City, Maryland, to know what it meant to take an open stand against it. I also knew what it meant for a Catholic priest and a Jesuit to take that stand. He would not get support from the Catholic church or the Jesuit Order. He would be supported only by his faith in God and his belief that his faith required him to take a stand against the evil of racism.

As Dan spoke out and wrote in support of the civil rights movement, I was proud of him not only because he was a Jesuit and a priest, but most of all, because he was fully human. He was willing to stand up and take the brunt of the attack against his faith and his belief that we are all children of the one God. He took a position which I knew from my own experience was the right position to take, but also a dangerous and painful position. It required risking his life for his faith. Dan was offering leadership the church badly needed, leadership it had lacked for many years. He also offered the same leadership to the Jesuit Order, which lacked it as well.

By his willingness to risk his life for the faith, by his leadership as a Jesuit and a priest, I was proud of him, proud to be his brother. As a believer in Christ, I saw Dan, along with his brother Phil and Martin Luther King, Jr., as one of the few Christ figures of my age. They all risked their lives for their faith. They were willing to take a stand.

At the time of the Freedom Rides I was already out of my parish and teaching at Georgetown University. In my small parish I had been warned by Jesuits in nearby parishes that I should keep my mouth shut on the racial issue and just say nothing. It took a good deal of time and prayer for me to decide to take a stand against segregation in my parish. But I took a stand, and I saw what happened. Now here was Dan, speaking out for civil rights and writing about it, not like me in a little parish, but on the national scene. I was cheered and greatly encouraged in my faith by Dan's example. He quickly became one of the best-known Jesuits in the country. I knew some of the loneliness of "going it alone," and that Dan would have to go through much more in his commitment to racial justice in the church and in society. But that was all the more evidence that his leadership was sorely needed.

By 1965, the Vietnam war was well under way and so was opposition to it. Dan was beginning to be a national leader against the war. He had helped found the Catholic Peace Fellowship. Along with Rabbi Abraham Heschel and Lutheran Pastor Richard Neuhaus, Dan organized the Clergy and Laity Concerned About Vietnam committee. Then, when Cardinal Spellman asked the New York Jesuit provincial to get Dan out of New York City, the provincial sent Dan to Latin America. Dan phoned me and asked me to take his place on the committee. He told me he was going to South America, and that he would tell anyone who wanted a speaker to talk against the war to call me. By his example, Dan led me to consider the Vietnam war; now, by his invitation, he pushed me into doing something.

On his way to South America, Dan came to Georgetown. Monsignor George Gingwash and Father George Joyce of St. Augustine's Church, who had both struggled for racial justice in Washington, D.C., wanted to give a party for Dan. I had to borrow a car to take Dan to the party, and as I was driving along, I remember him saying with amusement, "I am in exile and yet here I am driving in a Cadillac to a party."

Dan went to Latin America and saw firsthand the aggression of the wealthy and the powerful against the poor and the powerless. He traveled to Mexico, Brazil, Chile, Peru, and elsewhere. He wrote about it and made the connections between the oppression of the poor in Latin America and first-world war-making. He returned more famous than ever, a well-known writer, a spokesman for peace. He taught me and the country that the struggle for peace and the struggle for justice are very much the same struggle. There was a comprehensive parallel between the two. The people opposed to racial justice were in favor of the war. Southern senators who opposed the Civil Rights Bill were now pushing for financial support of the war. The same arguments used against racial justice were used against peace. White racists who said that black people were not really human now said neither are the Vietnamese. Meanwhile, the same theology that supported racial justice, supported peace and opposition to the war. This theology teaches that we are all children of one God, sisters and brothers of one another. This was the theology of Martin Luther King, Jr., and Daniel Berrigan, a theology that says when we kill any of our brothers and sisters, we offend God. The gospel that says that we should love one another, including our enemies, means we are to love everyone of every color and of every land, including Vietnam.

Dan's example and Dan's writings helped me fill in the details of that comprehensive parallel between the struggle for racial justice and the struggle for peace. So did Martin Luther King, Jr. I remember the day I stood in front of the bulletin board at Georgetown and read a notice that told of Dr. King's decision to speak out against the war. In a speech in front of the United Nations, King said he was not going to spend his life opposing segregation and then stop at the three-mile limit. He said he had been advised by his friends and supporters that if he turned against the war, he would lose support for the civil rights movement. He would no longer be welcome at the White House. He would no longer receive funds. He took all this into account, and he still spoke out against the war. He called it "a racist war"; there were twice as many black men in the US military (compared to their percentage in the US population) as whites, and Americans were killing people of color in Vietnam. They too were no less than the children of God. The racism and the war must stop, he declared.

When I finally realized that all three leaders who had been Christ figures in my life, Dan and Phil Berrigan and Martin Luther King, Jr., had turned against the war, I knew I too had to stand completely against the war. In 1967, when Dan and Phil were the first Catholic priests to be arrested for opposing the war, I supported them.

I remember Dan and Phil and their friends standing trial in Baltimore for the Catonsville Nine action. I sat inside and was amazed at the way the judge acted. Later I read Dan's play, *The Trial of the Catonsville Nine*, with great interest. Dan was leading the way in the church's opposition to the war.

Years later, during the 1970s, my young niece and I drove to a nearby jail early one morning to pick up Dan, who was supposed to be released. We arrived at about 8 A.M. and I asked the sheriff, "Is Father Berrigan released yet?"

The sheriff replied, "We don't have any fathers here. What's his name?"

"Daniel," I said.

"What's he done?"

"He poured blood on the temple of death."

"What does that mean?"

"You ought to know," I answered. "You have him in here for doing it."

Dan appeared a little later. As we were riding to the train station to send Dan on his way back to New York, my niece asked from the back seat, "Why did you do this?" Dan had been in jail for pouring blood on the Pentagon.

He turned around to her. He understood it was a serious question, and he gave this answer: "You get to reading scripture a little bit, and you soon find that Christ was a suspect of both the church and the state, and then you ask yourself, 'Am I a suspect of the church and the state?' That's really the reason for it, but that's not the way it is always understood."

I thought that was the clearest explanation given by him for his peace activities.

Dan told us a story. "One Jesuit said to me, 'I understand why you destroyed draft records, but I don't understand this business of opposing nuclear weapons.'" Dan said to the Jesuit, "I destroyed draft records in 1968. How long did it take you to understand that?" The Jesuit answered, "About 1973." Dan replied, "Well in about five more years you may understand about opposing nuclear weapons."

I remember Dan telling me that a Jesuit friend once said to him, "Dan, you'd be welcome to teach literature or poetry at one of the twenty-eight Jesuit colleges and universities in the country if you'd just stop talking about this darn peace business. You are the most prolific of all Jesuit writers."

Dan replied, "If I stopped this darn peace business, what would I teach?"

Dan has made me question myself all during my life. I've felt very small compared to him. I went to jail a few times for minor things, like blocking the hallway of the Capitol, refusing to leave the Rotunda when told to, and remaining to pray and sing in opposition to nuclear weapons, but I was not in jail long. Dan challenged me and many other Christians to answer the question: "Do you accept the call of God to get your hands dirty like Martin Luther King, Jr., Mahatma Gandhi, and Oscar Romero, as well as Jesus himself? How seriously do you commit yourself to practicing God's compassion and witnessing to God's mercy in a world of sin?" These are the questions that Dan's life puts before us.

As Dan celebrates his seventy-fifth birthday, he still offers the example of being a Christ figure to me and everybody who has eyes to see.

A Letter from Your Brother in El Salvador

JON SOBRINO, S.J.

Dear Dan,

I am writing this letter to give thanks to God and to celebrate with your friends your seventy-five years of life, most of them lived as a member of the Company of Jesus.

As you know, I have never lived with you, and for that reason I only have a few personal memories of you. The first time that I saw you, when I was a philosophy student at Fusz Memorial in St. Louis and you came to speak to us in the early 1960s, I recall something special about what you told us. The last time that I saw you was thirty years later in El Salvador, after the assassination-martyrdom of our brothers of the Central American University. Between both dates I remember when Father Arrupe went to visit you in prison, a gesture that made me happy because of what it said about him and because prison, given the situation of our world, is not a bad place for a Jesuit to be. Of course I know about your dedication to peace, your prophecy and utopia, your times in prison, and something of your writings.

From all of this I have come to think of you as a *witness,* a brother Jesuit who has joined faith in God to human responsibility in an untiring and incorruptible work for peace. For that reason—because you are a witness—I am inspired to share with you some reflections that I have made these days about our witnesses, the Salvadoran martyrs. I make them thinking about our world, but also with the future of the church and the Company of Jesus in mind.

By coincidence, at this moment the General Congregation of the Jesuits is being celebrated in Rome. We don't know yet what will come from it, but I remember some words expressed by Father Kolvenbach at the end of last year—with concern but also with his usual composure—that the Jesuits had not yet found the "spark" for the General Congregation.

Well, I hope that our brothers have by now found in Rome the spark that will give us light and warmth, so urgent in a world which oppresses the truth with lies and in a world with a heart of stone that kills the poor. But for us here—said with total simplicity—that situation is clear: the martyrs and the beatitudes that they express are this spark. And you will understand this very well, with your long life of testimony and struggle for peace: we need witnesses and we need beatitudes, both of which are ignored and despised by our badly named "civilization," which not only does not feed the poor but does not humanize—or civilize—anyone.

So if there is something that we have, here and there, it is witnesses and martyrs. Salvadorans, like Archbishop Romero, as well as less-well-known *campesinos*, like Polin and Ticha, Julia Elba and Celina, until we come to our brothers Ellacu, Lolo, Nacho, Juan Ramon, Amando, and Segundo. And there are North Americans like Martin Luther King, Jr., Ita and Maura, Dorothy and Jean, and many others. There is where the spark is, and, if you allow me to remember the obvious, it has been there from the beginning in the cross of the martyr Jesus.

But let us go now to the reflections. The first is this: I have come to the conclusion that martyrs are an obstacle, and for that reason there hovers over them a great silence which I want to denounce. This silence makes me indignant because it expresses ingratitude—one of the sins to avoid according to St. Ignatius—and above all because it impoverishes this already destitute civilization.

"They" want to deprive the martyrs of reality, as though they were things of the past, relegated to museums, not of interest to a world that "has arrived at the end of history." The silence is notorious in the official realm. Government officials, military officers, politicians, the U.S. Embassy, and the United Nations do not mention them. Nor do many bishops, with the exception of Archbishop Rivera and the dedication with which he put forward the canonization of Archbishop Romero. Only the poor, this is sure, remember the martyrs with affection.

But the most important thing is to discover how the analysts of the system justify this silence. To synthesize, they say that *really* to remember the martyrs and to make of them our best tradition would bring to the actual moment more bad than good: social traumas, intolerance, aggressiveness, all things that should disappear in the new, pragmatic, neoliberal "global village." The "real" democracies (we must not only speak of "real" socialisms in order to discredit socialism, but of "real" democracies) need a psychological-social environment that is quite distinct from that which generated the martyrs. They need pluralism, tolerance, dialogue, and the memory of the martyrs appears to be more of an obstacle than a help. And as the problem is serious, and because we also in the church and in the Company of Jesus can fall into this aberration, allow me to say a word about this.

Certainly toleration is good, but it is also certain that it's only a small step from toleration to indifference. And in this way the tolerant democracies of the North of the planet can contemplate without blinking how twenty to thirty million human beings die of hunger each year, and they can never give a second thought to what is occurring in Rwanda, Haiti, Chad, El Salvador or Nicaragua. Certainly democracy can be good to moderate the aggressiveness of liberating, revolutionary, and religious ideas, but it is also certain that it is only a small step to numbness, and as we are going in the world, the prophetic/utopic potential of the religious is ever more necessary to spur democracies without compassion. Certainly diversity in ways of thinking and believing should be respected, but it is also certain that we cannot reduce to pluralism the fundamental difference between those who take life for granted and those who cannot take precisely life itself for granted. The rich Epulons and the poor Lazaruses of our days should not be presented as models of pluralistic coexistence, but as those who are in need of conversion and those who are condemned to death.

The reason that is given for silencing the martyrs is, while unjust, very logical. The martyrs are obstacles and continue to be dangerous. Even after their death, they continue to live. They bring to the light of day the truth about our world today, but they also illuminate how we can build a world on truth, compassion, love, and justice. That's how the poor see it, which leads me to the second reflection.

Many times I have asked the humble people here in El Salvador who Archbishop Romero was for them, and the unanimous response has been: "Archbishop Romero spoke the truth, he defended the poor, and that's why they killed him." They are saying that a martyr is one who is killed for very precise reasons: for speaking the truth and for defending the poor.

That's what happens in reality. In El Salvador, many years ago a process of truth was established, and in that process there have been authentic witnesses and false witnesses. Among the false witnesses have been government officials and generals, many communications media, powerful financial groups, judicial administrators, politicians, ambassadors—and sadly, some bishops. They have manipulated the truth to the extreme of trying to blame the poor for everything bad, while the powerful have been presented as the source of everything good. They presented Archbishop Romero as the bad person, and the one who ordered his killing as good. Neither the current president nor the previous one has ever retracted this, and his assassination has never been seriously investigated. Today, despite some attempts to improve, there still does not exist the slightest willingness to seek the truth.

Those who have given their lives for the truth, the authentic witnesses, have been the martyrs. They have not become martyrs simply by virtue of an intellectual conviction, if we can be allowed to speak this way, but because they were full of compassion and mercy. They have spoken the truth in order to defend the oppressed. Martyrdom has above all been the expression of a great love for those who suffer poverty, oppression, repression and death. The martyrs, and this must be emphasized, have not given their lives in order to gain something for themselves, neither power nor riches, but in order that the poor majority might live.

Why the best and the most generous ones are assassinated is one of the great enigmas of history, the *mystery of evil*. But this is also the great existential question for every human being and every Christian: whether to continue to defend the poor or not, whether to struggle against monopolizers and executioners only "from without," with the weapons of the word, and social, political and diplomatic power, or to struggle also "from within," bearing the sin of this world.

If some Christians have been martyred, it is because they have loved greatly, shown mercy and compassion—and called for justice. From a Christian perspective, love is necessary to become a human being. But action for justice is also needed. "To know me is to do justice," Yahweh says. Love, in the form of justice, is necessary to shape a human society.

Everyone proclaims how good and necessary democracy is, but it isn't clear what real good this means for the majority of the poor or what foundations are necessary for democracy to become a reality. True, the Western tradition has formulated it as "liberty, equality, and fraternity." In reality, however, "liberty," economic liberty, especially for the few, almost always is used for their own benefit and against the majority. Very little is said of equality, and nothing of fraternity. And so in our democracy there is no fraternity or love. The following are some data about our democratic world which I just read a few weeks ago:

> In 1960, the poorest 20% of the people of our planet shared 2.3% of the world's income. This percentage has diminished to 1.7% in 1980 and 1.4% in 1990. At the same time the richest 20% have increased from 70.2% in 1960, to 76.3% in 1980 and 82.7% in 1990.

In our so-called democratic world the cry of the poor doesn't reach the ears of the rich. There is no conversion of those who live in scandalous wealth to the welfare of those who live in scandalous misery.

When it is announced as good news that the day will come when the crumbs of the rich man, Epulon, will reach the poor man, Lazarus, it is with the desire that the situation of Epulon need not change very much. The poor continue to wait. The rich have still not taken a serious step toward reconciliation.

When one looks at the disparity, the words of Paul to the Romans come to mind. We could paraphrase the words in the following way: "Who will liberate us from so many lies and cover-ups? Who will liberate us from so much hatred and injustice?" Politicians and legislators can offer some help, but in order to turn around this history of lies and death, we need martyrs of truth and of life, faithful witnesses to the end.

This is the difficult and risky function of the martyrs—to defend truth, love, compassion, and justice in our society. But they also generate hope, because they tell us that truth and love are possible. They tell us that we can live in another way, and that we can try to turn around history.

Dear Dan, this is what I would like to share with you. I have spoken to you, witness to peace, about our brothers and sisters, martyrs of truth and justice. You well know that all this leads to the same thing: the truth and justice for which our martyrs gave their lives and the peace to which you have dedicated your life. You know as well that martyrs and witnesses are those upon whom we have to keep our eyes fixed, because they are the ones who keep our hope alive so we can continue working in this world, in the church, and in the Company of Jesus. As Ignacio Ellacuría told us: "All the blood of the martyrs shed in El Salvador and Latin America, far from bringing discouragement and despair, has instilled a new spirit of struggle and a new hope."

My wish is that you will continue to be faithful "in following the poor and humble Jesus," and that you rejoice in the "disgrace and abuse" that bring you near to the poor of this world and not in "the mundane and vain honors," about which St. Ignatius advises us in his *Spiritual Exercises.*

And lest I forget Jesus: "Not every life is an occasion for hope, but the life of Jesus, who out of love bore the cross, truly is." May this hope accompany you all the days of your life.

Your brother,
Jon Sobrino, S.J.

Crossing the Line

LUIS CALERO, S.J.

I remember well the detention cell in which we were temporarily placed. It was small, like a bird cage, with two long cement benches on each side. I looked around and recognized each one of the friendly faces in the room: university students, fellow faculty, Pax Christi members, and brother Jesuits, all of whom had joined in the action against death in El Salvador. It seemed like the natural place to be, a place of choice, a room that symbolized opposition to murderous government policies that had killed people in the name of democracy and freedom in Central America. As I sat down I thought of the more recent casualties—of my own Jesuit brothers and friends. I thought of Nacho Martín Baro playing the guitar and singing after community meals—he was no longer with us. But we were still around, and we had to continue their work.

Dan had been with us all along: cheerful, radiant, putting his life on the line as he had done so many times before, addicted to denouncing lies. His presence gave us strength and vigor, his words commanding hope. I never thought that crossing the line of civil disobedience could be so simple, effortless, freeing. I don't recall a single moment of hesitation. And it was not as if we were doing a great thing. No big splash; it was just right and nothing else. The great frustration came not from being under arrest but in knowing that this symbolic statement amounted to very little in pragmatic terms, that policies of sending weapons to brutal military officers would continue killing many more. Our temporary discomfort was nothing in the light of the tragedy of this war of terrorism against the poor. Dan taught me about the rightness of civil disobedience as a sign of loving the other nonviolently. For me it was a gradual process of learning, accompanied by reflection and prayer and, sometimes, resistance in my inner self. The most difficult thing about crossing the line was not the fear of being beaten, arrested, rejected by family or friends, but the realization that we could be arrested a hundred times, a thousand perhaps, and this country's policy in El Salvador would remain the same—targeting defenseless *campesinos* whose crime was only to struggle and demand a life of dignity, like anybody else.

I had encountered Dan several times during my Jesuit life. He once taught at Berkeley, California, when I was a student at the Jesuit theologate. At that stage of my training he appeared to me a rare combination of Jose Marti, Che Guevara, and Miguel Pro—three very different people. Marti was a poet, Che was a visionary, Pro was a committed apostle. I vividly remember when Dan took time to have a cup of espresso with me. He seemed more interested in my studies and concerns than in discussing himself. That was at the time of the Central American crisis, and we talked about refugee communities in Mesa Grande who were dreaming of returning to their homeland.

But it was in the fateful year of 1989, at Loyola University of New Orleans, that we became friends. He was a visiting professor in religious studies, and I was teaching Latin American studies. We lived together in community, took walks in Audubon Park next to the university, discussed the strengths and shortcomings of Jesuit life. I had heard stories about his stubbornness and persistence in community, driving his points across at the dinner table. I never found the slightest trace of rudeness in him, not the slightest. He spoke softly and with care, addressing friends and opponents with the same attentiveness and compassion. He spoke to us with the conviction and humility of one who had been to the mountaintop—and in prison for years.

That day, November 16, remains clearly ingrained in my mind, as it combines tragedy and light. Yes, death and resurrection. I had just finished teaching my "Peoples of Latin America" class when a student approached me and asked if I had heard the terrible news. I thought she was referring to the FMLN offensive in the capital city of San Salvador, which had unleashed indiscriminate killings against civilians. "No," she said, "I am talking about the murders at the UCA last night—I am afraid that some of your Jesuit friends may be dead." I was disconcertingly quiet, astonished. I rushed to the phone in my office to check the validity of the report. The facts were confirmed from the Jesuit provincial residence: names were read, one by one. I put the telephone down and wept.

In my mind I saw the UCA campus with its many trees and familiar faces. I had known all along that it could happen, yet I did not know. My memory fails me when I think about subsequent events on that day. I remember walking downstairs from my fifth floor office at Loyola, across campus, and into Dan's office—hoping desperately that he would be there. He was, thank goodness, and he listened to my narration of the events of horror in distress and unbelief. The telephone on his desk kept ringing, but nothing could turn his attention from attending to my pain, his pain. Blessed are those who comfort the sorrowful, for they shall be comforted. We spoke about the insanity of dollars, weapons, communist paranoia. Eventually we made our way to a coffee shop, where we sat silently to grieve our loss.

The Loyola University community was stunned by the news. That evening we organized a prayer vigil at Ignatius Chapel, where friends in faith and solidarity brought song and support. A picture of St. Oscar Romero adorned the front of the chapel reminding us of the long list of martyrs, some known and many unknown. In prayer we were led to understand that evening that something of profound consequence had happened—a call to conversion—and that we were invited to make a strong statement against the apathy that had promoted such death. In soothing words Dan invited us to reflect on the seeds of life planted in martyrdom, on the magnitude of the evil empire, and on the need to bring about personal and collective change. I left that chapel still stunned and confused, but hopeful that those seeds could grow.

In the next few days, as we gathered to reflect on our response to the events, Dan, whose experience and insight we valued and trusted, emerged as the natural leader of the group. He had confronted many times the dehumanizing power of militarism, political mindlessness, and violence. The group grew in size and fortitude. As meetings went on we clearly understood that the logical outcome of our reflection was to join in civil disobedience, dissociating ourselves from a government that insisted on making murder the order of the day.

Our strategy was to block the entrance to the first floor set of elevators at the Federal Building in downtown New Orleans. We wore jeans, suits, clerics—about a hundred people of whom some twenty-five were involved in civil disobedience. As I sat on the ground of the elevators I looked to my right and saw a well-dressed professor of Loyola's law school and to my left a student who appeared glad to be out of class but even more glad to join in this public statement. As alarms went off in the building, we sang songs, accompanied by those gathered in support. We paused to pray and ask God for our own conversion and that of the world.

At one point the district attorney came down from his office and gave us a reprimand for blocking the elevators and paralyzing the building. Addressing all of us, but looking at Dan in particular, he attempted to persuade the crowd to disperse voluntarily. He indicated that he was Jesuit-educated and that Jesuits had taught him to respect the law. "That was a bad thing," Dan replied. Frustrated and unconvincing, the attorney informed us that he had been trying to get in touch with the Jesuit provincial, so that he would order us to leave the building by the force of his moral authority. "Fr. Provincial?" Dan said with a smile on his face. "Well, he is right here with us—why don't you speak to him?" The attorney turned around, irate and confused. "Is Fr. Provincial in the crowd?" he asked. After establishing his credentials as a Jesuit product and sympathetic to the cause of justice, he asked the provincial to order us to leave. That was a mistake. The provincial responded that we were adults and aware of the consequences of our actions. "Moreover," he added, "I have to tell you that I consider U.S. policy in El Salvador murderous and bankrupt." We were hand-cuffed and taken to the cell with the cement benches. That day I felt grateful and proud to be a Jesuit.

I was tried in court, along with many others, and sentenced to some forty hours of community service. My probation officer timidly mentioned that he was proud of our action. My sentence consisted in working with Salvadoran refugees in New Orleans, not a punishment but a reward. Dan was brought to trial from New York at a later date. He had missed his previous court dates, and I was among those who served as a character witness in the trial. I told the judge that Dan was an inspiration to me and others in the Society of Jesus, that he was an agitator of love for God and neighbor, that I had met few people with such a great sense of integrity and compassion. I meant what I said.

Sometime later Dan was invited to New Orleans, this time to receive an honorary doctorate from Loyola University—at that time the first Jesuit institution to honor him for his service and in recognition of his scholarship. His words of acceptance still ring in my mind. "This is the second most important public recognition I have received in this marvelous city of New Orleans," he said. What could be the first? people wondered. "The first and most important recognition," he continued, "was the day I was arrested at the Federal Building for denouncing the moral wrongness of U.S. policy in El Salvador." Yes, Dan, that was more important. Thank you for teaching us how effortless it is to cross the line.

Servants of Christ's Mission in a World of War

PETER-HANS KOLVENBACH, S.J.

Long before Ignatius of Loyola founded the Society of Jesus, he was an ambitious soldier. After he was wounded in battle, he spent many painful months recuperating. During that time, he read the lives of the saints and the gospels, and he decided to renounce his military career in order to follow Jesus as the saints had done. To mark his conversion, he spent a long evening in prayer in a church before a statue of Mary with the child Jesus, and then early the next morning, he laid down his sword before the statue, exchanged his military clothes for the clothes of a beggar, and embarked upon his new spiritual quest of discipleship to Jesus and his way of humble service and boundless love.

The Society of Jesus continues today to commit itself to Ignatius's vision of discipleship to Christ. The Thirty-Second General Congregation of the Society of Jesus said that to be a Jesuit "is to know that one is a sinner, yet called to be a companion of Jesus as Ignatius was." It continued:

> What is it to be a companion of Jesus today? It is to engage, under the standard of the cross, in the crucial struggle of our time: the struggle for faith and that struggle for justice which it includes. . . . The mission of the Society of Jesus today is the service of faith, of which the promotion of justice is an absolute requirement. For reconciliation with God demands the reconciliation of people with one another.

The Thirty-Third General Congregation confirmed our commitment to the faith that does justice and makes peace:

> As an international body, the Society of Jesus commits itself to that work which is the promotion of a more just world order,

greater solidarity of rich countries with poor, and a lasting peace based on human rights and freedom. At this critical moment for the future of humanity, many Jesuits are cooperating more directly in the work for peace as intellectuals, organizers and spiritual leaders, and by their witness of nonviolence. Following the example of recent Popes, we must strive for international justice and an end to an arms race that deprives the poor and threatens to destroy civilization. The evangelical call to be genuine peacemakers cautions us to avoid both naivety and fatalism.

In our recent Thirty-Fourth General Congregation, the Society of Jesus once again recommitted itself to be "servants of Christ's mission." We know that we are sinners and that we have failed, but we know that the crucified Christ continues to call us to follow him as he walks the way of peace.

To be a companion of Jesus in our times is to be a voice for peace, an advocate for justice, a servant of the whole human family. Our world continues to be ravaged by war, starvation, poverty, and oppression. The international sale of weapons promotes the death of millions. The ongoing maintenance of nuclear weapons in the face of massive poverty and hunger remains a crime against God and humanity. The countless deaths in Rwanda, the former Yugoslavia, and elsewhere demand the laying down of our weapons and the cessation of war. Pope John Paul II, in a recent letter commemorating the fiftieth anniversary of the end of the war in Europe, recalled with deep regret that we have not yet entered into the promised land of peace. "In human hearts, including those of believers, there is a strong temptation to hate, to despise others and to deceive them."

The Lord, however, does not fail to help us. He can and does bring about in the human heart attitudes of love, understanding, and peace, and a sincere desire for reconciliation and unity. Now, more than ever, we need to follow his way of the cross, the way of nonviolent love and reconciliation, the way of Jesus the peacemaker. In these times, if we are to be faithful to the God of peace, we must rededicate our lives, in the name of the gospel, to the struggle for disarmament, justice, and reconciliation.

The voice of Christ speaks clearly to us from the gospels: "Love your enemies, do good to those who hate you, bless those who curse you, pray for those who mistreat you" (Lk 6:28). As followers of Jesus, we are called to be people who love our enemies, instruments of Christ's own reconciling love. To do that, we walk in solidarity with the poor, speak out against injustice and systemic violence, and are willing to suffer for our Christian conviction. But we pledge never to retaliate, never to hate, never to respond with further violence. Our Christian vocation as apostles of peace in a world of war and oppression demands that we be people of peace, people who trust in the God of peace, people who insist that a world without war is possible.

And so, it is right that we celebrate Father Daniel Berrigan, because peace took root in his heart, as it has in the hearts of so many others, opening them to God. I join my brother Jesuits and Fr. Berrigan's many other friends in thanking God for Fr. Berrigan's lifelong service of Christ's mission of peace. And I send him my blessings on his seventy-fifth birthday. May his example encourage all of us to be faithful to Christ, who continues to invite us to forge new paths in God's reign of justice and peace.

THE WRITER

A Social Critic with Humor and Mystery

MICHAEL TRUE

Gore Vidal has said that American culture "handles" its social critics in one of three ways. The first is to try to "black out" a critic
altogether, by denying him or her an audience, as it did Noam Chomsky
until recently. The major media—MacNeil/Lehrer, for example—pre-
tend that Chomsky doesn't exist; they seldom invite him as a com-
mentator, though he remains one of the best-informed persons in the
world on American foreign policy. And the *New York Times* and *Boston Globe*, even before they became Siamese twins, consistently ignored his numerous books of investigative reporting since 1969.

A second way is to demonize the critic, as it does Jesse Jackson,
treating him as if he were possessed or harmful simply because he
keeps reminding us of obvious injustices: homelessness and racial dis-
crimination and unemployment and violence in our midst.

A third way that American culture deals with its critics is to call
them outrageous or to trivialize them, as it does Gore Vidal—regarding him as a television entertainer (a kind of left-wing William Buckley),
rather than as one of the most knowledgeable, distinguished men of
letters in English. His *United States: Essays 1952-1992* already claims
a rightful place alongside the collected essays of George Orwell and
Virginia Woolf.

Until he became a social critic, about 1965, Daniel Berrigan was
treated with respect by reviewers—lionized, one might say—as poet,
beginning with the Lamont Poetry Prize in 1958, and as a religious
writer, especially by fellow Catholics. Little by little, however, after
his time in Eastern Europe and particularly after Francis Cardinal
Spellman exiled him to Latin America, Berrigan's poetry became more
satiric and his prose became more precise. Even during the early 1970s,
years of protest and imprisonment, however, the literary prizes
mounted, with the Melcher and Thomas More prizes and the Obie
award for his popular and only play, *The Trial of the Catonsville Nine*.

167

Then Berrigan had the gall to criticize not only his native land, but Israel as well, pointing out complicity between the two war-making states. At that point, the roof fell in, as Berrigan became *persona non grata* among columnists and literary journalists. The editor of a well-known journal of opinion, for example, excised from my review any reference to Berrigan's 1973 speech before the Association of Arab University graduates.

The attitude of some commentators on Berrigan the writer reminds me of the attitude of one of my academic colleagues, an alumnus of three Catholic colleges and universities. Speaking with his secretary, who suggested that the professor might wish to hear Father Berrigan speak on campus some years ago, Professor Machiavelli said, "Not only will I not be there, I think it's a disgrace that Daniel Berrigan is allowed to speak on a Catholic college campus." Such a view is a minority opinion, but an entrenched one. For academics especially, ideas in conflict with the political and religious status quo have no place in "educated" discourse, little right to exist. I mention this incident because of its relevance to the present status of "Daniel Berrigan the writer."

As a critic, Berrigan continues to be subjected to rough handling for criticizing the "guvmint." Not satisfied with living under William Clinton, Berrigan recently reminded readers of a religious journal, in a letter to the editor, about ongoing agonies of unemployed and hungry Americans, maimed Iraqi children, and others living and dying under the heel of the U.S. arms trade. For doing so, the journal's editors dismissed him, snootily, as a "prophet," a code word meaning "ungrateful citizen of the U.S. of A., who fails to understand the big picture." So it goes.

As with earlier writers who noted the American emperor's nakedness—the faithful, persistent Paul Goodman (1911-72), for example—Berrigan has been trivialized and vilified, but never for long blacked-out. His reading public remains large and appreciative. He has published ten books in prose and poetry since my *Daniel Berrigan: Poetry, Drama, Prose*, selections from his first forty books. Although I see no need to alter my perspective on him as a writer as expressed in that anthology, I do want to emphasize a couple of points mentioned there and to call attention to his best book in recent years.

In the introduction to *Daniel Berrigan: Poetry, Drama Prose*, I tried to suggest why he has a special claim on our attention, not only as a public figure, but also as an artist. Yes, he is known and regarded as an influential person, as a priest, teacher, and war resister, but that is something a bit different from his claims on our attention as a writer, a person drawn to the power of art in conveying his sense of the world and his relationship to it. And while no one can or wants to separate the man and his work, his writing has a heft, weight, and distinction of its own. It may even be how history remembers him, as we remember earlier pamphleteers who lived vigorous public lives while making distinctive contributions to the language. Writing on religion, as well as public issues, he belongs among a lively company, including Goodman—but also Thomas Merton, Dorothy Day, John Henry Newman, and Thomas Paine.

Long interested in the poet, essayist, and religious writer, I have reviewed Berrigan's books over the years in *New Republic, Cross Currents*, and similar periodicals. In doing so, I pointed to what I regarded as well or poorly written, incisive or repetitious—that is, where, from my point of view, he succeeded or failed as a writer and where his rather Zen attitude toward publishing rendered him less accessible to readers than he might be. I did so out of respect for the man and the artist, but also out of respect for his audience, for the issues he dealt with, and—since he is a poet—for the tradition within which he chooses to write.

Surveying reviews of his (now) fifty books, a thoughtful reader has to be struck by how seldom commentators indicate any awareness of him as a craftsman, as an artist at work, before moving on to praise or to criticize the person (at times for rather idiosyncratic reasons).

When Berrigan's autobiography, *To Dwell in Peace*, appeared in 1987, I realized how serious the situation had become and how unlikely it was that he would be given a decent shake by people responsible for literary culture. A remarkable book by any standard, *To Dwell in Peace* was treated with disdain, linked by one reviewer with the autobiography of Jerry Falwell; subjected by another to pop-psychology analysis; and savaged by another. In the latter case, a well-known religious journalist seized the opportunity to settle accounts with Daniel Berrigan, Catholic war resister.

Whatever disagreements one might have with him on particular issues, Berrigan's life has been enormously productive, diverse, risky—in a word, *interesting*. Equally interesting is the manner in which he told his story, in a style that is exactly appropriate with his understanding of his various vocations, as priest, teacher, poet, religious writer.

Among many attitudes that he might have adopted, Berrigan chose to tell his tale rather formally, as if he were observing his life from some distance. It's a perspective that he has lived, in a highly personalized era, with some insistence. And he obviously had some choice, amid numerous possibilities, because of obvious "perks"—intelligence, good looks, education, travel, and wide associations. In his dedication, he reminds one of other radicals who chose to live "against the American grain," rather than amid comfort and popular acclaim: Elizabeth Gurley Flynn (1890-1963), Dorothy Day (1897-1980), Thomas Merton (1915-68). Perhaps more to the point, since the comparison offers numerous points of reference, is John Henry Newman (1801-90), the great Victorian controversialist who resigned his post as an Oxford don in the established Church of England for a life of turmoil and uncertainty in the immigrant and "English gothic" Church of Rome.

Berrigan, like Newman, had a sizable and appreciative public by his early forties. "I was becoming known here and there through my books," Berrigan wrote in *To Dwell in Peace*, "was teaching, leading retreats, lecturing, offering poetry readings: working like a demon and loving it. . . . My peers and I had an influence that went beyond formalities. We were quasi gurus of the college: we walked in light."

Soon, however, the scene, as well as the life, was fundamentally altered. He left LeMoyne College, Syracuse, in 1964, to spend a sabbatical year in Europe among worker priests in France and behind the Iron Curtain. Decades later he looked back in "grief and gratitude (I in the minor mode, surely) of a Newman departing Oxford." Without fully realizing it, he was moving into a larger world of radical possibility and pain:

> Never again would I be, for any appreciable time, a member of a Jesuit faculty. Never again dwell fondly on the thought, as I did in those days, of "my college." The satisfaction, achievement, devotion to study, the communality of faith with the young, these were gone. I lost my aura; more grievously, I lost a home. Henceforth I would be a wanderer on the Earth; here and there, an overnight dwelling; and only of late years, folded in a Jesuit community at last.

The story of his interim years is recorded in various literary forms—poetry, drama, prose—at times casual, even careless, at other times eloquent, terse, moving. In *To Dwell in Peace*, however, the man and the writing are one, shaped and clarified to a purpose, for anyone who takes the trouble to listen with mind, heart, and psyche.

Among various passages, this one, near the end of his autobiography, conveys the humor and mystery of the past thirty years:

> We had to improvise as we went, in a tactical sense. So we improvised and went. There resulted an element of trial and error—and, on occasion, of hilarious lefthandedness. But in the deeper sources, where resolution is forged and blessed, where motives have their mysterious start, there was no improvising at all. One does not improvise a tradition (and tradition, in season and out, was our point): one received it with open hands, all undeserving.

So, as a writer and person, as social critic and radical, Berrigan is a traditionalist after all.

In a culture and among people "who remember nothing past last Tuesday" (Gore Vidal, again), few may understand what Berrigan means by "a tradition." But for anyone familiar with the writers whom he resembles in various ways, he offers essential insights and valuable riches. Moving backward in history, one thinks again of Merton, Goodman, Day, Newman, Paine—not to mention that wider and deeper literary net that gathers Gerard Manley Hopkins and Edmund Campion.

As a writer, Berrigan not only reminds us of that tradition. He also contributes to it, strengthening it and offering that literary choice to us once again.

THE TEACHER

Mev Puleo

Teacher of Peace

COLMAN McCARTHY

In the late 1980s, and after an exchange of letters about the teaching of peace, Dan Berrigan sent along a snapshot of his students at Loyola University in New Orleans. From the looks on the faces of them all—about fourteen women and eleven men, and with Dan in the back row—it appeared as if they had just had a couple of hours of vibrant discussion and spirited thinking. Most were smiling, with one or two looking as if they were clowning for the camera. A merry group, I remember thinking.

And why not? What undergraduates wouldn't be joyful to have Dan as their teacher: in the classroom regularly and faithfully, to nudge a couple of students toward the writings of Dorothy Day or the Acts of the Apostles, to suggest to a few others that they read Merton or Amos, and at the end of the course see them awaken to the possibilities of peacemaking in their own lives and communities.

I've kept that picture in my office, placed on a shelf where I keep peace books that I use for my own classes on nonviolence.

That year in New Orleans, Dan was the model professor at Loyola. Six of his brother Jesuits had been slain in El Salvador. Many of the killers had been educated in the ways of death at Ft. Benning, Georgia, at what is called "the School for Assassins." Priests have been arrested there for obstructing good order. There, too, governmental violence is resisted, and lessons taught and learned. On the last day of the semester, Dan took his students on a field trip that twinned as their final exam. They went to the Hale Boggs Federal Building to demonstrate against the White House-Congressional-State Department-CIA-Pentagon-inspired war in El Salvador. The media reported the event—a couple of paragraphs on the AP wire—as another Berrigan "brush with the law." He and the students were arrested on charges of obstructing the entrances, corridors, and elevators of the Boggs building. What the AP didn't report was Dan calling out to his students as they were packed into the police wagon: "Everybody gets an A!" Has Catholic higher education ever had as stirring an academic moment?

I imagine that the members of that class, wherever they are scattered now, have often looked back on that day as a resource in their lives, remembering with moral recall the rareness of the event as a perfect match with the uniqueness of their teacher. Give them a final exam? Poke them like slow-moving cattle to see if they could belch up the intellectual fodder of the course, as though only memorized ideas are the goal of education?

Not for that professor. As with all teachers who look on student braininess as a possible character defect—as in Walker Percy's line that you can make all A's and go out and flunk life—Dan Berrigan knew that the great gift he could give his class was to practice what he taught. He knew, also, that too many people leave our colleges and universities idea-rich but experience-poor.

Getting arrested on the field trip was perhaps a quickly passing event in the lives of his students, but it surely put them in touch with what Kierkegaard believed in his essay "For Self Examination": "In our age they talk about the importance of presenting Christianity simply, not elaborately and grandiloquently. And about this subject they write books, it becomes a science, perhaps one may even make a living of it or become a professor. But they forget or ignore the fact that the truly simple way of presenting Christianity is—to do it."

Dan's teaching at Loyola was one of many stints in the classrooms of colleges and universities—from LeMoyne to Cornell to Berkeley to Villanova to DePaul. Except for his enjoying the warm company of his students, I can't imagine that those stays on campuses were comfortable moments for him. The schools of his own order—the twenty-seven Jesuit colleges and universities—are all but annexes of the Pentagon, some taking research money to hone Caesar's weaponry, others cajoling the young to march, obey, and learn to kill as ROTC cadets.

Dan reports from the front lines of the quad:

> The Catholic campuses offer little relief. One cannot but marvel at the gap between religious rhetoric and public conduct. It could even be argued that on the matter of pretension to a higher moral code, the Catholics come off worse than their secular counterparts. It is probably no news that the showcase Catholic universities boast prestigious theology departments even while the military march on their commons. . . . In the past five years, I have been invited to the campuses of at least five religious orders, including my own: Vincentians, Holy Cross, Franciscans, Benedictines, Jesuits. On each campus, theology looms large; on each campus also, ROTC. The Big Buck stalks the Little Book,

all but slams it shut. The theologians who consider such matters to be morally grotesque are few and far between.

No fewer and farther, either, than the campus mahatmas, the university presidents. While visiting Notre Dame in the mid-1980s, I saw so many students wearing military garb that I thought I was at Fort Hesburgh. It was no illusion; 10 percent of Notre Dame students are enrolled in ROTC. No college or university has a higher percentage. I sought out General Hesburgh for an interview. With five-star pride, he boasted of Notre Dame's being at the top of the ROTC heap. Ever patient with those of lesser intellect, he instructed me on the pedagogical soundness of having Air Force, Army, and Navy units at Notre Dame: "Colman, you have to understand: we must Christianize the military." Alas, I didn't understand. In my ignorance, I asked a question: "Oh? There's a Christian way to slaughter people?"

It was a brief interview.

Notre Dame has never awarded Dan Berrigan its hallowed Laetare Medal. Nor has Georgetown brought him in for an honorary degree. Nor has J. Peter Grace, William Simon or Peter Flanigan—moneybag Catholic laymen all—endowed a Berrigan chair for peace studies. When I lecture at Catholic campuses, I give a spot quiz at student assemblies. Identify these six people: Robert E. Lee, U. S. Grant, Paul Revere, Dorothy Day, Thomas Merton, and Daniel Berrigan. All hands go up on the first three. The last three draw blanks. The kids know the peacebreakers but not the peacemakers.

Occasionally, a hand or two does go up on the name of Berrigan. I think to myself, well, there's probably a professor on the loose around here who has slipped a Berrigan book or two onto the required reading list, and hoped the department chair won't learn of it. Let Catholic kids read about Daniel Berrigan and next thing you know they end up becoming Christians.

Seeking Wisdom by Living the Truth

ROBERT LUDWIG

"I attended Jesuit schools, and they always taught me to obey the law," an angry federal prosecutor John Volz shouted, as the news cameras panned the Loyola students engaged in a sit-down, blocking the elevators at the Federal building in New Orleans. Face flushed and arms waving, he bellowed, "I wish I could talk to your provincial," pointing his finger at Daniel Berrigan.

"He's right behind you," came the reply from a smiling and soft-spoken Berrigan.

Surprised and taken off-guard, Volz turned around to see Jesuit Provincial Father Gerald Fagin, dressed in black suit and collar. The cameras, still rolling, focused now on Fagin: "I'm sorry that's what you thought you learned from the Jesuits," he spoke directly into the living rooms of New Orleanians watching the evening news, "because we've always taught that you must follow your conscience even when it conflicts with civil law. That's exactly what Father Berrigan and these students are doing, and I'm here to support them."

The exasperated Volz threw up his arms and ordered the protesters' arrest, exercising his civil responsibility but no longer able to hide behind the respectability of religious authority. As Berrigan the teacher was pulled away, he waved to the students and said, "You all get A's!"

The occasion for the protest was the murder of six Jesuits and their housekeeping staff by Salvadoran military personnel at the University of Central America. Berrigan was at Loyola in the fall semester of 1989, teaching a course entitled "The Acts of the Apostles," and he and many of his students decided to protest American military aid to El Salvador in the wake of the Jesuit massacre. Even the students who chose not to engage in civil disobedience gained profound insight into the dissonance between Christian faith and cultural conventions. The New Testament suddenly became contemporary, its witnesses confronting them with choices—about life and death, about the implications of faith in Christ's resurrection.

Several years earlier, Dan had come to Loyola for a similar semester-in-residence stint. His engaging personality, affable style, and unwavering commitment to social justice made him a welcome guest at the Jesuit residence, where he was enthusiastically received. The New Orleans Province (and particularly the community at Loyola) had been tempered during the civil rights era, when men like Louis Twomey, David Boileau, and Joseph Fichter had taken great risks in their work for integration and labor justice. Their legacy was Jesuit solidarity with the New Orleans underclass in their struggle for equality.

After returning to New York at the end of this first semester-in-residence at Loyola-New Orleans, Dan wrote to the university's president, Father James Carter, saying that, despite a wonderful and enriching experience with "some of the most courageous and committed students" he'd ever known, it would be his last such stint at Loyola. He felt that, in conscience, he could not return because of the university's sponsorship of ROTC. Father Carter responded in a letter in which he stated that criticizing from the sidelines was always easier than being in the hot seat where decisions had to be made. All things considered, Father Carter thought that "given the reality of the military, it is better to have officers who have the benefit of a Jesuit education."

Dan's response in a second letter to Father Carter is classic Berrigan: "I love your logic. It seems to me that, given the reality of abortion, Loyola should sponsor an institute for abortionists, and given the reality of capital punishment, you should sponsor an institute for executioners!" Chagrinned but still in charge, Father Carter did nothing to challenge the existence of ROTC at Loyola. Within a year's time, however, dropping student enrollments in ROTC allowed Loyola to phase it out, arranging for interested Loyola students to participate in Tulane's program. So informed, Dan returned again, this time to lead the student protest against military aid to El Salvador. This time, however, at the end of the semester Father Carter informed Dan that the Loyola Board had voted unanimously to confer an honorary doctorate on him at the May commencement. Months later, Dan returned for that ceremonious event, quipping that he had apparently been "fully rehabilitated," but then in seriousness said this: "Today is the second most satisfying day I've spent in New Orleans. The most satisfying was last December when I was arrested with my students."

In 1992 and again in 1994, Dan spent semesters-in-residence at DePaul University in Chicago, where he taught "The Prose and Poetry of Resistance" to a class made up of both graduate and undergraduate students. His DePaul students speak of Dan as both a challenging teacher and an encouraging mentor. They felt his strong and inspiring presence in the classroom and "hanging out" over coffee. He seemed equally comfortable discussing technical aspects of writing and the authors' human struggles within their life-contexts and listening to students' own personal stories of family difficulties, getting serious about life, and figuring out what to do with their postgraduate futures.

"Dan is always a teacher, whether in the classroom or out," says Lyman Millard, who had been encouraged to sign up for the Berrigan course by his mother, who had herself been influenced by Dan when she was a student protesting the Vietnam war while studying at the University of Connecticut. Lyman found Dan to be personally challenging, urging him to rethink his stance toward Catholicism: "One of the reasons I'm a Catholic again is because of Dan. He wasn't a hypocrite. His life was consistent with the gospels." Dan had responded to his self-described atheism by telling him that he was "the most Christian person I know."

"Phenomenal" is music major Anthony Burton's description of Dan the teacher. He had heard of Dan's history of protest and resistance from his father, a Methodist minister who had used his chapel to harbor AWOL soldiers during Vietnam. "He was so astute at picking up where each individual person was coming from. He knew that my life was music, and he talked about how I could use music to make the world a better place. He gave me a copy of Pete Seeger's musical autobiography—autographed by Seeger!"

Courtney Peterson had never heard of Dan before she took his course but was intrigued that here was a radical priest. "I had never seen a priest do anything except say the Mass. He was able to help us evaluate poetry in light of experience—the authors' experience and our own. To take it in and *feel* it." She was particularly impressed by the way he led the student Mass: "Everyone was there to pray, and he was there *with us*. Stories are handed down, not read. That's how it was with Dan. It was so real, not reading prayers."

Dan's peaceful, mellow air led some DePaul students to speculate about whether "he was high all the time." "People who didn't know him were sort of distrustful of his peacefulness. They thought he was aloof. But really he was salt of the earth. All his teachings are rooted in experience, telling about his own and asking you about yours."

My own experience of Dan as a teacher, observed both in New Orleans and at DePaul, is dominated by one word, *awareness*. Dan notices. He listens. He doesn't *try* to be attentive; he just is. Attentive to the readings, to his own experience and thoughts, and most of all attentive to the students. He takes teaching very seriously, spending lavish amounts of time preparing for class by going over the readings. He takes at least as much time reading students' papers and making comments on them. He's demanding, asking a lot of students, challenging them, chiding them, inspiring them to think and to express their depth, to be honest, to put something of themselves into their writing and into the class discussions.

Most academics are intimidated by him—not by anything he does, but by his honesty and his perspective. He cuts through the sanctimonious rhetoric of abstractions to the human, to experience, to life. No tweed jacket, no tie. Usually blue jeans and collarless shirts picked up at second-hand shops. No briefcase brimming with bibliography, no ponderous lecture, no sharp-edged questions, no ready critique snapping from his academic ego. No willingness to pay homage to academic convention. Just a profound respect for truth—and a passion to live it. With courage and humor, with humility and presence, with respect and love. This can be unsettling in the academic milieu, where ideas are often subtle weapons and copious words used as shields to hide behind.

Over the years—I have known Dan since 1972—my respect for him as a teacher has deepened. I wish the universities were filled with Dan Berrigans. Not clones. Not political dissenters. Not people who have been jailed for conscience. But people who combine intelligence and knowledge with humility and love—people who seek after wisdom by trying to live the truth and who reach out to the young with lived truth. I wish the universities were filled with men and women of courage and—here comes that word again—awareness.

THE RETREAT MASTER

Sowing Seeds of Peace
for Future Generations

ROBERT RAINES

Daniel Berrigan led his first retreat at the Kirkridge Retreat Center in Pennsylvania in 1978, and he is still leading two retreats a year. I have participated in most of them over those years, and thus have had the opportunity to observe him "close up" as a retreat master. Whatever the title of a given retreat, Dan always does Bible study. And what Bible study! He prepares carefully, often in typed manuscript, referring occasionally to it, while opening up the biblical text under review. His language is rich with metaphors and images from the text, provocatively, poetically connected with our own lives and the public scene.

Dan practices what Barth preached: live life with the Bible in one hand and the daily newspaper in the other, engaging word and world. One of my last retreats with him was on Ezekiel. When Ezekiel's wife died, God commanded him *not* to mourn, as a public sign of what was to come to all: a time of inability to mourn over the death even of children. Berrigan's images—death of the heart, dead hearts, tearless eyes, numbing of hearts over the loss of humanity on a huge social scale—wakened us to our own numbed hearts. God commanded Ezekiel (and always, Berrigan suggested, us too), to shock people into resurrection of heart. Talk these days of orphanages, cutting school lunches, reservations of the poor, and harsh blaming of the most vulnerable, bespeaks such inability to mourn the loss of an entire generation. So, Berrigan asked, pointedly but gently, what would God have you do to shock people into resurrection of heart?

For Berrigan, partisan politics has been of less interest than the ongoing, inevitable confrontation of the biblical God with the powers that be. For him, biblical people are always being called to struggle for peace and justice in the midst of oppression and injustice. Hebrew prophets and the apostles were often in trouble with the authorities, religious and political, and often in jail. So it is not surprising that those who take such a God and such texts seriously in our time are likewise embroiled in costly witness.

In the early 1980s, following the Plowshares witness of the Berrigan brothers and others at the General Electric weapons plant near Philadelphia, many friends were being arrested in similar nonviolent civil disobedience actions around the country. In one of Dan's retreats in that period, we were considering Acts (a biblical book to which he returns frequently). He pointed out that when Peter was arrested and put in jail for preaching the resurrection in the name of Jesus (Acts 5), an angel came that night, opened the prison door, and told him to go back to the temple and keep right on preaching in the name of Jesus. Berrigan named that night visitor the "angel of recidivism," the "unrehabilitated angel." It is clear to me that the unrehabilitated angel has been working overtime in the decades of Berrigan's words and deeds; that there is an elfin, obdurate resistance to unjust authority in Dan that abides to this day. Some of us learned in these retreats that that spirit of resistance is contagious and can get you in trouble. Berrigan's words about Isaiah might well apply to him as well: "He refuses to let us rest easy in the world—any more than he himself came to a banal adjustment to wicked times. No, he stirs the blood, he urges us on, he places the burden of peace and justice where it rightly belongs: on the conscience of the believing community."

Berrigan draws believers and those who want to believe to be with him on retreat—people who admire the integrity of his word and deed, the long-haul commitment of his peacemaking witness. Most of the beginning session of a retreat is given to hearing from participants how it is going with them in their lives and ministries. Amazing people—teachers, parents, Catholic Worker folk, people living in resistance communities, others working with prisoners or the poor, ministers, lawyers, business people—all seeking God's will for their lives. Dan often invites along some young person just getting involved in peacemaking, some worker with the poor who needs rest and renewal.

At a retreat in the spring of 1991, during the Gulf War slaughter, the room was filled with the anguish of many who had been unable to prevent that war and that killing field. There was comfort in acknowledging our sorrow, and mutual encouragement to keep on keeping on. Berrigan was nourished by the stories of these people of faith, struggling in their lives to be faithful to the gospel. A Jewish lawyer who never missed a Berrigan retreat said to me, "He's my Bible teacher." Berrigan encouraged people not to be tied to outcomes, but to do the work of peacemaking with non-attachment, planting the seeds, making the witness, leaving the results to God. Over the weekend, with sessions, meals, and late night singing and storytelling, the community deepened. On Sunday morning, participants designed and led the liturgy, concluding with eucharist concelebrated by Berrigan and others, women and men. You felt you had spent a few days at an oasis of the commonwealth of God.

I think Dan Berrigan is at his best in the small, intimate community of the faithful gathered on a residential retreat. In such a context, his own ease is reflected in marvelous wit and wisdom pressed out of decades of consistent witness, his fierce passion deepened into magnanimity, and even humility! He loves the large, high-ceiling living room space in our Kirkridge home, where he and close friends and family would gather after hours on Friday night. One such night he breathed a sigh of relief and delight, saying, "If I die, I will return to this room." A long-time colleague in peacemaking replied to him, "*If* you die?"

Dan speaks of "the fear of human variety" that causes governments, churches, institutions to exclude or condemn one group or another. He stretches our hospitality to include any and all people, especially outsiders. Jews, Buddhists, gay and lesbian folk, all know they are welcome. He is respectful of opinions different from his own— gentle, ironic, funny, self-deprecatory—while enjoying the reality of his own celebrity, whether a cameo appearance in the film "The Mission" or eating ice cream on a Ben and Jerry's poster. Laughter erupts often, and sometimes tears. Always the community of faith has been reconstituted, and for many, the eyes of our hearts have been enlightened that we might know afresh the hope of our calling.

His authority comes not only from his scholarship, wit, and poetic gifts, but most deeply from the integrity of word and deed in his life. He has been "walking the walk" of peacemaking witness for decades, and so the talk comes through clear and true. If, as William Stringfellow put it, vocation is the name for the discernment of the coincidence of the word of God in history with one's own selfhood, Berrigan is one who has found and is living his vocation. His encouragement to retreatants is not to espouse *his* vocation, but to discover and live one's own. His teaching and presence are not combative or preachy, but suggestive, invitational, evocative. He is a hearer and a doer of the word in our midst, a powerful impetus to go and do likewise.

Berrigan has led hundreds of retreats in dozens of places over the fifty or so years of his ministry. I am one of those who has been nourished again and again, my own flagging faith and witness revitalized. Who knows how many have been nudged to the edge of their estate in concern for the poor and involvement in peacemaking: some who had been silent speaking out; others who had spoken or written now engaging in nonviolent civil disobedient protest at the Pentagon, weapons-centers, submarine or air bases. Not only individuals have been nourished, but some institutions have been profoundly leavened by his retreat ministry. Over the years at Kirkridge, many staff and board members participated in his retreats, so that serious peacemaking has become an abiding commitment of the leadership of the place. Art on the walls reflects this priority to all retreatants who come to Kirkridge. Our communications have been salted and peppered with stories of peacemaking. Along with a few others, he has seeded two generations of peacemakers in this country. A lot of the seeds of this "Danny Appleseed" have been planted in the hearts and lives of people on retreat with him.

Blessed and blessing is Daniel Berrigan, who may rightly be called one of the children of God.

THE MENTOR

A Life Both Comforting and Challenging

SHELLEY DOUGLASS

Jim's mother sent a clipping from Seattle this week—Dan Berrigan had been speaking there. The reporter was happy: Dan had avoided arrest in New York on this Ash Wednesday 1995 so that he could make the trip to Seattle University. He was postponing his next arrest to Good Friday. During this Lent, it was noted, Dan continued his concern for the poor and the outcast, continued to call government to accountability, and was particularly concerned with the people who called themselves Christians but showed no compassion for the poor. I could almost hear the reporter thinking, "Same old Berrigan!" as she filed her story and went on to the next one.

Same old Berrigan. Somewhere between 1965 and 1968, I went with a group of students from Wisconsin to a peace march in New York, one of those marathon twenty-four-hour drives with several hours for demonstration sandwiched in between two halves. I remember standing in a cavernous empty street with a crowd of other people, waiting for the march to start. Someone said, "There's Dan Berrigan!," and we all turned to look.

I saw a middle-aged man with a mop of dark hair, a mobile, expressive face, eyes that sparkled with life. He was surrounded by young men, all intent on some discussion. Our group wandered on; none of us knew what to say to a famous stranger.

I was a new Catholic, unfamiliar with the ways and scandals of the 1960's church. I knew the Berrigan name was controversial, and I had the sense that truth-telling lay behind the controversy. I had really not paid much attention. This gathering in the streets of New York left me with a vivid impression: You could tell the truth and have a sense of joy and vibrancy; you could suffer and yet be free. You could focus community through risk. Good lessons, learned from a distance.

Later I was to learn more about Dan's sense of community, his suffering and his joy. In 1972, Dan came to Hawaii to speak at a series of evening gatherings in support of the Hickam Three, men who had entered Strategic Weapons Facility Pacific and poured blood on top-secret air-war files. My husband, Jim, was one of them. They were originally charged with felony crimes that made them liable for ten years or more in prison. Dan's presence in Honolulu in support of the Three helped to galvanize broad concern, even from outside the state.

I remember the night before the trial began. With a full and ex-hausting day of meeting and strategizing behind us, Jim wanted to go home and work on his opening statement, to get it word-perfect so that he could read it in court the next morning. Dan wanted to cook dinner for us. Dan won. We went to his cramped hotel room, and he served us, surrounding us with warmth and care, giving comfort in many senses of the word. He offered us wine, and Jim refused. Wine puts him to sleep, and he wanted a clear head to write his statement when we finally got home.

Dan pressed. Jim declined. Dan said finally, "Come on, Jim. Have some wine. Scripture says, Don't worry about what to say before the authorities, because the Spirit will give you the words." Jim had some wine, went to sleep, and made a fine extemporaneous opening state-ment the next day.

I remember too that one of our volunteer lawyers wanted to give us a marvelous gift, so he took two of us—Dan and me—flying high over the island of Oahu in a tiny prop plane. I sat in a tiny bucket seat in the back, Dan up front with the pilot, both of us white-knuckled as our pilot/lawyer rolled us over the right and then the left, showing us military bases and scenic wonders. When we landed both passengers were green and a bit shaky, but Dan was still able to say a graceful thanks.

Dan Berrigan, the mentor. Dan's poetry has been a most important source of courage for me. Poetry can be written down in words, typed or printed. Poetry can also be acted out in napalm on files, sojourns underground, hammers on missile parts, lonely climbs over fences at abortion clinics and weapons factories. Each kind of poetry illumi-nates, elucidates, the other.

Dan the poet was part of actions known in movement circles for their "macho" flavor, going up against the powers to the limit of one's ability. Unlike others in those circles, Dan always admitted the tre-mendous price of those actions. Admitted, putting into hard words, accounting for each tear or drop of blood. Dan's heroic actions gave hope just because he was not heroic. He suffered, despaired, cried aloud in anguish. Like the rest of us, he was hanging on by his finger-nails, hanging on to hope and sanity. His shared anguish made my anguish easier to bear.

There is a plaque hanging on our wall here in Birmingham, a carved wooden head of Christ crucified that Dan found in the trash one day outside a church that was being renovated. He picked it up, took it home, and wrote on it everywhere: verses from the psalms, names of suffering friends, events of horrific magnitude. "My God, my God, why hast thou forsaken me? Philip . . . My Lai . . . " Words all over this station making visible, concrete, the modern way of the cross, situating it in salvation history, claiming its meaning. Claiming thereby the terrible cost of speaking truth in tangible fashion, deadly serious, a matter of life and death.

If I respect Dan for his honesty about the cost of living out gospel values, I love him for his sense of fun and for the deep joy he radiates. Dan telling stories of past actions; Dan enjoying food and wine; Dan cooking for us, getting everything just right; Dan watching the children and lighting up at their antics. It's all a matter of life and death, and Dan's example is one of choosing the life offered, experiencing the suffering and embracing the joy. It is a kind of living as if each moment were the last amid health problems, systemic injustice, community problems, world in crisis: still rejoicing in the solitary blooming flower, seeing the hope in a fragile community, the light of one ray breaking through the clouds.

Dan's is an enigmatic kind of leadership, humorous, sometimes impatient and critical, parabolic in the sense that he raises questions by his life instead of giving answers by his words. The wild flash of public, symbolic action simply intensifies the glowing flame of his everyday life. Community, simplicity, love for the poor, service to the dying, fidelity to the gospel: these create a life both comforting and challenging, a light to see by in very dark days. Same old Berrigan. *Deo gratias.*

Inspiration and Invitation

JOYCE HOLLYDAY

I was a young associate editor at *Sojourners* magazine when Dan Berrigan sent us a poem for a special issue. It was accompanied with a note that went something like this: "Here's the poem—my first effort on my word processor. Seems a bit jumbled. Maybe I got a food processor by mistake."

I will always remember that message. It was classic Berrigan, reflecting several of the qualities of Dan that over the years I have come to so appreciate.

First of all, there's that droll sense of humor. I save my greatest admiration for folks who look the reality of the world in the face—those who see its worst inhumanities, who understand its unlimited capacities for destruction—and can still laugh. I picture a mischievous Berrigan grin behind the composing of the words.

Second, the note speaks of Dan's commitment to simplicity. He, like me, was among the last to take the leap from paper and pen to computer. Somewhere along the line, I said to myself, "If Dan Berrigan has a computer, I guess it's OK for me." A role model in more ways than he knows.

The note mentions food. Ahhhh. I remember a delectable pasta dish that Dan whipped up in his apartment in New York—just one course in a meal that seemed never to end. Then there were the seafood specialties he lavished upon guests to his cottage on Block Island. Long evenings, good food, good company—Dan is someone who has mastered the art of hospitality and fine entertaining; one who believes that simplicity and justice don't demand austerity and stinginess. His is a "welcome table"— there's always room for one more to share the soup and the soul.

I have returned again and again to Block Island and the cottage that stands on a bluff overlooking the surf. I've written a book there, watched a red moon rise from the porch, fallen asleep to the sound of the lighthouse's horn in fog. Once two friends and I were invited by an islander to go out in his boat and help pull lobster traps, a feat that was followed by the consumption of twelve lobsters among the three of us—a feast never to be forgotten.

One visit to the island was delayed by Hurricane Gloria, another interrupted by Hurricane Bob. Salt spray lashed the vegetation, and heavy rains washed away a piece of the bluff. Gale winds set into frantic motion the colorful lobster buoys that hang along the porch railing, collected here and there like the memories of a lifetime.

It is fitting that this cottage is Dan's. It is a place of rest and prayer and inspiration, sitting on the edge of the world, taking whatever blasts come its way. It is a survivor.

The cottage, like Dan, is humble. And it is this about him that touches me perhaps most of all. The numbers of lives he has changed by his writing and speaking, by his courageous and compassionate presence, are beyond measure. I consider myself blessed to be among that fortunate throng.

My faith formation began in the First United Methodist Church on Chocolate Avenue in Hershey, Pennsylvania. I was a high school student—writing papers with titles such as "Stopping Communist Aggression in Vietnam" (well researched from a wide variety of issues of the *Reader's Digest*)—when Dan and several others went on trial in Harrisburg, just thirteen miles away. I've come a long way, thanks in part to Dan's witness over the years.

I was a searching seminary student when I first heard Dan speak. It was in Connecticut the day before the launching of a Trident submarine. The next day, he joined others in a resistance action and was carted off to jail.

This has been going on for decades, always with peaceful persistence. I recall years later, after the first Plowshares action, watching a "Sixty Minutes" segment in which Mike Wallace was commenting on how desperately Dan must want peace. With characteristic aplomb, Dan said quietly, "I'm not desperate about anything."

Total commitment, yes. Desperation, no. A life lived as if anything is possible. That is the gift.

One of the most enjoyable of my assignments at *Sojourners* was editing Dan's journal from his brief acting career on the set of "The Mission." When the movie was screened in Washington, I went with others from Sojourners Community to see it. Dan spoke one word in the film. That word was "No."

The "No," according to Dan's autobiography, began almost thirty years ago with saying no to the Vietnam war by burning draft files in Catonsville. He confesses that he wasn't sure at first, that he was following the lead of his brother Philip.

"In place of eyes, or sight," he writes, "I had only faith to go on, or trust, which perhaps comes to the same thing. . . . Instead of evidence or logic, there was something better to go by—a hand in mine, someone to walk with. Enough, and more."

Dan Berrigan has spent a lifetime saying no—no to injustice, to despair, to war, to death. But I am even more moved by what he says yes to. With all the odds stacked against him, he still says yes to community and compassion, to peace and possibility.

And so he helps us to say yes as well. I remember sitting in a room in Philadelphia with twenty-four friends and soon-to-be friends in October of 1983. President Reagan was rattling sabers toward Nicaragua, the contras were being secretly trained and outfitted by the CIA, and we were trying to figure out what to do about it.

A delegation from North Carolina had been to visit the tiny Nicaraguan town of Jalapa, near the Honduran border, which was suffering under contra raids. The members observed that while they were present, the raids stopped. What if we maintained a permanent presence of North Americans in Nicaragua—to pray, to document contra activities, to stand beside our sisters and brothers there in nonviolent witness?

It seemed foolish, crazy. As one person in the room put it, "Sure—people are going to beat down the doors to put out their own money to go stand in a Nicaraguan war zone next to strangers and risk their lives."

People did beat down the doors. Thousands went—and were transformed. And the propaganda makers in this country had to contend with a constant flow of U.S. citizens telling the truth.

One group was kidnapped on a river by contras, another boldly floated into Corinto harbor to confront ships laying mines. Witness for Peace went on for years, beyond our wildest hopes and dreams. More than one policy analyst has said that plans for a U.S. invasion of Nicaragua were thwarted by this faithful host of witnesses.

A few weeks after I returned from Nicaragua with the first Witness for Peace team, I was leading a retreat at Kirkridge. Dan Berrigan was the other speaker that weekend. He listened intently as I spoke about the sorrows and hopes that I had found in that brave country.

When I was done, he walked toward me with a beaming smile and gave me a warm hug. He didn't have to say a word. There it was—that "hand in mine, someone to walk with." Enough, and more.

Dan has always walked ahead, shining a light on the path, reaching back to help us weaker, or slower, or younger ones along. He helps us to be braver than we are. The kids are turning out all right, Dan.

We at Sojourners were honored to have Dan do a poetry reading for us several years ago. Afterward, I wrote in my journal that I hoped some day to combine writing and resistance so creatively and coura-geously. I fall short. It seems that we all do in the presence of this gifted and determined brother. But I will always remember that evening as inspiration and invitation.

Thank you, Dan—for all of it.

A Letter from Prison

FRANK CORDARO

Greetings from Club Fed Yankton. I'm writing from the federal prison camp in Yankton, South Dakota. I am completing a six-month prison term for "crossing the line" at the Strategic Nuclear Command (StratCom) Headquarters at Offutt Air Force Base, just south of Omaha, Nebraska. This is the fourth six-month prison term I've done for trespassing at Offutt since becoming a Catholic priest in 1985. It would not be too far afield to say I have Father Dan Berrigan to thank for these opportunities to be imprisoned for my faith.

From very early in my faith-based peace-and-justice formation, I have looked upon Dan and Phil Berrigan as icons and heroes. They are two men whose vision and leadership in the ways of Christian peacemaking in the U.S. Catholic community have helped set the mark for what goes for being faithful to the nonviolent spirit of Jesus in the last years of the twentieth century. As the years have passed, Dan and Phil Berrigan have also become good friends and mentors for me in my journey.

I got to know Dan and Phil in the early 1970s, when I was close to dropping out of the seminary after becoming active in the Catholic Worker movement. While still in the seminary, I spent the summer of 1975 at the Davenport Catholic Worker. I fell in love with the Catholic Worker movement. The following fall, I fell in love with a wonderful woman. That next summer I dropped out of the seminary and helped start the Des Moines Catholic Worker. It was early in this process that I first became a student of the Berrigan brothers, learning of their story and their witness, first through their writings and then by attending their talks.

In those early years, I made every possible effort to attend Dan Berrigan's presentations in the region, no matter what the sacrifice. I'd drop whatever I was doing, clear my calendar. I sometimes drove all night in order to be in that audience to hear Dan Berrigan. In Iowa alone, I heard Dan in Cedar Rapids, Dubuque, Ames, and Davenport. I also traveled to Minneapolis, Chicago, Kansas City, Omaha, and South Bend to hear Dan speak.

It did not matter what the subject of Dan's talk was or whether he was the featured speaker or on a panel, whether it was a reading of his poetry or his giving a lecture. I just wanted to be there, in his presence, to absorb what I could. For years I did not understand much of his poetry. Half the time I missed the meaning of his prose. Yet I knew down deep in my "unsophisticated ways" that this high-sounding, well-educated Jesuit poet was to have a profound and lasting effect on my life. After each presentation I would patiently wait my turn in line with other admirers just to shake his hand and thank him for his good words and for being a faithful witness.

My first real personal encounter with Dan happened when I was visiting the New York Catholic Worker. Dan came to St. Joseph House to celebrate the Friday night Mass. It was right after the evening meal. Dan appeared very informal, with workman's trousers, black turtle-neck shirt, and a medallion around his neck. A simple soup-kitchen cup and bowl on a dining table served as chalice and paten on the altar. A small candle and crucifix completed the liturgical setting. A Bible was used for the readings. There was nothing else: no sacramentary, no vestments. Just twelve people around a soup-kitchen table. The gospel told about the feeding of the multitudes. There was a dialogue homily. Dan talked first; others shared. I remember talking longer than Dan, but saying much less. I was embarrassed afterward.

It was one of the highlights at the Des Moines Catholic Worker when I helped bring Dan to town in 1979 for a dramatic reading of his play, *The Trial of the Catonsville Nine*. It was a fundraiser for the Catholic Worker. Dan, of course, played himself during the reading of the play. It was a great success. (We repeated the performance with Dan in 1994 at Dowling High School in Des Moines, the same Catholic high school that hosted the 1979 performance.) Dan charged us nothing for his time and effort, and asked only if we could cover his expenses.

The best gig involving Dan was having him give one of the keynote addresses at the first Faith and Resistance Retreat held in Glenwood, Iowa, in February 1985. This retreat was hosted by the late Bishop Maurice Dingman. More than 600 people attended. The three-day effort ended with 240 of those at the retreat "crossing the line" at Strategic Air Command at nearby Offutt. I shall never forget the touching introduction Bishop Dingman gave Dan, and how Bishop Dingman embraced him as Dan approached the speaker's podium. (An enlarged framed photo of that embrace now hangs on my office wall.)

One of the things that attracted me to Dan and Phil Berrigan was their uncompromising reading of the scriptures. The New Testament serves as their primary source for interpreting reality. Everything from their personal understanding of themselves to the larger world in which they live is seen through the lens of the New Testament. Their sense of church—its traditions, dogmas, and structures—is measured by these scriptures as well as the larger social, economic, and political structures and institutions that rule the world.

From this uncompromising reading of the New Testament came a clarion call to follow the ways of the nonviolent Jesus. Dan and Phil took on the no-killing, love-your-enemies directive explicit in the New Testament, which was already made known and claimed in U.S. Catholic circles by Dorothy Day and the Catholic Worker movement. They gave it new form and focus during the Vietnam war years. It was during this time that Dan and Phil taught us an important lesson on how to get the church to face up to the nonviolent spirit of Jesus. They helped clarify for U.S. Catholic peacemakers the focus and direction our efforts should take in confronting U.S. militarism and warmaking.

In the beginning of their anti–Vietnam war efforts, the Berrigans directed much of their attention and energies toward the church—individual Catholics, parish congregations, religious communities, and bishops. Their reasoning: If the Catholic community knew the sobering facts about the Vietnam war, and our government's murderous and unjust participation in it, and applied a basic reading of the gospels, the U.S. Catholic community would rise up and condemn the war. The U.S. Catholic bishops would declare the war unjust and forbid any Catholics from participating in it, and that would put an end to it.

They soon found out that the roots of imperial militarism and violence run very deep in the U.S. Catholic faith community. The church as a whole was not ready to sever its ties with our nation's warmakers. (It still is not.) Dan and Phil figured the most direct and quickest way to get the church on the right side of the anti-war, anti-imperial struggle was to take responsibility upon themselves to act. They turned their attention and energies to confronting the nation's warmaking structures and institutions.

Their refocused direction took shape when they entered the Catonsville draft-board offices, walked out with bundles of draft-card files, and burned them. They did this bold act in broad daylight. They even stuck around to "'fess up" to the crime. They let the symbolism of their action and the testimony of their convicted persons explain the meaning.

With the burning of the draft-card files at Catonsville, the ways of the Catholic peacemaking in the United States were changed forever. A whole new form of faith-based nonviolent resistance was born. The same basic principles and faith reasoning lead Dan and Phil to participate in the first Plowshares action, which took place at the General

Electric Nuclear Weapons facility at King of Prussia, Pennsylvania. They made sound gospel sense at Catonsville in 1968, and the same sound gospel sense rang equally true at King of Prussia in 1980.

One of the moral pitfalls for us peace-and-justice folks who spend a great deal of time and energy condemning unjust social, economic, and political structures is that we tend to become self-righteous. We don't always distinguish the social sins and evils of the systems we are confronting from the people caught up in the fallen structures and institutions. I have always admired how Dan has avoided this short-coming. Through the years he has spoken the harsh truths to the "powers that be," namely the social evils of our day, yet managed never to condemn the people caught up in them. In making critical judgments of systems and structures, Dan never puts himself above anyone who takes part in these flawed systems and structures.

Given Dan's history and the struggles fought through the years, given the powerful people who find his message altogether too much to bear (both inside and outside the church), this is no small feat. This nonjudgmental discipline reflects the basic humble spirit that has helped mold Dan Berrigan.

It is the same humble spirit that has greeted many of us, through the years, who have come to Dan for counsel and advice. He would take each of us, compassionately listen to our concerns, and give far more encouragement than advice. I know this to be true because I have been the benefactor of his wise counsel on more than one occasion. For this I am personally grateful.

In 1983, after seven years at the Catholic Worker and after numerous protests, arrests, and jailings, I explored the possibility of re-entering the ordination process. I had fallen out of love—it happens. Responding to a long-standing, sincere, and deep call to serve the church as an ordained priest, I asked the diocese to take a second look. Good Bishop Dingman took me back and sent me to St. John's Seminary in Collegeville, Minnesota. I did two years' time at St. John's. I raised what holy heck I could, making clear I was not relinquishing my Catholic Worker–resistance ways. And to the surprise of many, myself included, Bishop Dingman ordained me a priest into the Des Moines diocese in June of 1985.

I now consider myself a second generation "Berrigan-type" priest. As a beneficiary of Dan's priestly journey, I was ordained with my eyes open to the nonviolent resistance spirit of Jesus found in the gospels and to the imperial setting that we find our U.S. church in today. I consider Dan a role model for my priestly life.

As I approach my tenth anniversary as an ordained Catholic priest, a priest in good standing with the "big C" Church, I am particularly grateful for Dan's stick-to-it-ness in staying both a Jesuit and a priest during these last fifty-five years, no small accomplishment. Dan's perseverance and grace to stay within these institutional confines give me hope and reason to believe I might do the same, at least good cause to make every effort to do so.

On August 6, 1993, I got to do something I have wanted to do ever since being ordained. I was able to concelebrate the Eucharist with Dan Berrigan. The liturgy took place on the anniversary of the U.S. atomic bombing of Hiroshima at the entrance of the Nevada Nuclear Test Site just before a trespassing as a civil disobedience witness. There was nothing dramatic about the liturgy. The symbols were simple: a rock mound, a piece of art, a wooden cross, a makeshift table for an altar, a Bible, some bread and wine. The Nevada desert on an already hot early August morning served as worship space. There were seventy-five nonviolent peace-and-justice–Catholic Worker types in a circle around the altar. As Dan led the opening prayer I thought to myself how blessed I've been to know this good and faithful man over the last twenty years. He has meant much to so many of my contemporaries in the U.S. resistance church. And I prayed that I make of my life in some measure the same faithful and generous witness Dan has with his.

Thank you, Dan Berrigan, for making a path! Happy seventy-fifth birthday!

THE FRIEND

Steadfast with a Smile

JIM WALLIS

"Christianity has nothing to do with racism or war." This I was told at the tender age of fourteen. Faith, the good church people said, had to do with the personal matters of salvation and living a life not conformed to the world around us. Of course, in the 1960s, white evangelical Christians in Detroit, Michigan, quietly supported both racism and the war in Vietnam but were able to keep such political matters separate from questions of Christian belief.

Nevertheless, my youthful heart was rising to the moral challenge of the civil rights movement and the emerging protest to the Vietnam war. It created a crisis of faith. When the questions I was asking couldn't or wouldn't be addressed in the comfortable world of my childhood and church, the hunger for answers took me into the inner-city and to the black churches. In the black community I began to find the honest answers I was looking for, and I also found a new community of friends that would last the rest of my life. But those new learnings and new friends were not welcome back in the little Bible church that had raised and nurtured me.

The clash was too great, and it led to painful separation. I left the church, lost my childhood faith, and found my home in the civil rights and anti-war movements. Years of activism and organizing followed during those turbulent years. I acted out of conscience, but not out of faith, and was unsuccessfully evangelized by every Christian group on the campus of Michigan State University—most of them also supported the war. The church and faith had once been my second home and family, the context of my whole life. But now I felt hurt and betrayed.

So I was angry at the church and at Christians in those days. But there were a few glimmers of hope that quietly kept me from giving up altogether on the possibility of faith. One was the persistence and perseverance of black Christians, whose faithful struggle was the moral foundation of the freedom movement. The other was a name I had only heard about—a name of two Christian brothers, two Catholic priests who opposed war in Vietnam . . . Berrigan. They had acted in resistance, had gone to prison, and there appeared to be others with them.

I was firmly entrenched in the secular student movement. We could put ten thousand people in the street in two hours time and were becoming more radical and alienated every day. Our experience of religion had turned us all away from it . . . but then there were those Berrigans. Looking back now, I really believe the prophetic witness of Dan, Phil, Liz and others literally kept hope alive for me.

After more demonstrations and tear-gassed confrontations with the police than I can begin to count, I slowly made my way back to faith by way of the New Testament. Our fledgling group of seminarians in Chicago began to put out a little tabloid we called *The Post American*, which later became *Sojourners*. I was reading *No Bars to Manhood* and other books by the Jesuit poet and activist who held out for me an alternative vision of Christian faithfulness. I can remember how eager I was to meet the one whose name had helped keep me from just giving up on Christian faith altogether and never coming back.

The opportunity came from another new friend, who was to become a spiritual mentor and father to me—William Stringfellow. It was at Bill's Block Island home where I first met Daniel Berrigan. The Island was, of course, the place where Dan had been arrested by the FBI. It had also become the place I went for retreat, renewal, and political discernment with the lawyer/theologian I considered the most incisive biblical critic of America. As others have also testified, the Stringfellow residence was a kind of monastic environment in the very best sense—deeply contemplative and integrally connected to the world. The radio was on, and the Bible was being read.

I met Daniel Berrigan around William Stringfellow's table. Never have I been around a table more nourishing than that one. The food, fellowship, prayer, and late-night conversation were to refresh my body, soul, mind, and spirit on many occasions. Without question, those of us who regularly gathered there found both the sustenance and discernment necessary for the biblical task of "discerning the times." There Bill and Dan helped nurture a new generation. Bill Kellermann and Scott Kennedy were also frequent visitors. Today, that table sits in my own dining room, and the tradition continues.

From our first meeting, it was unmistakably clear to me that Daniel Berrigan was, in the truest and most biblical sense of the word, a prophet. That word is so often misused and bandied about that one can easily lose its real meaning. The prophet is one who responds to a deep sense of call and, in the faithful fulfillment of his or her vocation, the word of God is announced. Daniel Berrigan would never confuse his every opinion with the word of God. It is indeed such authoritarianism that he has found so painful in his own church. Yet, when Daniel Berrigan prophesies, others hear the word.

Perhaps Dan spends so much time reflecting on the Hebrew prophets because he feels a kindred spirit with them. So many of us have been blessed to be led in retreat by Berrigan through Isaiah or some other prophetic sage. Sometimes it almost feels as though he and Isaiah are carrying on a conversation together, trying to discern what the word of God might mean in our contemporary circumstances. They seem to be quite at home in each other's company.

Even Dan's face and voice, now etched and tuned with time and struggle, portray a wisdom and clarity whose prophetic quality is evident to old and new listeners alike. A Sojourners' intern recently returned from her first retreat with Berrigan. Struck with the character and content of the prophet, she remarked, "But he also has such a wonderful sense of humor."

Indeed, the irony and satire of the poet have been a saving grace for the prophet. Daniel Berrigan has seen harshness in this world—from the bombed-out ruins in North Vietnam where he has walked, to the New York City streets of the broken and forsaken where he has lived, to the countless jail cells where he has been incarcerated, to the cancer wards and AIDS hospital rooms where he has ministered, to the ash heaps of the millions of nuclear victims that he has imagined. Yet, he has survived the pain without succumbing to the bitterness that sometimes overtakes those who allow themselves to take in the sufferings of the world. Berrigan's deep wells of passion are still capable of righteous anger, but also of much grace, mercy, and compassion.

Daniel Berrigan's mind and heart have always been more prophetic than ideological. That too has been a saving grace from pitfalls that others, so involved in life-and-death political struggles, have not been able to avoid. This prophet speaks in the language of a poet, which has always made it easier to listen to him.

But it is Dan's honest humanity that has always been so compelling to his friends. Being with him in places less public gives one a sense of how deeply Daniel Berrigan lives and celebrates life itself. There is a quality of delight and joyfulness about Berrigan that is often lost on those who see him only as prophetic critic. Berrigan, like Stringfellow, helped instill in me a love for wonderful cooking, bountiful feasts, and generous hospitality. Two of my favorite places in the world are Dan's apartment in New York City and the cliff-hanging cottage that Bill Stringfellow built for him on Block Island.

In the Jesuit community on West 98th Street, the walls in the two rooms of Dan's small apartment are literally filled with pictures and mementos of a life filled with commitment, meaning, and friendship. To study all the picture-framed treasures adequately takes several hours. Its history and warmth make Berrigan's apartment the most interest-

ing rooms in New York. Dan's place is also one of the city's best res-
taurants. When you are invited for dinner by Daniel Berrigan, you
know you are in for a meal as memorable as the evening.

It is on Block Island, however, that I will always picture Dan. The
simple cottage remains the last vestige of Stringfellow's property on
the Island, clinging precariously to the edge of Mohegan Bluffs and
overlooking the Atlantic Ocean. With its back to the Island and mainland beyond, there is the most spectacular view of the sea and, on a
clear night, a vantage point to see more stars than I ever imagined
existed.

Dan still goes there to rest and write, to walk windswept beaches
and quiet meadows, to pick wild blackberries and prepare evening
feasts for his friends. Some friends and family go there too and are
always greeted with shelves of wonderful books, more memories, and
pictures of Merton, Dorothy Day, Thich Nhat Hanh, Bill and Anthony, Phil and Liz.

Across the north wall of the cottage, Dan has written a poem in his
own hand. I don't think it has ever been published. A friend scripted a
beautiful copy for me, and it now hangs on my study wall:

> Where this House
> Dares
> Stand
> at Land's End
> and the Sea
> turns in Sleep
> Ponderous   Menacing
> and our spirit fails and runs
> —landward seaward askelter—
> we pray You
> Protect
> from the Law's
> Clawed
> Outreach
> From the Second Death
> From Envy's Tooth
> From Doom's Great Knell
> All
> Who Dwell Here

Under the poem are the names of spiritual pilgrims, Islanders, and
off-Islanders who have dwelt here. Add to them now many others—
Jesuits, those dying with AIDS, weary activists, honeymooning couples.
Both spirits are strong here—Berrigan's and Stringfellow's. Here and
in our hearts they will always be with us.

I've tried to tell Dan how much of a debt I owe to him. He will be cooking away in his New York kitchen while I rattle on about how just knowing he was there kept a spark alive in my young heart. He just smiles. Steadfast with a smile. "Can I fill your glass?"

Merton and Berrigan

An Extraordinary Friendship,
Two Extraordinary Spirits

MARY LUKE TOBIN, S.L.

I recall hearing that Dan Berrigan's response to the news of Thomas Merton's unexpected death on December 10, 1968, went something like this: "I feel as if I've lost my right arm." The two men—both poets, priests, peace-workers—shared a strong commitment to gospel values, lived out each in his own way, and a dedication to seeking justice and peace.

On several occasions in the early and middle 1960s, Berrigan visited Merton at the Abbey of Gethsemani in Kentucky. And from 1961 until the year of Merton's death, they carried on a very lively correspondence. The two developed a strong friendship, exchanging their thoughts about the church, religious life, the peace movement, the civil rights movement, poetry, the Vietnam war, and the predicament of being "silenced" (in Merton's case) or "exiled" (in Berrigan's case).

Merton clearly admired Berrigan. In a letter to W. H. ("Ping") Ferry about a Fellowship of Reconciliation group which was to gather at Gethsemani in November 1964, the monk wrote, "I do hope you will be able to make it. I especially want you to meet Fr. Dan Berrigan, a very live young Jesuit with great potentialities."

In confirming a future visit to the monastery by Rabbi Zalman Schachter, Merton wrote, "We will be looking for you August 8th. There may possibly be a Jesuit friend of mine, a poet, Dan Berrigan, here around then. If there is, you will like him."

It was not only to some of his regular correspondents that Merton indicated his high regard for Berrigan. Once, in a letter thanking Pope Paul VI for his encyclical on peace, *Mense Maio*, he took the occasion to write this paragraph of advocacy for Berrigan's peace efforts: "When

Your Holiness appeals for peace, it seems to me that priests and faithful everywhere ought to be able to support this appeal with words and
acts. Yet one of the priests [Daniel Berrigan] in this country who has
spoken out forcefully for a cessation of violence, torture and unjust
methods in Vietnam has been silenced by his religious superiors because of the opposition of certain newspapers and certain sectors of
public opinion."

To Dan himself, Merton wrote in the manner of one friend encouraging another, offering praise and support. "Your poems [*Encounters*] arrived. They are tremendous. You have great energy and discipline. I mean especially discipline of your poetic emotion and
experience." "I will write you up a litany of praises [for a Guggenheim
Foundation grant] that will knock them off their chairs. . . . Your last
book of poems deserves half a dozen Guggenheims. It is really splen-
did. . . . It is terse and even Zen-like, and it is the integrity of the
experience that above all comes through. Great, man, great." "Your
Polish tape arrived, was played, and passed on. Many thanks. It was
excellent." "Your statement on Vietnam was really fine! Very strong
and right on target."

Berrigan consulted Merton as his mentor. A reading of the latter's
letters to Berrigan suggests to me the wide range of topics about which
they were mutually concerned and on which Berrigan sought counsel
or information: What is Merton's opinion on civil disobedience? What
about church disobedience? What would Merton think about Berrigan's
plan to travel to Hanoi to deliver medical supplies? Would Merton
join in sending a cable to the pope asking the pontiff to condemn the
Vietnam war? Would Merton be one of an ecumenical clergy group
who would encourage young men to send them their draft cards? Could
Merton suggest materials for a course on nonviolence and religious
traditions that Berrigan would teach at Cornell University? What is
Merton's opinion about those who want to destroy "idolatrous
things"?

As friend to friend, Merton confided in Berrigan some of his doubts
about his own role in the peace movement, in which the Jesuit was so
highly active. In a letter to Berrigan explaining his concerns about the
self-immolation of Roger LaPorte (protesting the Vietnam war) and
his own initial negative reaction to this, Merton indicated that, having received a letter from Berrigan, he could better understand the
position of the Catholic Peace Fellowship. In November 1965, he wrote,
"My problem is different from any of yours by the simple fact that
you are, or have been up to now, there, fully informed, fully aware,
fully involved. I am at the other extreme and I felt that I was not
intelligently involved in something that was developing in a way I
knew nothing about and which I could not seriously participate in.
This still remains a problem. However, I do not want to do anything

abrupt about it, especially if it is going to be interpreted as a personal break [with the Catholic Peace Fellowship] which is the last thing I want. . . . And really I think you don't need me that much. I am pretty sure that I have outlived my active usefulness and that I can serve you much better by being a halfway decent hermit."

In another letter, Merton wrote, "I have come to the conclusion that the only thing for me is to speak out when I can, to sing on my own perch, and if they don't like the song, it will take them a little time at least to get all the way down to me to shut me up."

And again, "I think it is necessary for me to stay out of the lecture circuit and campus appearances, much more some of the other things . . . that would necessarily follow. I don't think I can do what God and the gospel demand of me personally unless I maintain the special kind of conditions I have been chosen for, that have been wished on me, and that I myself have chosen and prefer. . . . As regards peace movements, etc.: my job continues to be putting it on paper as best I can, I think, and, by letter or otherwise, helping individual C.O.'s with advice."

When answering requests for his counsel on next steps in Berrigan's work for justice and peace, Merton seemed always to urge clear thinking, analysis of motivation, a look at "the long haul," a setting of goals consistent with a gospel position. "In my opinion," he wrote, "the job of the Christian is to try to give an example of sanity, independence, human integrity, good sense, as well as Christian love and wisdom, against all establishments and all mass movements and all current fashions which are merely mindless and hysterical. But of course are they? And do we get hung up in merely futile moral posturing? Well, somewhere we have to choose. The most popular and exciting thing at the moment is not necessarily the best choice."

I recall two occasions when I witnessed firsthand the friendship between Dan Berrigan and Tom Merton. In the mid-1960s, Merton brought his friend over to the Loretto Motherhouse (about twelve miles from the Abbey of Gethsemani) to give a talk to our novices. I was delighted that these young women would hear a famous established poet, recognized by the literary world (Berrigan had recently received the Lamont Poetry Award). To my surprise, Berrigan spoke hardly at all of his poetry, but rather of his work with the students he was currently teaching at LeMoyne College. The Jesuit had helped motivate them to spend the previous summer engaged in a house-building project for needy black families in the South. This compassion for the poor surely resonated with Merton's own concern, expressed eloquently in his writings on racism.

The second occasion occurred in September 1979, eleven years after the death of Merton. For the formal opening of the Thomas Merton Center for Creative Exchange in Denver, I had invited Dan Berrigan to give an address. His talk, focusing on Merton's thoughts on nuclear weaponry and war, revealed splendidly both their friendship and their common dedication to peace.

Referring to his friend as "this extraordinary spirit, Thomas Merton," Berrigan used Merton's Cold War Letters to illustrate his urgently prophetic voice speaking against the buildup of nuclear weapons. Berrigan talked about Merton's contemplative work in the world, a work that impelled him to continue to criticize militarism and to criticize the church's silence on crucial issues. Insisting that the true contemplative must be aware of what is happening to people "in the world," Merton saw the monastery as a bridge to that world.

In his talk, Berrigan commented on Merton's reflections on sanity/insanity in his powerful essay, "A Devout Meditation in Memory of Adolf Eichmann." And, in his own poetic way, Berrigan himself described the balance required of a faithful person in the contemporary world:

> The life of the believing human being is a sort of high wire act in which one goes forward unsteadily, but goes forward, trying out a balance which can only be sustained if life is in movement; a balance between life within and life without; a balance between looking within and measuring the danger and the height from the ground; a balance between the distance to be covered and the distance covered, and going on. Somewhere on that high wire, Merton found his own sanity and recommended it to us.

Berrigan's address to those gathered to initiate the Thomas Merton Center spoke eloquently of his admiration for Merton, his embracing of Merton's thought, and his hope that we, like Merton and himself, would continue to resist the forces of death. I felt that his words testified to the gift of Merton as his mentor and friend as well as to the hope cherished, even in darkness, by both of them. In short, "this extraordinary spirit, Thomas Merton," was reintroduced to all of us that evening by another extraordinary spirit, Daniel Berrigan.

Keeping Me in the Church

MARTIN SHEEN

For years, I've been telling people, "Mother Teresa drove me back to Catholicism, but Daniel Berrigan keeps me there."

From the moment I met him in the summer of 1981, I have been challenged, nourished, and re-educated, with equal measure, in every aspect of my life: challenged to do those very often simple yet powerful nonviolent acts of witness that free our caged humanity and make us truly worthy of the long-promised blessing reserved for peacemakers; nourished by our own reclaimed spirit to whatever degree we might accept the challenge; and re-educated to the stark reality that in our bankrupt culture where greed, indifference, and fear foreclose any future and assure the ultimate triumph of death, a courageous and consistent nonviolent witness can redeem and reclaim with faith, hope, and love.

Following Dan's lead, I took my first public step toward that goal on a warm Friday morning in June 1986, at the Riverside Research Institute in mid-town Manhattan (where they are preparing laser-beam weapons for nuclear war).

It was my first act of civil disobedience, my first arrest, and it was the happiest day of my life. Without my being consciously aware of it at the time, Daniel Berrigan had taught me, just as he had taught so many others before, how to unite the will of the spirit with the work of the flesh.

Nothing will ever be the same again!

A Letter from Block Island

MARY DONNELLY

Dear Daniel,

Everyone knows I am no literary giant, but I want to be part of your seventy-fifth birthday book, so please know this is a labor of love.

I remember the night I first met you. I went to dinner at the Cottage with Frederick and Katherine Breydert. Bill Stringfellow and Anthony Towne were already there. Of course, you were there, too—you were the host! I have never forgotten that night. It was great fun listening to you, Frederick, Anthony, and Bill discuss religion and the politics of our country and the world, each a mental giant in his own right.

A lot has happened since that night in 1975. Katherine died. Frederick remarried and moved to Paris. He, too, has since died. Anthony, that giant of a man, died unexpectedly in 1980, leaving a void in all our lives. Bill had lost his best friend and had to set about making plans for his burial. You were in Berkeley teaching at the time. Since Anthony had been cremated, the ashes were put aside until you could get here to preside at the burial. That day will long be remembered as all of us gathered on the hill in front of Eschaton and weathered a raging Nor'easter while prayers were said and Anthony's ashes buried by the old anchor at the flagpole.

The next five years found Bill going between good and bad health. He lost his battle to survive in March of 1985. Again you were there to preside, this time at Bill's Requiem in St. Andrew's chapel. Do you remember the circus music playing as we left the chapel? You know Bill was smiling! Then the final burial. Two good friends, side by side. "Near this Cottage the remains of William Stringfellow and Anthony Towne await the Resurrection. Amen. Alleluia." So reads the plaque hanging in the Cottage, high above the sea.

I love to receive your latest literary works, always so specially inscribed. They are treasured gifts. I am forever grateful for your prayers and notes during my daughter Marguerite's illness. They truly helped to get her through that very difficult time. You probably don't remember the wonderful wooden apple you sent her from Appalachia, but we do—a constant reminder of your friendship.

We have had some great times. It seems to always be around the dinner table, but isn't it good to break bread and drink from the cup with good friends? Remember when we celebrated your fiftieth anniversary of entrance into the Jesuits? Some of us couldn't get off the Island for the celebration in New York, but the next time you were here, we gathered at my house and presented you with new pots and pans for the Cottage. Life can't get more exciting than that!

Your love for humanity is always apparent both in word and deed. I remember when you let a young couple stay at the Cottage for a few days so they could have a vacation, something they could never afford otherwise. Or the young fellow who had AIDS, who stayed at the Cottage with his mother, so they could celebrate his last earthly birthday together. You are a very special man, Daniel Berrigan!

Thank you, Dan, for the poetry reading you did in October 1993, for the Mary D. Fund. Money raised that night helped to keep our needy warm that winter. Thank you for tramping around Switzerland in those classy Block Island boots. Thank you for sharing in the Eucharist on Sundays at St. Andrew's. Thank you for phone calls and dinner shared and friends remembered and hope for things to come.

To me, you are the Beatitudes personified, and so I thank you for values shared and acted out. Most of all, I thank you for being my friend!

Happy birthday, Daniel!

Love and God bless,
Mary D.

Once and for All

JOSEPH ROCCASALVO

Among his systematic reflections on the church, Avery Dulles, S.J., suggests that development of doctrine is genuine only if it is true to its roots. All dogmatic formulation is nothing but the harvesting of what lay fallow in the beginning. "Origins are given once and for all," he writes with admirable quotability.

When I was asked to contribute to this volume in honor of Daniel Berrigan's seventy-fifth birthday, Father Dulles's aphorism came to mind. What better way to respond to a forty-year-old friendship, I thought, than to return to its origins, to a March day in 1955 when Dan and I first met. With the composition of place firmly fixed and my Ignatian energy mounting, I made an application of the senses. To my delight, I was able to summon the memory and enliven the tired cliché, "It seems like only yesterday."

As a member of Brooklyn Prep's Sophomore Sodality, I found myself in Father Berrigan's company taking a bus to the Gold Street Mission under the Brooklyn Bridge. Dan had been asked to substitute for the faculty moderator, who was confined to tutoring students in the lower mysteries of plane geometry. At the time of our meeting, I knew Dan by sight as the priest with the gracious manner and abstracted air, who did not so much traverse school corridors as waft through them. Though he had not yet won the Lamont poetry prize for *Time Without Number*, his repute as a consummate poet preceded him. His occasional preaching at the First Friday Mass was my sole exposure to his beguiling way with words.

Much of what he said was transparent, much obscure. Only later was I enlightened as a result of those bursts of insight his fresh metaphors had sparked. I still recall one sermon in which he warned the assembled students against "the illusion of the obvious." This phrase, opaque to me then, has since become perfectly clear. On that March day, as I sat on the bus beside him, in awe of the poet, I recall how deftly he put me at ease and how swiftly we seemed to arrive despite the tedious trip.

Dan and I walked a block to the mission and entered a ramshackle building. When I announced my purpose to the security guard, he directed us to the auditorium. Chairs in clusters encircled the room. A quorum of Catholic students were catechizing their captive charges. Dan left me to explore the building while I joined my Communion class to prepare them for the sacrament. The five students of the previous week were dutifully waiting. I noted a sixth had been added to the group—Winston. Five feet tall and wiry, he was dressed in over-sized clothes, hand-me-downs, I guessed, from an older brother or cousin. He was dark-complexioned with huge eyes and coal black irises. He did not so much sit in his chair as continually reposition himself. He muttered loudly as his eyes looked vacantly ahead. It took little to surmise that here was a needy child.

I began by reviewing the lesson: the reasons for bread and wine; the significance of eating together; the connection of food with life. I had hoped to explain how the Catholic Mass incorporates the Jewish Passover, but I never got that far. Throughout my efforts to teach, Winston squirmed or waved both hands or interrupted with irrelevant remarks. In short, he was being disruptive. My frustration was fast giving way to anger. When, to the cheers of the class, Winston landed on the floor with his collapsible chair alongside, I lost what patience I had. I did not notice Dan watching benevolently from a distance. He walked to where I stood and without explaining, asked Winston, "Would you like a soda?" He nodded yes, eager to exchange my irate presence for the friendly Coca Cola machine on the far side of the room.

With Winston gone, order returned and my class moved peaceably to its close. Occasionally, I glanced across the room to see him sipping his soda. Dan sat alongside with that Berrigan smile compounded of kindness and genial irony. As class ended, I gave my students their weekly assignment and dismissed them. I walked over to Winston, who was slurping the dregs from the bottle. Without soda to distract, I thought, would he again become unruly? Who would calm his antics? It was four-thirty, and the center remained open till five. Meanwhile, Winston had inserted a finger in the narrow neck of the Coke bottle and was banging it against his chair. Dan looked at me, still smiling, then turned to him.

"Winston, would you like to hear a story?"

"What story?" he asked, his curiosity aroused.

"About the genie in the Coca Cola bottle."

"What's a genie?"

I excused myself and walked away. I decided that Dan's improvisation was strictly between him and Winston. I regret now I did not stay within earshot of Dan's story, of a spirit locked in a Coke bottle eager for human form to benefit the one conjuring it up.

Promptly at five the security guard sounded the bell that signaled the close of the building. I saw Dan holding Winston's hand as they approached the boy's mother, who waited at the door.

"Were you good today, Winston?" she asked, expecting to hear the worst.

Winston nodded affirmatively, dilating his eyes, while Dan smiled in confirmation. We all left the building together. Winston waved good-bye, and Dan and I took the bus to Prep. I remember nothing of our conversation on the way back, nor do I recall being alone in his presence during the time I remained in high school. Not long after, he left Brooklyn Prep to teach theology at LeMoyne. In later years, we met on occasion in Jesuit Houses of Study: Bellarmine College, Loyola Seminary, Woodstock College; more frequently when I came down from Harvard; often when I resided in New York. Through all the years, the symbolic value of that first encounter has stayed with me as a distillation of Dan's manner of life as well as a blueprint of what was to come. I have been privy to his cumulative incarnations: priest, poet, theologian, peacemaker, playwright, consoler of the sick and dying—the names of the roster are legion. His genie—that Berrigan élan bottled up for years in Danbury prison and incarcerated in countless jails—has been summoned for the benefit of many, out of compassion for many.

In my own life, I have domiciled in palaces and hovels, have frequented the gold coast of Zurich and the slums of Bangkok. All of it is grist for the writer's imagination. But I can think of nothing more engaging than to sit with Dan in an outdoor cafe sipping cappuccino, a latter-day Winston, engrossed in a recent episode of that ongoing saga called his life. The New York tension mitigates as the lilt of his voice confirms all will be well. I leave his presence reinstated, reassured, revived. Origins are indeed given once and for all, but then all the best things are: poetry, music, friendship, holiness, Daniel.

Once and for all—how confident and solid a statement in this mutable world. No illusion this, and not for one moment obvious.

THE BROTHER

Dan My Brother

JERRY BERRIGAN

Dan Berrigan. Who is this post-modern man, this priest-poet? As our mother would put it, "Dan's not easy to describe, not easy to pin down!" It can be said though, that four decades or so ago, he glanced askance at the new superpower, the American empire. He was becoming skeptical of its official treatment of people elsewhere in the world. What he learned of the U.S. government and its policies led him to reject its PR, its blandishments. Eventually, he became and was to remain a resister of the White House, the Congress, and the Pentagon, places he considered world forces of lawlessness and disorder.

During these years Dan has, little by little, grown quietly subdued. In contrast to his earlier vocal and vociferous denouncings, he's become gradually aware of the deadly scope and tenacity of the forces he opposes. As one Catholic Worker put it, "Evil in the U.S. is riding high in the stirrups!" Dan's recognition of this has come to him through prayer, prison, and exile and has led him to develop a posture of firm but gentle wariness mixed with detachment. Teaching and lecturing, he's come by a style of understatement. He's learned, "I, we, concerned and caring though we are, can't do it overnight. Even together we'll not be able to reverse the duplicity and violence endemic to U.S. government and society today. If indeed the turnabout we work and pray for is ever to begin, it won't happen quickly; it won't happen even during our lifetime. All we can do is try to be faithful; all we can do is to keep on doing!"

I recall that Dan, even from boyhood, felt free enough to act on a sort of spiritualized instinct. To reach thoughtful conclusions, he'd broach this or that proposal and invite others to share their views. Dan was always one who valued dialogue.

Dan Berrigan, priest. Some years ago he, Carol, and I were in Ireland with our friend, Father Pat O'Brien. At a roadside, we drew up in

223

our car. "Here," pointed Patrick "is a priest hole, a place of life-or-death hiding for Irish priests hunted by Cromwell during Reformation times." I've seldom seen Dan more reverential than when he clambered down into the opening, remained quietly a minute or two, and emerged. Onlookers, we three gained a sense of his bonding, his mystical link-up with those Elizabethan martyrs. Later, returned to New York, Dan inserted into a frame with typically good taste, a fragment of porous rock he'd picked up in that Irish aperture. His gift to us, it hangs today on our study wall, a relic of the kinship Dan forms with any person, ancient or modern who lives "on the edge" for truth and justice.

Dan the priest has been there beside us family members. When Carol and I were married forty years ago, he, in company with Phil, helped celebrate our exchange of vows. Five years later, when our baby Marie was born, to live only two days, Dan baptized and afterward prayerfully buried her. When Tom's wife, Honor, died, Dan quickly ended his peace-speaking tour of England and returned to Rhode Island for her funeral. When word came of brother John's accident and hospitalization in Arizona, Dan flew to his bedside in tender support. For me, he's shown like concern in my several illnesses, as he has supported and suffered with stalwart Phil, locked away in many extended jailings.

For Dan, the word of God is essential, the final guide through the "human muddle." "By little and by little . . . serve self only to be able to serve others." Thus he takes that word to himself; thus he makes that word his own. In this I'd like to compare him briefly to fellow-poet and fellow-Jesuit Gerard Manley Hopkins, about whom Dan has written a book-length poem of tribute. Of Hopkins's life, that of the very Hopkins whose "sprung rhythm" energized like a new flame the sedate writings of his fellow Romantics, Robert Lowell has written "it was a continuous, substantial progress toward perfection." (I claim that the same can be claimed of Dan and his life.) Continues Lowell, "He [Hopkins] knew nature but he did not know too much about people." Ah, but whatever the accuracy of Lowell's discernment of Hopkins, a searching glance at Dan's life shows that he does indeed know "about people," a lot!

I'd not make that claim if Dan had not for so long studied and tested himself, and learned in the doing. As a result, he is a just and impartial man who's trained his ego into an instrument to create and to serve! He's taken seriously the classic, "First and foremost, know thyself." At "knowing," he's become adept. The result is that he's skilled at "knowing" people; this can be seen through the forge and flames of rebuff and forgiveness in his own life. For all the caprices of the power figures who've oppressed him through his years of being shunted and shifted and shunned, Dan holds no grudge. Take, for example, his boyhood rejection by his dad; with time that turned into a sort of gradual, maudlin acceptance by father of son, especially as Dan entered the Jesuits and "stuck it out." By 1969, our father, then in his ninety-first year, was dying. Meanwhile, Carol and I were engaged with four small children whom we'd adopted as infants. To us both he gave a gentle adjuration: "Stay with the kids; I'll sit with Pop." So it happened that during our father's last night Dan was present at his bedside—to soothe, to comfort, to sustain. At dawn he phoned us: "Dado died peacefully; are you both okay?" Typical: first, concern for others; first, concern for the living. Context: a large-minded, open-handed forgiveness.

The summer of 1982 I spent in federal prison at Allenwood, in Pennsylvania. During those weeks I composed some pieces of verse; in them I spoke in a serious, slightly portentous voice of concerns about the chaplain's conduct, the inmates' work details, the regimentation, the lack of privacy, and so on. Returned to teaching that fall, I was invited to read these compositions before various student audiences. As I recall, they listened in a sort of somber puzzlement but applauded dutifully.

In time, I shared these same writings with Dan. His response to them was a kind of ratifying silence. To my credit I picked up on and with time accepted his cue. "I affirm your 'muse,' Jerry, your attempt to create, your tone of indignation, your ideas; if I fail to compliment you it's in the name of artistic truth." Neither because of kinship nor fraternal affection could Dan water down his response. "I love you enough, Jerry, to lay on you what I honestly see in your writings; I've given them my best shot; you deserve no less." So much for my poetic artistry.

As a brother of Dan Berrigan, poet, however, I own a type of "disadvantage in my advantage." Let me explain. The former position comes as a part of my limitless respect for Dan's poetic talent, but that is at the same time mixed with my deep brotherly affection. Thus I'm likely to be influenced in any critical views I may offer of his writings. On the latter note, the "advantage," I can only consider that it emerges from the experience of forty years of "teaching" the works of many poets, from the study and interpretation of many more, and from the attempt/failure (and insight so gained) to write poetry myself.

Thus it is: I claim that Dan Berrigan is an unusually gifted poet. Indeed, because of a blend of his high talent, his versatility of words-as-truth, and his spiritual commitment, his writings are remarkably superior to the kind of self-conscious, ego-bristly, merely clever verses being produced today. Yet, apart from the Lamont Prize won for his first book of poems, *Time Without Number*, Dan has gone in the past and today goes unrecognized. Why? Mainly, I think, because of his "life as politics," superficially viewed as abrasive, as "radical." For their part the critics pen their evaluations of Dan's poetry (when at all) with sidelong squints at the major media and presses, most of which have become profitable adjuncts of multinational corporations. Dan's contempt, of course, for Exxon, Coca Cola, Ligget and Meyer, and such like, is well known. As a result, he had eschewed the major publishers and turned instead to the minor, home-industry presses. End result: no widespread sales of his work, a development he accepts as enhancing his simple life and tastes.

Dan Berrigan, brother. Peter and Andrew, James and John . . . biblical, of course. Such fraternal bondings help me clarify what I mean by Dan's and our kinship. It's mainly in scripture that I find his quality: loyalty, respect, affection, acceptance, and more, the stuff seen in our eyes and heard in our voices, the faces we turn to each other. Dan has himself been the cementer of our singleness of mind and heart; our unity is a rich product of his life; it's his aura, his radiance, what he exudes.

How can all this be, you ask? Dan believes in scripture as a model for living humanly. Believing, he lives that belief; in consequence, his relationships, loyalties, and personal and priestly choices are directed toward acquitting himself in biblical ways. Yet for all his accepting the portentous note of Bill Stringfellow's "Principalities and Powers," Dan moves with a light step, with good humor and grace. To the flatterings ("You're a world figure, Dan!") of the "demons," he gives a dismissive glance. You get a sense of his long-since-formed resolve: "There's really only one way to live, isn't there—simply and modestly." Then, with a puckish smile, "Here, let me help!" or "Call if you care to," or "Will you let me do some of that?" Actions speak louder than words—a truism Dan's made his own.

Reflecting on our early years together, I think that Dan, even as a teenager, fell in love with the will and word of God. Thenceforward his acting, speaking, thinking, praying, and writing all seemed done with distinctive grace. Today I can recall watching his growth, his emergence. Of course, for him there were pitfalls, setbacks. One was our father's early-formed aversion, evident in word and manner, toward Dan. That was for everyone a tough family reality, but the central easement was Dan's response. Even at so early an age—8, 10, 12, 15?—his sense of the fall as a prime ingredient of life was clear. "Here's some evidence of it in my family, in me personally," he seemed to say. Dan rode it out. On his knees beside Mama saying the rosary before the statue of the Virgin at "Jerry Knoll," our boyhood home, Dan was more than pious—he was explicit in prayer-intentions.

Devoutly he asked blessings for Pop, for the family, for the world, for himself. He grew in a sense of his own need. He, at the same time, sowed seeds of faith, germination not only of his priestly vocation and future membership in the Jesuits, but also of his loyalty to the church for the sixty years to follow.

Worth noting is a side of Dan's makeup that shows how he deals personally with the hard-core vanity of the American culture. Boyhood snapshots show Dan with neatly parted, slicked hair. Later and to the present, he appears with uncombed locks worn in bangs. Knowing him we can hear his unspoken, "Hey, my clothes are neat and simple, and so are my whiskers and hair. Take me as I am—with you I'll do the same."

Despite the really traitorous state of his back, Dan shows only casual concern for his physical well-being. On it he expends merely the energy to "keep going": no excesses, no fads or fetishes or gimmicks to enhance or extend life. Only a *sanus mens in sano corpore*; only the strength needed for generous service to others.

In people there are few quirks or fallacies that Dan finds intolerable. Only when he sees clear signs of ill-will, of hypocrisy, of power-brokering (e.g., Clinton's pre-election garnering of tainted votes; his return to Little Rock to witness the capital punishment of a retarded criminal) does Dan from his violated sense of justice cry "No! No!" Typically he is impartial, kind, indulgent of human foibles. "Most motives are obscure, are mixed. That being the case why should I or anyone use them as a basis for judgment?" Simply because of his firm grasp of his own dignity, Dan offers that same asset in tender and inviting ways to each person he meets.

Dan, the faithful one. Has Dan ever been tempted to "leap over the traces," forsake his vows, quit the priesthood and the church? Perhaps once. In the beginning of the American involvement in Vietnam, Dan was exiled by Cardinal Spellman of New York (Dan's Jesuit provincial acceded) to Latin and South America. Lasting three months, this period was for Dan one of cruel privation, of barren justice. The power-brokers' decision, "Kick him out! Get rid of him!," had been made simply because Dan had resisted the U.S. military, of whose chaplaincy Spellman was the head. During his banishment and after his return to the United States, Dan reflected, prayed with vision, with patience. For him, growing and maturing in the spirit, truth underlay his conscientious, reasoned actions. "Truth is durable because truth is the Supreme Good." He looked before and after; he mused, "This violence done me will inevitably be seen for what it is." He knew, and was assured by friends, that he had been victimized not so much for acts of resistance as by authority illegally and immorally exercised. So, submissive to long-range Good, he elected to remain a Jesuit, to stay in the church. Today, years afterward, Dan Berrigan, man of wisdom, knows as perhaps never before that to love and serve the truth is not only to pay love's price but inevitably to vindicate love.

Now, ending this chapter, I have a view of Dan's reading what I've penned, and of the half-amused, self-deprecatory play on his lips. His sense of the comic is deep and developed. Always, whether he is telling or listening to a pregnant joke, Dan's sense of paradox is at work. Ever the poet/visionary, he applies his sense of the incongruous to himself. "I think it's great that you think highly of me," he'll quip, "but try not to get carried away. Why all the fanfare?"

But finally, his sense of the other will show inevitable and pristine; he'll turn to me, the writer, and with a twinkle say, "Well, what you've written, Jerry, is very nice, and, thanks for the interest!"

With a Word to the Weary

ELIZABETH McALISTER

The Sovereign God has given me an instructed tongue, to know the word that sustains the weary. He wakens me morning by morning, wakens my ear to listen like one being taught.
— Isaiah 50:4

For thirty years, Dan has been, for me, the instructed tongue who knew the word that sustained my weariness, that disciplined my excitability, that shepherded it to human scale.

In 1973, Jonah House and the CCNV (the Community for Creative Nonviolence) had a campaign at the White House. Each day through that summer, people entered the White House, knelt in prayer for an end of the slaughter in Indochina, and were arrested and carted off to jail. In trying to fill the calendar, I met with Dan and friends in New York City to see if they would take a day. I shared what people had been doing and began to extrapolate on what people might do by way of upping the ante. Gently, but firmly, Dan asserted that it was the witness that was important, people putting themselves there, saying what needed to be said. Human effort, human scale witness.

Dan's book *Absurd Convictions, Modest Hopes* was relatively new. He believed what he wrote. He practiced what he said. And he was right. As he had been right some years earlier when a small group of us, outraged at some new atrocity of the Johnson Administration, wanted to do a draft-board action with little to no planning, with little to no prayer, with little to no weighing the cost and our capacity to endure the consequences. It was Dan who admonished that the spirit, indeed the fabric of nonviolent action is maligned by such knee-jerk reaction as we contemplated.

At the end of Albert Camus's *The Plague*, the doctor ruminates on the question: "Why did it happen?" Dan's directives have been the essence of the doctor's response: "They forgot to be modest!" They forgot to be modest, which is to say, human. But unlike Camus, who withholds further comment, Dan fleshes out the limits and the possibilities of the human, which are identical with the limits and possibilities of nonviolence. "Who can tell us?" I've heard him ask. "The culture can't. It can tell us about the sub-human! It can tell us about the super-human! These it knows. The human it does not." Ceaselessly, he points to Christ as the model of the human and reflects on the conduct of Christ in the scriptures. If Christ is the model of the human, Dan is its ardent advocate. He stresses human scale over against those who laud the super-human and become sub-human in their every venture.

If being human means, at least in part, being modest, Dan has been urgent in reminding us that modesty distinguishes every phase of a nonviolent struggle. We know that we are human beings who are incomplete, vulnerable, waiting for what humans cannot bring to pass. Building a just and peaceful society is beyond us. Building the kingdom of God is beyond us. But it is a tragic parody of modesty that elects only the task it calculates "do-able." It is a pitiable excuse for the human to assume that "we don't have to go too far into this business of transformation after all. Just get this little piece of the task done so we can say we did something!" Modesty requires that we give our all. We do all we can do. We suffer all that is required of us. We imagine alternatives seventy times seven times. And when the end is still not achieved, we assent. The acid test of modesty!

"We are not about building an empire!" He holds up the model of Dorothy Day, who built a community (and kept rebuilding it) to do what could be done—small, real, with every individual involved, with every part of his or her humanity touched and challenged. Keep it human. Empire building is about numbers and dollars and weights and measures; it counts and uses and abuses and, ultimately, crushes people.

A man of stories. Dan loves stories, especially stories that don't get in the imperial press, stories of the so-called little people. He weaves stories, enlightening, enlarging, enhancing the glimmers the scriptures give us. In opening Acts for us, he said: "A real understanding of Acts means the book is open and we are in it; our acts are part of it. The teaching of Acts has to do with lives being lived now, by the likes of us. Which suggest that an aspect of fidelity to the living is that we encourage stories—the scriptures of our lives. And that we listen! So many lives are unconsidered in the culture. People go down without a cry; their stories of no moment, because their lives are of no moment, like dust filling the cracks."

Acts, he told us, especially those of us living in the whirlwind of community, goes from the great exhilaration of the first communities to the worst aspects of a local community, the deception and subsequent death of Ananias and Saphira. "Unfaithfulness is as close at hand as the community's own life. We have these fevers and chills in community. We're forever picking up the pieces and wondering if it is all worth it."

I asked Dan: "Why then are we so dismayed, so undone by this roller coaster aspect of community? Is it that we don't understand our own tradition, our own humanity, our own dependence on God?"

"All that," he answered, "and also that we are in a vortex of difficult times. We're not only observers to it but we're part of it as well. So we need to begin with some compassion—for ourselves and others. It's humiliating to learn that we're so underdeveloped humanly and emotionally."

How are we to act as humans and as Christians? It has to do with arranging our lives so that something about a new humanity can flourish. The implications of a new humanity can be translated in nonviolent community. The community, vulnerable and clumsy as it might be, is yet evidence of the power of the Spirit. We have, as it were, two stages of the human—before and after Pentecost. We know and we will know both rhythms—in the Spirit on the one hand; and incomplete, vulnerable, and waiting for the Spirit, on the other hand. Maybe community life is an awakening in the Spirit, to the Spirit, a process that takes time. We should give ourselves and each other time.

Let us imagine ways of being human together, Dan says to us. Let the life that flowed from Pentecost enrich our imaginations. What are the elements of the common life of the early community? We begin with overturning material arrangements, holding property in common, developing a new understanding of private property. What is the meaning of private property to people of faith? Luke had the promise of Deuteronomy 15:4 in mind. An understanding "that there be no poor among you" also meant that there be no wealthy among you. This was not a law within the community but a choice, a choice that his insight and encouragement enable us to make again and again.

In 1973, Dan sat with the community at Jonah House. He invited, encouraged and prodded us to publish a newsletter. Call it *Year One*. He wrote the piece that gave it its name. We still put it out, four times a year or as close to that as events and personnel allow. We are still at "Year One" in the sense of beginnings. But we are doing something and saying something and living what we say—or trying to. As humanly as we can.

Words. I've watched Dan play with a word. I could almost see him roll it in his mouth and mind, stretch it, feel its tone, weight, and measure. A poet at work! A mystic! A love affair with the right word, a word to the weary! And when he gives his word, he stands by what he says. He believes it, is accountable for it, is willing to act on it. His word is a promise, a promise that binds him to all of us. He is speaking where he stands in faith. And he shall stand afterward—in the presence of what he has said.

A Testimony to My Brother

PHILIP BERRIGAN

Who is my brother Dan Berrigan? Very simply, Dan Berrigan is what Dan Berrigan has done, is doing, does. According to Gandhi, conduct is the best yardstick of a person's life. Dan's identity is the excellence of his life. He is one of those remarkable people who has narrowed the gap between word and deed, who has put flesh on his words.

St. John's prologue—"the Word became flesh!"—infuses his biblical scholarship and theology. I have read over the years the best of theological schools—European, North American, Latin American liberation theologians. None of them writes with Dan's authority about nonviolence or resistance to a criminal state. Few of them teach the God of the Bible as unarmed toward us and creation—the God who commands us to disarm ourselves and the violent structures of state and church. Few of them comprehend that Jesus Christ, the "image of the invisible God," rejected the sword categorically, preferring an agonizing and ignominious death rather than to pick it up. "A son cannot do anything on his own, but only what he sees the Parent doing; for what she does, her son will do also" (John 5:19). Few have risked so much in calling an illegitimate State to accountability, provoking its wrath, and the wrath of a servile church. None of them has been hunted by the hounds of the FBI; none of them has nearly died in prison.

Like other clerics, Dan learned his theology from books. But unlike them, he tested it in the cauldron of civil resistance, in the kangaroo courts and faceless prisons of the empire, in compassionate care for those with cancer and AIDS. Experience, prayer, and study became a colander to sift the word of God and to open it up as Christ opened the scriptures for the disciples on the road to Emmaus. I have heard him open the scriptures many times and teach them with rare authority. Not many of his confreres have learned their text from "the road less traveled," the way of the cross.

Dan will claim none of the above—all the more reason why others should. Rarely will he speak of himself in the retreats he gives, or in his writing or resistance. There are more important things to do than to speak of himself. There is the word of God to contemporize, live, and teach. There is the empire to denounce—its pomps, circumstances, and crimes. There is nonviolence to assert and community to champion. There is violence and war to resist, its American stripe and export. There is friendship to uphold and honor. There is availability to high and low, and constancy of kindness and generosity to everyone. There is, above all, Jesus Christ to love and to follow, in humans and in creation.

Dan tells an ironic story, a commentary on the Jesuits and their opacity toward his convictions and writing. He drew it from the fifties and early sixties, when religious were required to submit their writings to Society and diocesan censorship. The Jesuit censor remarked to him about an early manuscript: "Dan, it looks to me like you're written out!" Thirty years and forty books later, Dan finds the story delicious and tells it with relish.

I knew both Dorothy Day and Thomas Merton, but not well enough to appreciate them fully at the time. But I have learned to acclaim their work since. No one influence has so enriched the American church as the Catholic Worker. And one cannot mention the Worker without reference to Dorothy—her vision, lucidity, and example. Regarding Thomas Merton, his singular contribution was, to my mind, not just a defense of monasticism, but an early condemnation of nuclear possession and brinksmanship, and of the Vietnam war. Merton also published essays and books bolstering Christians faced with the widening madness of the American empire.

I do not hesitate to rank my brother with these two great Christians. Comparisons are odious, and prophets have little credit in their own time. But I have witnessed the lives of all three, and I can't help but judge their comparable example and influence.

Dan has struggled with uncertain health for years, dating back to the late sixties. This fact became strikingly apparent as we prepared for the King of Prussia Plowshares Eight action and the disarmament of the Mark 12A.

A group of us, including both Dan and Jerry, had just spent a week in Ireland, supporting Irish political prisoners and "The Dirty Protest." Before audiences and press, Dan was, by far, our best spokesperson. He knew Ireland and its political snarls from previous visits. Furthermore, the Irish loved him, as a human being, priest, and resister. Unknowingly, our hosts exploited him mercilessly, shoving him forward to meetings, interviews, and press conferences. Even before we returned home, this regimen left him depleted and half-sick.

Once back in New York City, he faced a brace of speaking commitments, at Cornell and elsewhere. Once finished with them, exhaustion and the flu set in, forcing him to bed and rest. After several days, he left his sickbed, barely able to walk, to join us in Pennsylvania. With clear and unalloyed faith, he told the remainder of the Plowshares Eight: "I want to go with you (to the G.E. plant in King of Prussia) if you'll have me." We would have him indeed, knowing he would supply singular gifts to action and community. But his health worried us. We had many reservations about it. These he brushed aside as inconsequential. He accepted us; we accepted him. Sick as he was, he set to work on last details.

Before our testimony at G.E., we had no illusions about consequences. This robber corporation dominated the economics and politics of Pennsylvania's Montgomery County—the courts being its faithful servant. On September 9, 1980, the court indicted us on thirteen felony counts, refused bail for Dan and myself, and set bail of $250,000 on our six friends. The next spring, after trial and conviction, Judge Salus punished Dan, myself, John Schuchardt, and Carl Kabat with three- to ten-year sentences. Nor did our lawyers, including Ramsey Clark, escape Salus's wrath: all were cited for contempt.

Eventually, consequences became smoke, but one could never judge that at the time. As subsequent sentences of Plowshares militants proved, the war-managers take their bloody business seriously; they treasure weapons more than people and usually protect them with deadly force. Tampering with these lethal toys is a grievous affront, treachery of the highest kind. Dan knew this when he took his faithful plunge.

My own faith, feeble and decrepit as it is, will never forget my brother's faith and his trust in God.

When Carl Kabat came to Jonah House in 1977, we asked him what he expected from community. He answered promptly: "Fraternal correction!"

That Carl has since mellowed about fraternal correction is neither here nor there. Any of us would. We cling to our moral lesions with a blind tenacity. In any case, of all those I love, only two have dared to confront me with my purple patches, Elizabeth and Dan. Only two have dared to point out my anger at the alleged faults of others, my confusion over rage and outrage, my frequent ruthless treatment of community members, my tendency to invert Gandhi's order of priority, a concave lens toward myself, a convex lens toward others, maximizing their faults, minimizing my own. I made a practice of condemning the "injustice" of my friends, sometimes even discarding them. Justice became a buzz word with me, a camouflage under which to hide. I was the "just" person. Others were lame, or at best, striving.

Dan loves me, and I try to return that love in my limping way. Certainly, I respect him as I respect no one else, and I honor his gifts and his life. But because he loves me, he will, on rare occasions, lay bare my arrogance and runaway ego, dragging them into the light and hanging them up to dry like wet laundry. This usually evokes protest. I rant and rave and argue. But reflection later on states that he is right. I have no secrets with God, and few with him. The upshot is that I learn, slowly and painfully.

Love requires fraternal correction; so does community. Others see us with far greater clarity than we see ourselves. They can penetrate our illusions, expose our sullenness, comprehend our hidden agendas. In my better moments, I have longed for an evaluative practice in community, where one's conduct is subject to the light of the gospel and to nonviolent principle. Alas, occasions when others tell me the truth about myself are too infrequent. Dan understands this. He understands this as part of relationship, part of brotherhood. We must honor the little or large heroisms of others; but we must also resist the breaches of truth and trust in one another—the tendency to acculturate, control, and oppress. We must bind the Strong Man (Mark 3:27) on that level also.

Dan the theologian and biblical scholar, Dan the faithful one, Dan the counselor, Dan the brother—all become brief and episodic references to a life so rich and varied, so compassionate and just, so profound and practical, that one is helpless to assess it or gauge its excellence.

In those who know him, Dan inspires something like awe—such is the sublimity of his life and his thought. Apropos of this, I heard a remark once from a man who heard him lecture: "Jesus Lord, this guy is too good to be true!"

Yes, too good to be true, but good enough to be true—the truest person I've known. As he approaches his seventy-fifth birthday, I give him a brother's love and wish him many years of struggle and service. That is to say, I wish him ongoing familiarity with our Lord's cross. I wish him the peace of Christ.

THE LAST WORD

Less Than

DANIEL BERRIGAN

The trouble was not excellence.
I carried that secret,
a laugh up my sleeve
all the public years
all the lonely years
(one and the same)
years that battered like a wind tunnel
years
like a yawn at an auction
(all the same)

Courage was not the fault
years they carried me shoulder high
years they ate me like a sandwich
(one and the same)

the fault was—dearth of courage
the bread only so-so
the beer near beer

I kept the secret under my shirt
like a fox's lively tooth, called
self knowledge.

That way
the fox eats me
before I rot.

That way I keep measure—
neither Pascal's emanation

naked, appalled
'under the infinite starry spaces'
nor a stumblebum
havocking
in Alice's doll house.

Never the less!
summon
courage, excellence!
The two, I reflect, could
snatch us from ruin.

A fairly modest urging—
don't kill, whatever pretext.
Leave the world unbefouled.
Don't hoard.
Stand somewhere.

And up to this hour
(don't tell a soul)
here I am.

Contributors

Elizabeth Bartelme is a former editor with Macmillan Books and Doubleday Books and former adjunct professor of English at Hofstra University. She was the editor of fifteen of Daniel Berrigan's books. She lives in New York City.

Frida Berrigan attends Hampshire College in Massachusetts, and lives at the Jonah House community in Baltimore, Maryland, with her parents, Elizabeth McAlister and Philip Berrigan.

Jerry Berrigan, like his brothers born in Minnesota, is the fourth of the six Berrigan sons. He and Carol Rizzo Berrigan have been married for forty years. They live in Syracuse, New York, where they are both professors—Jerry of English and Carol of special education. They are parents of four children and grandparents of three.

Philip Berrigan lives with his wife, Elizabeth McAlister, and their children, Frida, Jerry, and Katie, at the Jonah House community in Baltimore, Maryland. He was a member of the Baltimore Four, the Catonsville Nine, the Plowshares Eight, the Nuclear Navy Plowshares, and the Pax Christi–Spirit of Life Plowshares.

Luis Calero, S.J., is a priest and anthropologist who spends half of each year teaching at Santa Clara University in Santa Clara, California, and at the University of Central America in San Salvador, El Salvador.

Joan Chittister, O.S.B., is the former prioress of the Benedictine Sisters of Erie, Pennsylvania. She is a noted public speaker on issues of justice, peace, and feminism, and the author of several books, including *Wisdom Distilled in the Daily*.

Ramsey Clark is lawyer, peace advocate, author, and a former attorney general of the United States. He lives in New York City.

Robert Coles is a psychiatrist on the faculty of Harvard University. His many books include *The Spiritual Life of Children* and *Children of Crisis*, and with Daniel Berrigan, *The Geography of Faith*. He lives in Concord, Massachusetts.

Frank Cordaro is a Catholic priest and pastor of St. Patrick's Church in Council Bluffs, Iowa. He has spent many months in jail for crossing the line at the Strategic Air Command Base.

Earl Crow is a professor at High Point University in High Point, North Carolina.

John Dear, S.J., is a Jesuit priest, peace activist, and the director of the Sacred Heart Center, a neighborhood center for the poor in Richmond, Virginia. A member of the Pax Christi–Spirit of Life Plowshares, his books include *The God of Peace: Toward a Theology of Nonviolence*; *Disarming the Heart: Toward a Vow of Nonviolence*; *Seeds of Nonviolence*; *Peace Behind Bars*; *Our God Is Nonviolent*; and *The Sacrament of Civil Disobedience*.

Richard Deats is the former executive secretary and director of interfaith activities of the Fellowship of Reconciliation and is currently the editor of *Fellowship* magazine. Prior to joining the FOR staff in 1972, he taught at Union Theological Seminary in the Philippines for thirteen years. He has taught nonviolence in over a dozen countries, and lives in Nyack, New York.

Mary Donnelly is a widow, a mother of seven, a grandmother of six, and the visiting nurse on Block Island, Rhode Island, for thirty-eight years.

Jim Douglass is a peace activist and the author of *The Nonviolent Cross*; *Resistance and Contemplation*; *Lightning East to West*; and *The Nonviolent Coming of God*. With his wife, Shelley, he founded the Ground Zero Center for Nonviolent Action in Bangor, Washington. He and Shelley live in Birmingham, Alabama.

Shelley Douglass is a peace activist and director of Mary's House, a Catholic Worker house in Birmingham, Alabama. She co-authored, with her husband, Jim, *Dear Gandhi: Now What?*

Jim Forest is a former editor of the *Catholic Worker* and former secretary of the International Fellowship of Reconciliation. A member of the Milwaukee Fourteen, he is the author of several books, including *Making Friends of Enemies*; *Living with Wisdom: A Life of Thomas Merton*; and *Love Is the Measure: A Biography of Dorothy Day*. He directs Peace Media Service and lives with his wife Nancy in Holland.

Tom Fox is editor of *The National Catholic Reporter* and lives in Roeland Park, Kansas.

Thomas Gumbleton is a Catholic bishop and the former president of both Pax Christi and Bread for the World. Co-author of the U.S.

Catholic Bishops' pastoral letter *The Challenge of Peace: God's Promise and Our Response*, he lives in Detroit, Michigan.

Thich Nhat Hanh is a Vietnamese Buddhist monk, poet, retreat leader, and the author of over seventy-five books including, *Being Peace*, *Touching Peace*, *The Miracle of Mindfulness*, and with Daniel Berrigan, *The Raft Is Not the Shore*. Nominated for the Nobel Peace Prize by Martin Luther King, Jr., he has lived in exile since the mid-1960s in Plum Village, France.

Joyce Hollyday is a retreat leader, activist, former associate editor of *Sojourners* magazine and author of *Turning Toward Home* and *Clothed with the Sun*. She lives in Atlanta, Georgia.

Mary Evelyn Jegen is the former national coordinator of Pax Christi USA, the former chairperson of the Fellowship of Reconciliation, and a professor of theology at Trinity College in Washington, D.C.

Peter-Hans Kolvenbach, S.J., is superior general of the Society of Jesus.

Denise Levertov is a poet who lives in Seattle, Washington. Her latest book, *Tesserae*, a collection of prose memoirs and vignettes, is published by New Directions.

Robert Ludwig is director of university ministry at DePaul University in Chicago and the author of *Reconstructing Catholicism for a New Generation*. He was director of the Loyola Institute for Ministry at Loyola New Orleans from 1982 to 1989. His doctoral dissertation, *Theology and Politics in America: Daniel Berrigan as a Contemporary Profile*, was completed in 1973 for the Aquinas Institute of Theology, St. Louis, Missouri.

Elizabeth McAlister, a peace activist and organizer, lives with her husband, Philip Berrigan, and her children, Frida, Jerry, and Katie, at the Jonah House community in Baltimore, Maryland. She was a member of the Griffiss Plowshares and the co-author, with Philip, of *The Time's Discipline*.

Colman McCarthy is a columnist for *The Washington Post* and the director of the Center for Teaching Peace. He teaches at three schools and universities in Washington, D.C., where he lives. His books include *Disturber of the Peace* and *All of a Peace*.

Megan McKenna is a retreat leader and public speaker who lives in Albuquerque, New Mexico. Her books include *Not Counting Women and Children; Parables: The Arrows of God;* and *Mary: Shadow of Grace*.

William Hart McNichols, S.J., spent many years working with AIDS patients in New York City and now lives in Albuquerque, New Mexico, where he is an artist and iconographer.

Richard McSorley, S.J., directs the Center of Peace Studies at Georgetown University in Washington, D.C. He is the author of *New Testament Basis for Peacemaking* and *It's a Sin to Build a Nuclear Weapon.*

Anne Montgomery, R.S.C.J., is a sister of the Sacred Heart, a peace activist, and a member of the Plowshares Eight, the Pershing Plowshares, and the Kairos Plowshares. She is the co-author of *Swords into Plowshares*, and lives in New York City.

Don Moore, S.J., is an author, a professor of theology at Fordham University, and the religious superior of the West Side Jesuit Community in New York City.

Ched Myers works with the American Friends Service Committee in Los Angeles, California. His books include *Binding the Strong Man* and *Who Will Roll Away the Stone?*

Robert Raines, author, lecturer, and retreat leader, was the director of the Kirkridge Retreat Center in Bangor, Pennsylvania, from the late 1970s until 1993. He lives in Guilford, Connecticut.

Richard Rohr, O.F.M., lectures and gives retreats on justice and spirituality and is the animator of the Center for Action and Contemplation in Albuquerque, New Mexico. His books include *Simplicity*; *Quest for the Grail*; *Near Occasions of Grace*; and *Radical Grace.*

Joseph Roccasalvo teaches at the Institute of Pastoral Studies, Loyola University, Chicago, and is the author of *Portrait of a Woman: A Novel.*

Rosemary Radford Ruether is on the faculty of the Garrett School of Theology in Evanston, Illinois. Her books include *Sexism and God-Talk.*

Molly Rush is a wife, mother, grandmother, peace activist, member of the Plowshares Eight, and staff member of the Thomas Merton Center. She lives in Pittsburgh, Pennsylvania.

Martin Sheen is an actor and peace activist. His films include "Gandhi," "Apocalypse Now," "Da," "Gettysburg," "An American President," and "Blind Ambition." He lives in Los Angeles, California.

Jon Sobrino, S.J., is a Jesuit priest and a theologian on the faculty of the University of Central America in San Salvador, El Salvador. His books include *Christology at the Crossroads, Archbishop Romero, Companions of Jesus, Jesus the Liberator,* and *The True Church and the Poor.* He was speaking in Thailand at the time his Jesuit community was massacred in El Salvador on November 16, 1989.

Walter Sullivan is the Catholic bishop of Richmond, Virginia, and the president of Pax Christi, the national Catholic peace movement.

Mary Luke Tobin, a Sister of Loretto, a former president of the US Leadership Conference of Women Religious, was one of the few women observers at the Second Vatican Council. A friend of Thomas Merton, she traveled twice to Vietnam. At eighty-seven years old, she currently directs the Thomas Merton Center for Creative Exchange in Denver, Colorado.

Carmen Trotta is a member of the *Kairos* peace community and St. Joseph's House, the Catholic Worker in New York City.

Michael True, professor of English at Assumption College in Worcester, Massachusetts, is the author of *An Energy Field More Intense Than War: The Nonviolent Tradition and American Literature; To Construct Peace;* and *Ordinary People: Family Life and Global Values;* and the editor of *Daniel Berrigan: Poetry, Drama, Prose.*

Jean Vanier is the founder of L'Arche, a movement that offers hospitality to the disabled. His books include *Community and Growth* and *Be Not Afraid.* He lives in Trosly, France.

Jim Wallis is editor of *Sojourners* magazine and lives in Washington, D.C. His books include *The Soul of Politics; The Call to Conversion; Agenda for Biblical People;* and *Revive Us Again.*

Walter Wink is a theologian at Auburn Theological Seminary and leads workshops on nonviolence. He is the author of *Naming the Powers; Unmasking the Powers;* and *Engaging the Powers.* He lives in Sandisfield, Massachusetts.

Bill Wylie-Kellermann is a United Methodist pastor teaching at the Robert H. Whitaker School of Theology in Ferndale, Michigan. He is the author of *Seasons of Faith and Conscience* and the editor of *Keeper of the Word: Selected Writings of William Stringfellow.* He lives in Detroit, Michigan.

Howard Zinn is a historian who teaches at Boston University. His books include *A People's History of the United States; Disobedience and Democracy; Postwar America; The Politics of History;* and *You Can't Be Neutral on a Moving Train.*